ENVIRONMENTAL REMEDIATION TECHNOLOGIES, REGULATIONS AND SAFETY

TOXIC SUBSTANCES CONTROL ACT: SUMMARY, CHALLENGES AND REFORM PROPOSALS

Environmental Remediation Technologies, Regulations and Safety

Additional books in this series can be found on Nova's website under the Series tab.

Additional e-books in this series can be found on Nova's website under the e-book tab.

Chemical Engineering Methods and Technology

Additional books in this series can be found on Nova's website under the Series tab.

Additional e-books in this series can be found on Nova's website under the e-book tab.

ENVIRONMENTAL REMEDIATION TECHNOLOGIES, REGULATIONS AND SAFETY

TOXIC SUBSTANCES CONTROL ACT: SUMMARY, CHALLENGES AND REFORM PROPOSALS

SHANNON M. MCDONNERY
AND
CINDY L. ELROY
EDITORS

Nova Science Publishers, Inc.
New York

For permission to use material from this book please contact us:
Telephone 631-231-7269; Fax 631-231-8175
Web Site: http://www.novapublishers.com

Library of Congress Cataloging-in-Publication Data

Toxic Substances Control Act : summary, challenges, and reform proposals / editors: Shannon M. McDonnery and Cindy L. Elroy.
p. cm.
Includes index.
ISBN 978-1-62100-783-8 (hardcover)
1. United States. Toxic Substances Control Act. 2. Hazardous substances--Law and legislation--United States. 3. Poisons--Law and legislation--United States. 4. Chemicals--Law and legislation--United States. I. McDonnery, Shannon M. II. Elroy, Cindy L. III. Schierow, Linda-Jo.
KF3958.T692 2011
344.7304'622--dc23

2011038571

Published by Nova Science Publishers, Inc. † New York

Contents

PREFACE

Thirty-five years of experience implementing and enforcing the Toxic Substances Control Act (TSCA) have demonstrated the strengths and weaknesses of the law and led many to propose legislative changes to TSCA's core provisions. The basic structure of the Toxic Substances Control Act (TSCA) of 1976 has never been amended, but recent legal, scientific, and technological changes are prompting some policy makers to reexamine the law. This book summarizes the Toxic Substances Control Act (TSCA) and the major regulatory programs dealing with chemical production and distribution in U. S. commerce.

Chapter 1 - This report summarizes the Toxic Substances Control Act (TSCA) and the major regulatory programs dealing with chemical production and distribution in U.S. commerce. The President's Council on Environmental Quality proposed comprehensive federal legislation in 1971 to identify and control potentially dangerous chemicals in U.S. commerce that were not adequately regulated under other environmental statutes. President Ford signed TSCA into law on October 11, 1976. Subsequently, five titles were added to address specific concerns—asbestos in 1986 (Title II, P.L. 99-519), radon in 1988 (Title III, P.L. 100-551), lead in 1992 (Title IV, P.L. 102-550), environmental and energy issues in schools in 2007 (Title V, P.L. 110-140), and formaldehyde emissions from composite wood products in 2010 (Title VI, P.L. 111-199). In 2008, Congress added provisions to Title I, Section 6 and Section 12, banning certain activities with respect to elemental mercury (P.L. 110-414).

TSCA authorizes EPA to identify potentially dangerous chemicals in U.S. commerce that should be subject to federal control. The act authorizes EPA to gather and disseminate information about production, use, and possible adverse effects to human health and the environment of existing chemicals, and to issue "test rules" that require manufacturers and processors of potentially dangerous chemicals to conduct and report the results of scientific studies to fill information gaps. For chemicals new to U.S. commerce, TSCA requires pre-market screening and regulatory tracking of new chemical products.

Chapter 2 - The basic structure of the Toxic Substances Control Act (TSCA) of 1976 has never been amended, but recent legal, scientific, and technological changes are prompting some policy makers to reexamine the law. The Kid-Safe Chemicals Act (H.R. 6100/S. 3040 in the 110th Congress) would have reshaped risk assessment and management of industrial chemicals in U.S. commerce. TSCA currently regulates potential risks based on three policies: (1) Chemical manufacturers are responsible for testing chemicals to determine their potential effects on health and the environment; (2) EPA should regulate chemicals that present an unreasonable risk to health or the environment; and (3) EPA's implementation of the law should not create unnecessary economic barriers to technological innovation. Few have expressed concern about the last TSCA purpose, but TSCA's progress in achieving the first two goals has been debated: where some see success, others see failure, and both groups point to EPA's history of implementation and voluntary initiatives in support of their views. EPA has compiled an inventory of roughly 82,000 chemicals that have been produced in, or imported into, the United States at some time since 1976. The agency has promulgated regulations to restrict production or use of five chemicals under TSCA.

Chapter 3 - Thirty-five years of experience implementing and enforcing the Toxic Substances Control Act (TSCA) have demonstrated the strengths and weaknesses of the law and led many to propose legislative changes to TSCA's core provisions. Stakeholders appear to agree that TSCA needs to be updated, although there is disagreement about the extent and nature of any proposed revisions. S. 847 in the 112th Congress legislation would amend core provisions of TSCA Title I. This report compares key provisions of S. 847, as introduced, with current law (15 U.S.C. 2601 *et seq.*).

Generally, S. 847 would increase the amount of information about chemical toxicity and usage that chemical manufacturers and processors would be required to submit to the U.S. Environmental Protection Agency (EPA), and would facilitate EPA regulation of toxic chemicals. The bill directs EPA to establish, by rule, varied or tiered minimum data set requirements for different chemical substances or categories of substances. Data would be required from chemical manufacturers and processors for all chemicals within 5 years of the date of enactment of S. 847, earlier for high-priority chemicals. All chemicals already in commerce are to be placed on a list and prioritized by EPA into three groups based on the need for risk management. A chemical must be included in the highest priority class if it "is, or is degraded and metabolized into, a persistent, bioaccumulative, and toxic substance with the potential for widespread exposure to humans or other organisms." EPA is required to determine whether chemicals in the top two priority classes, as well as all new chemicals, meet a stringent new safety standard, given the imposition of any needed restrictions on manufacture, processing, distribution, use, or disposal. The bill would prohibit any activities with respect to an evaluated chemical substance that the EPA had not specifically allowed in the safety standard determination.

Chapter 4 - On April 15, 2010, Senator Lautenberg introduced legislation (S. 3209) to amend the core provisions of the Toxic Substances Control Act (TSCA) Title I. Representatives Waxman and Rush introduced comprehensive legislation to amend TSCA (H.R. 5820) on July 22, 2010. This report compares key provisions of S. 3209, as introduced, H.R. 5820, as introduced, and current law (15 U.S.C. 2601 *et seq.*).

Both bills would amend the 35-year-old law to shift the burden of demonstrating safety for chemicals in commerce from the U.S. Environmental Protection Agency (EPA) to manufacturers and processors of chemicals. Both bills also would prohibit manufacture, processing, and distribution of any chemical substance or mixture for which safety has not been demonstrated. Although they propose somewhat different safety standards for EPA to enforce, both bills suggest a health-based standard. In contrast, current law requires that a chemical not pose "an unreasonable risk of injury to health or the environment," and that any regulation should control unreasonable risk to the extent necessary using the "least burdensome" means of available control. This TSCA standard has been interpreted to require cost-benefit balancing. To facilitate safety assessment, the proposals would require data development and submission to EPA for all chemicals in commerce.

In: Toxic Substances Control Act
Editors: Shannon M. McDonnery and Cindy L. Elroy ISBN: 978-1-62100-783-8

Chapter 1

THE TOXIC SUBSTANCES CONTROL ACT (TSCA): A SUMMARY OF THE ACT AND ITS MAJOR REQUIREMENTS*

Linda-Jo Schierow

SUMMARY

This report summarizes the Toxic Substances Control Act (TSCA) and the major regulatory programs dealing with chemical production and distribution in U.S. commerce.

The President's Council on Environmental Quality proposed comprehensive federal legislation in 1971 to identify and control potentially dangerous chemicals in U.S. commerce that were not adequately regulated under other environmental statutes. President Ford signed TSCA into law on October 11, 1976. Subsequently, five titles were added to address specific concerns—asbestos in 1986 (Title II, P.L. 99-519), radon in 1988 (Title III, P.L. 100-551), lead in 1992 (Title IV, P.L. 102-550), environmental and energy issues in schools in 2007 (Title V, P.L. 110-140), and formaldehyde emissions from composite wood products in 2010 (Title VI, P.L. 111-199). In 2008, Congress added provisions to Title I, Section 6 and Section 12, banning certain activities with respect to elemental mercury (P.L. 110-414).

TSCA authorizes EPA to identify potentially dangerous chemicals in U.S. commerce that should be subject to federal control. The act authorizes EPA to gather and disseminate information about production, use, and possible adverse effects to human health and the environment of existing chemicals, and to issue "test rules" that require manufacturers and processors of potentially dangerous chemicals to conduct and report the results of scientific studies to fill information gaps. For chemicals new to U.S. commerce, TSCA requires pre-market screening and regulatory tracking of new chemical products.

If EPA identifies unreasonable risks associated with existing or new chemicals, TSCA requires the agency to initiate rulemaking to reduce risks to a reasonable level. EPA may regulate the manufacture, importation, processing, distribution, use, and/or

* This is an edited, reformatted and augmented version of a Congressional Research Service publication, CRS Report for Congress, RL31905, from www.crs.gov, dated July 29, 2011.

disposal of chemicals. TSCA provides a variety of regulatory tools to EPA, ranging in severity from a total ban on production, import, and use to a requirement that a product must bear a warning label at the point of sale. However, TSCA directs EPA to use the least burdensome option that can reduce risk to a level that is reasonable, given the benefits provided by the chemical product or process.

Title I of the original statute establishes the core program, directs EPA to control risks from polychlorinated biphenyls (PCBs), and bans certain activities with respect to elemental mercury. Title II directs EPA to set standards for asbestos mitigation in schools and requires asbestos contractors to be trained and certified. Title III directs EPA to provide technical assistance to states that choose to support radon monitoring and control. Title IV provides similar assistance with respect to abatement of lead-based paint hazards. Title V addresses environmental issues at schools, including energy efficiency. Finally, Title VI directs EPA to set standards for emissions of formaldehyde from composite wood products.

Introduction

The Environmental Protection Agency (EPA) is responsible for identifying and regulating toxic substances in U.S. commerce under the authority of the Toxic Substances Control Act (TSCA). This report defines key terms, provides a brief history of toxic substances control law, and describes key provisions of TSCA. In addition, this report lists several references for more detailed information about the act and provides a table that cross references sections of the *U.S. Code* with corresponding sections of the act. The report is descriptive rather than analytic, highlights key provisions rather than providing a comprehensive inventory of the act's numerous sections, and addresses authorities and limitations imposed by statute, rather than the status of EPA implementation or other policy issues.

Overview

The Toxic Substances Control Act (15 U.S.C. 2601 *et seq.*) authorizes the EPA to screen existing and new chemicals used in manufacturing and commerce to identify potentially dangerous products or uses that should be subject to federal control. EPA may require manufacturers and processors of chemicals to conduct and report the results of tests to determine the effects of potentially dangerous chemicals on living things. Based on test results and other information, EPA must regulate the manufacture, importation, processing, distribution, use, and/or disposal of any chemical that presents an unreasonable risk of injury to human health or the environment. A variety of regulatory tools is available to EPA under TSCA, ranging in severity from a total ban on production, import, and use to a requirement that a product bears a warning label at the point of sale. TSCA directs EPA to use the least burdensome option that can reduce risk to a level that is reasonable, given the benefits provided by the chemical product or process.

Federal legislation to control toxic substances was originally proposed in 1971 by the President's Council on Environmental Quality. Its report, "Toxic Substances," defined a need for comprehensive legislation to identify and control chemicals whose manufacture, processing, distribution, use, and/or disposal was potentially dangerous and not adequately regulated under other environmental statutes. The House and Senate each passed bills in both the 92nd and 93rd Congresses (in 1972 and 1973, respectively), but controversies over the scope of chemical screening prior to commercial production and distribution, level of costs, and the relationship to other regulatory laws stalled final action. Episodes of environmental contamination—including contamination of the Hudson River and other waterways by PCBs, the threat of stratospheric ozone depletion from chlorofluorocarbon (CFC) emissions, and contamination of agricultural produce by polybrominated biphenyls (PBBs) in the state of Michigan—together with more exact estimates of the costs of imposing toxic substances controls, opened the way for final passage of the legislation. President Ford signed the TSCA into law on October 11, 1976. The original legislation included a single title, which has since been designated Title I.

Table 1. Toxic Substances Control Act and Major Amendments (codified as 15 U.S.C. 2601-2671)

Year	Act	Public Law Number
1976	Toxic Substances Control Act	P.L. 94-469
1986	Asbestos Hazard Emergency Response Act	P.L. 99-519
1988	Radon Program Development Act	P.L. 100-551
1990	Radon Measurement	P.L. 101-508, § 10202
1990	Asbestos School Hazard Abatement Reauthorization Act	P.L. 101-637
1992	Residential Lead-Based Paint Hazard Reduction Act of 1992	P.L. 102-550
2007	Energy Independence and Security Act of 2007, subtitle E - Healthy High-Performance Schools	P.L. 110-140
2008	Mercury Export Ban Act of 2008	P.L. 110-414
2010	Formaldehyde Standards for Composite Wood Products Act	P.L. 111-199

TSCA (Title I) directs EPA to

- require manufacturers and processors to conduct tests for existing chemicals if (1) their manufacture, distribution, processing, use, or disposal may present an unreasonable risk of injury to health or the environment; or they are to be produced in substantial quantities and the potential for environmental release or human exposure is substantial or significant; (2) existing data are insufficient to predict the effects of human exposure and environmental releases; and (3) testing is necessary to develop such data (Section 4);
- prevent future risks through pre-manufacture screening and regulatory tracking of new chemical products (Section 5);

- control unreasonable risks already known, including risks from polychlorinated biphenyls (PCBs), as well as risks for existing chemicals that may be discovered in the future (Section 6); and
- gather and disseminate information about chemical production, use, and possible adverse effects to human health and the environment (Section 8).

Authorization for appropriations for these activities and a state grant program for control of toxic substances in the environment expired on September 30, 1983, although appropriations for these programs have continued.

In October 2008, Congress amended TSCA Title I when it enacted the Mercury Export Ban Act of 2008 (P.L. 110-414). It prohibits certain activities with respect to elemental mercury.

Subsequently, five titles have been added to TSCA to address specific concerns—asbestos in 1986 (Title II, P.L. 99-519), radon in 1988 (Title III, P.L. 100-551), lead in 1992 (Title IV, P.L. 102-550), schools in 2007 (Title V, P.L. 110-140), and formaldehyde in 2010 (Title VI, P.L. 111- 199). Title II directs EPA to set standards for asbestos mitigation in schools, and requires asbestos contractors to be trained and certified. Title III directs EPA to provide technical assistance to states that choose to support radon monitoring and control. Title IV provides similar assistance with respect to abatement of lead-based paint hazards. Title V addresses environmental issues at schools, including energy efficiency. Finally, Title VI establishes limits on emissions of formaldehyde from composite wood products.

TITLE I

Testing of Chemicals

Many chemicals, even some in widespread use, are not well characterized in terms of their potential health and environmental effects. One of the major goals of TSCA was to induce the development of test data by producers (i.e., manufacturers, importers, and processors) of chemicals in commerce. Section 4 of TSCA directs EPA to require the development of test data on existing chemicals when certain conditions prevail: (1) the manufacture, processing, distribution, use, or disposal of the chemical "may present an unreasonable risk," or (2) the chemical is produced in very large volume and there is a potential for a substantial quantity to be released into the environment or for substantial or significant human exposure. Under either condition, EPA must issue a rule requiring tests if (a) existing data are insufficient to resolve the question of safety, and (b) testing is necessary to develop the data.

Because there were more than 55,000 chemicals in U.S. commerce at the time EPA was to begin developing test rules, Congress established a special interagency committee to help EPA determine which chemicals should be considered first, and to coordinate testing needs and efforts among government agencies. At least every six months the Interagency Testing Committee (ITC) must consider candidate chemicals for inclusion on a list of substances that the ITC recommends to EPA for development and promulgation of test rules. TSCA directs the ITC to "designate" a subset of chemicals on the list for EPA action within 12 months. The list can contain no more than 50 "designated" chemicals at any time. When a chemical is designated, EPA has one year to respond by issuing a proposed test rule or a notice explaining why no testing is needed.

TSCA requires the ITC to consider the following factors when it makes listing decisions: (1) quantity of the substance to be manufactured, (2) quantity of the chemical in environmental releases, (3) number of people who will be exposed occupationally and the duration of exposure, (4) extent of non-occupational human exposure, (5) similarity of the chemical to any other chemical known to present an unreasonable risk, (6) existence of data concerning environmental or health effects of the chemical, (7) the quantity of information to be gained by testing, and (8) the availability of facilities and personnel for performing testing. Chemicals known or suspected to cause or contribute to cancer, gene mutations, or birth defects are to be assigned a higher priority. In response to information that indicates "there may be a reasonable basis to conclude that a chemical ... presents or will present a significant risk of serious or widespread harm to human beings from cancer, gene mutations, or birth defects," TSCA requires EPA action to prevent or reduce that risk or publication of a finding that the risk is not unreasonable.

Pre-manufacture Notification for New Chemicals or Uses

TSCA (Section 5) requires manufacturers, importers, and processors to notify EPA at least 90 days prior to producing or otherwise introducing a new chemical product into the United States. Any information or test data that is known to, reasonably ascertainable by, or in possession of the notifier, and that might be useful to EPA in evaluating the chemical's potential adverse effects on human health or the environment, must be submitted to EPA at the same time. TSCA also requires EPA to be notified when there are plans to produce, process, or use an existing chemical in a way that differs from previously permitted uses, if the Administrator has determined by rule that new uses of the chemical may produce significant changes in human and environmental exposures and therefore require notification. The 90-day notice provides EPA with the opportunity to evaluate the chemical use and, if necessary, to prohibit or limit such activity before it occurs to prevent unreasonable risk of injury to human health or the environment.

EPA has 45 days after notification (or up to 90 days if it extends the period for good cause) to evaluate the potential risk posed by the chemical. If EPA determines that there is a reasonable basis to conclude that the substance presents or will present an unreasonable risk, the Administrator must promulgate requirements to protect adequately against such risk. Alternatively, EPA may determine that the proposed activity related to a chemical does not present an unreasonable risk; this decision may be based on the available data, or, when no data exist to document the effects of exposure, on what is known about the effects of chemicals in commerce with similar chemical structures and used in similar ways.

The purpose of EPA's screening procedure is to identify potential hazards, and control them before use of a chemical becomes widespread. If data are inadequate to make an informed judgment and (1) manufacture, processing, distribution in commerce, use, or disposal may present an unreasonable risk, or (2) a chemical is to be produced in substantial quantities, and the potential for environmental release or human exposure is substantial or significant, EPA may issue a proposed order to prohibit or limit such activities until sufficient data are submitted.

Although the legislative history of TSCA includes a presumption that testing of new products would take place before they were widely used, either as the chemical was developed, or as its markets grew, TSCA also forbids promulgation of blanket testing requirements for all new chemicals. This reflects concern that uniform testing requirements might stifle innovation in the chemical industry. Thus, EPA must decide which chemicals, or which categories of chemicals, warrant the costs of pre-market testing. EPA reviews approximately 1,000 new chemical manufacturing notices annually.

Regulatory Controls for Hazardous Chemicals

TSCA requires EPA to regulate manufacturing, processing, distribution in commerce, use, or disposal of a chemical if it will present an unreasonable risk of injury to health or the environment, and the risk cannot be reduced to a sufficient degree under another federal law administered by EPA. The alternative means available to EPA for controlling chemical hazards that present unreasonable risks are specified in Section 6 of TSCA. EPA has the authority to

- prohibit or limit the amount of production or distribution of a substance in commerce;
- prohibit or limit the production or distribution of a substance for a particular use;
- limit the volume or concentration of the chemical produced;
- prohibit or regulate the manner or method of commercial use;
- require warning labels and/or instructions on containers or products;
- require notification of the risk of injury to distributors and, to the extent possible, consumers;
- require record-keeping by producers;
- specify disposal methods; and
- require replacement or repurchase of products already distributed.

EPA also may impose any of these requirements in combination or for a specific geographical region. However, EPA is required by TSCA to regulate only "to the extent necessary to protect adequately" against a risk, and to use the "least burdensome" regulatory approach, even in controlling unreasonable risks.

Two chemical substances are directly addressed in Title I: PCBs and elemental mercury. TSCA directs EPA to regulate PCBs and to ban most uses. In addition, TSCA prohibits the sale, distribution, or transfer of elemental mercury by federal agencies.

Information Gathering

Section 8 of TSCA requires EPA to develop and maintain an inventory of all chemicals, or categories of chemicals, manufactured or processed in the United States. The first version of this inventory identified approximately 55,000 chemicals in commerce in 1979. All chemicals not on the inventory are, by definition, "new" and subject to the notification provisions of Section 5. These chemicals must be added to the inventory if they enter U.S. commerce. Chemicals need not be listed if they are only produced in very small quantities for purposes of experimentation or research.

To aid EPA in its duties under TSCA, the agency was granted considerable authority to collect information from industries. EPA may require maintenance of records and reporting of: chemical identities, names, and molecular structures; categories of use; amounts manufactured and processed for each category of use; descriptions of byproducts resulting from manufacture, processing, use, and disposal; environmental and health effects; number of individuals exposed; number of employees exposed and the duration of exposure; and manner or method of chemical disposal.

Manufacturers, processors, and distributors of chemicals are required to maintain records of significant adverse reactions to health or the environment alleged to have been caused by a substance or mixture. Records of adverse effects on the health of employees must be retained for 30 years from the date of reporting. Industry also must submit lists and copies of health and safety studies. Studies showing adverse effects previously unknown must be submitted to EPA as soon as they are completed or discovered.

Imminent Hazards

Section 7 provides EPA authority to take emergency action through the district courts to control a chemical substance or mixture which presents an imminent and unreasonable risk of serious widespread injury to health or the environment.

Relation to Other Laws

Section 9 requires EPA to report cases of chemical risk to other federal agencies with the authority to prevent or reduce the risk. If the other agency determines that the activity does not present the risk described by EPA in its report, or initiates action under the law to protect against the risk, TSCA prohibits EPA from taking regulatory action with respect to such risk. For statutes under EPA's jurisdiction, TSCA gives the Administrator discretion to decide if a risk can best be handled under the authority of TSCA.

Enforcement and Judicial Review

Section 11 authorizes EPA to inspect any facilities subject to TSCA requirements and to issue subpoenas requiring attendance and testimony of witnesses, production of reports and documents, answers to questions and other necessary information. Section 13 mandates TSCA enforcement at the national borders by the Treasury Department.

Section 15 identifies acts prohibited under TSCA, while Section 16 describes penalties for acts violating these prohibitions, as well as recourse available to anyone accused of such violations. Section 16 authorizes civil penalties, not to exceed $25,000 per violation per day, and affords the defendant an opportunity to request a hearing before an order is issued and to petition for judicial review of an order after it is issued. Criminal penalties also are authorized for willful violations. Section 17 provides jurisdiction to U.S. district courts in civil actions to enforce TSCA Section 15 by restraining or compelling actions that violate or comply with it, respectively. Chemicals may be seized and condemned if their manufacture, processing, or distribution violated the act.

Section 19 authorizes any person to file a petition for judicial review of specified rules within 60 days of issuance under TSCA. The court is directed to set aside specified rules if they are not supported by substantial evidence in the rulemaking record taken as a whole.

Section 20 authorizes civil suits by any person against any person in violation of the act. It also authorizes suits against EPA to compel performance of nondiscretionary actions under TSCA. Section 21 provides the public with the right to petition for the issuance, amendment, or repeal of a rule requiring toxicity testing of a chemical, regulation of the chemical, or reporting.

Confidential Business Information

Section 14 provides broad protection of proprietary confidential information about chemicals in commerce. Disclosure by EPA employees of such information generally is not permitted, except to other federal employees, or when necessary to protect health or the environment. Data from health and safety studies of chemicals is not protected unless its disclosure would reveal a chemical process or chemical proportion in a mixture. Wrongful disclosure of confidential data by federal employees is prohibited, and may result in criminal penalties.

Chemical Categories

Section 26 allows EPA to impose regulatory controls on categories of chemicals, rather than on a case-by-case basis. However, EPA cannot regulate a group merely because it is composed of new chemical substances.

State Preemption

TSCA Section 18 preempts state actions that establish or continue in effect requirements applicable to a chemical substance or mixture that is regulated under TSCA Section 5 or 6, unless the state requirement is identical to the federal requirement, implements another federal law, or prohibits use of the substance or mixture within the state. However, a state may ask EPA to allow a state requirement that provides a significantly higher degree of protection from risk than does the federal requirement.

Other Provisions

TSCA Section 10 directs EPA to conduct and coordinate among federal agencies research, development, and monitoring that is necessary to the purposes of the act.

Section 12 excludes chemical products manufactured for export from TSCA requirements except for reporting and record keeping requirements in Section 8. In 2008, Congress excluded elemental mercury from this exemption, banning its export beginning in 2013, with the exception of mercury contained in coal. Other exemptions for essential uses may be granted by rule.

Section 22 waives compliance when in the interest of national defense.

Section 23 provides protection of employees who assist in carrying out the provisions of the act (i.e., "whistle-blowers").

The potential effects of TSCA rules on employment must be monitored by EPA, according to Section 24.

Section 25 mandates study of the need for indemnification of people affected by federal laws administered by EPA and of the feasibility of establishing a standard classification system for chemical substances and of storing and retrieving information about them.

Section 26 authorizes data sharing and cooperative action to facilitate TSCA implementation between EPA and other federal agencies. It also authorizes collection of fees for EPA processing of data submitted in response to an order under Section 4 or 5. EPA is directed to establish an office to assist the regulated community. The agency also must establish a procedure to ensure disclosure of financial interests in the regulated community by EPA employees. Final orders issued under TSCA must contain a statement of basis and purpose. Finally, Section 26 established within EPA a new Assistant Administrator for Toxic Substances.

TSCA Section 27 authorizes research and development of test methods for chemicals by the Public Health Service in cooperation with EPA.

Grants to states are authorized by Section 28 to establish and operate programs to prevent or eliminate unreasonable risks to health or the environment.

Section 29 authorized appropriations through 1983. An annual report is mandated by Section 30.

Title II (Asbestos in Buildings)

Growing public concern about the presence of potentially hazardous asbestos in buildings, especially in schools, led to congressional efforts to address this problem. Title II of TSCA, the Asbestos Hazard Emergency Response Act (AHERA), was enacted in 1986 (P.L. 99-519) and amended in July 1988 (P.L. 100-368). It required EPA to set standards by October 1987, for responding to the presence of asbestos in schools. The standards, set at levels adequate to protect public health and the environment, identify appropriate response actions that depend on the physical condition of asbestos. Schools, in turn, were required to inspect for asbestos-containing material, and to develop and implement a plan for managing any such material. Plans for managing asbestos were to be submitted by schools before May

1989, and implementation was to begin by July 1989. The law contains no deadlines for schools to complete implementation.

Title II requires asbestos contractors and analytical laboratories to be certified, and schools to use certified persons for abatement work. Training and accreditation requirements also apply to inspectors, contractors, and workers performing asbestos abatement work in all public and commercial buildings. EPA may award training grants to nonprofit organizations for asbestos health and safety programs. However, authorization of appropriations for this grant program expired September 30, 1995. Other Title II requirements (such as mandates that buildings be inspected for asbestos) have not been extended to non-school buildings.

To enforce requirements, TSCA authorizes EPA to take emergency action with respect to schools if school officials do not act to protect children. The act also authorizes citizen action with respect to asbestos-containing material in a school and to compel action by EPA, either through administrative petition or judicial action. Civil penalties not to exceed $5,000 are authorized for violations such as failing to conduct an inspection or to develop a school management plan.

Concern about how schools would pay for required actions was addressed in separate legislation (the Asbestos School Hazard Abatement Act of 1984, or ASHAA, P.L. 98-377). It established a program offering grants and interest-free loans to schools with serious asbestos problems and demonstrated financial need. Although EPA for several years did not request funding for this program, Congress appropriated funds. Authorization of appropriations for this program expired September 30, 1995, and Congress has not appropriated funds since FY1993; a total of $382 million in grant and loan funds were appropriated from FY1984 through FY1993. Repaid ASHAA loans are returned to an Asbestos Trust Fund, established in TSCA Title II, to become a dedicated source of revenues for future asbestos control projects.

Title III (Radon Programs)

In October 1988, Congress amended TSCA by adding Title III—Indoor Radon Abatement (15 U.S.C. 2661 *et seq.*, P.L. 100-551). The basic purpose of Title III is to provide financial and technical assistance to the states that choose to support radon monitoring and control; neither monitoring nor abatement of radon is required by the act.

Title III required EPA to update its pamphlet "A Citizen's Guide to Radon," to develop model construction standards and techniques for controlling radon levels within new buildings, and to provide technical assistance to states. EPA is to provide technical assistance by: establishing an information clearinghouse; publishing public information materials; establishing a national database of radon levels detected, organized by state; providing information to professional organizations representing private firms involved in building design and construction; submitting to Congress a plan for providing financial and technical assistance to states; operating cooperative projects with states; conducting research to develop, test, and evaluate radon measurement methods and protocols; developing and demonstrating new methods of radon measurement and mitigation, including methods that are suitable for use in nonresidential child care facilities; operating a voluntary program to rate radon measurement and mitigation devices and methods and the effectiveness of private firms and individuals offering radon-related services; and designing and implementing training seminars. The proficiency rating program and certification for training programs collect fees for service, and therefore are meant to be self-supporting, but Congress authorized $1.5 million to be appropriated to establish these programs. Congress authorized $3 million to be appropriated for each of three years beginning in 1989 for the other provisions of Sections 303, 304, and 305.

A matching grant program was established for the purpose of assisting states in developing and implementing programs for radon assessment and mitigation. For this program, $30 million was authorized to be appropriated over three years, with funds targeted to states or projects that made efforts to ensure adoption of EPA's model construction standards and techniques for new buildings; gave preference to low-income persons; or addressed serious and extensive radon contamination problems or had the potential to reduce risk or to develop innovative assessment techniques, mitigation measures, or management approaches.

Other sections of Title III require EPA to: conduct a study to determine the extent of radon contamination in schools; identify and list areas of the United States with a high probability of having high levels of indoor radon; make grants or cooperative agreements to establish and operate at least three regional radon training centers; and provide guidance to federal agencies on radon measurement, risk assessment, and remedial measures.

All authorizations for appropriations specific to this title expired September 30, 1991, although appropriations have continued.

TITLE IV (LEAD EXPOSURE REDUCTION)

The 102nd Congress added Title IV to TSCA when it enacted the Residential Lead-Based Paint Hazard Reduction Act of 1992 as Title X in the Housing and Community Development Act of 1992 (P.L. 102-550). TSCA Title IV aims to accelerate federal efforts to reduce risks to young children who daily are exposed to lead-based paint in their homes. In addition, it was intended to stimulate development of lead inspection and hazard abatement services in the private sector, while ensuring that the services provided and any products employed are reliable and effective in reducing risk. To these ends, Title IV directs EPA to

- promulgate definitions of lead-contaminated dust, lead-contaminated soil, and lead-based paint hazards;
- ensure that people engaged in detection and control of lead hazards are properly trained and that contractors are certified;
- publish requirements for the accreditation of training programs for workers;
- develop criteria to evaluate the effectiveness of commercial products used to detect or reduce risks associated with lead-based paint;
- establish protocols, criteria, and minimum performance standards for laboratory analysis of lead in paint films, soil, and dust;
- establish a program to certify laboratories as qualified to test substances for lead content; and
- publish and distribute to the public a list of certified or accredited environmental sampling laboratories.

Title IV explicitly applies these requirements to federal facilities and activities that may create a lead hazard.

In addition, Congress directed EPA to conduct a study of lead hazards due to renovation and remodeling activities that may incidentally disturb lead-based paint. EPA is required to promulgate guidelines for the renovation and remodeling of buildings or other structures when these activities might create a hazard.

Title IV directs EPA to establish a clearinghouse and hotline to distribute information about the hazards of lead-based paint, how to avoid exposure and reduce risk, and new technologies for removing or immobilizing lead-based paint. In addition, Congress mandated development of a lead hazard information pamphlet; public education and outreach activities for health professionals, the general public, homeowners, landlords, tenants, consumers of home improvement products, the residential real estate industry, and the home renovation industry; and information to be distributed by retailers of home improvement products to provide consumers with practical information related to the hazards of renovation where lead-based paint may be present.

Title IV authorizes states to propose programs to train and certify inspectors and contractors engaged in the detection or control of lead-based paint hazards. States also may develop the required informational pamphlets. TSCA requires EPA to promulgate a model state program that may be adopted by any state. Congress gave EPA the authority to approve or disapprove authorization for state proposals and to provide grants for states to develop and implement authorized programs. A federal program must be established, administered, and enforced by EPA in each state without an authorized program.

The Department of Health and Human Services also has responsibilities under Title IV of TSCA. It mandates a study by the Centers for Disease Prevention and Control (CDC) and the National Institute for Environmental Health Sciences to determine the sources of lead exposure to children who have elevated lead levels in their bodies. The National Institute for Occupational Safety and Health is directed to study ways of reducing occupational exposure to lead during abatement activities.

The act established a rule-making docket to ensure the availability to the general public of all documents submitted to agencies that are relevant to regulatory decisions pursuant to this legislation. The docket is required to include the drafts of all proposed rules submitted by EPA to the President's Office of Management and Budget (OMB), written comments on the drafts, and written responses to comments. In addition, the agency must provide an explanation for any major change to a proposed rule that appears in the final rule, and such changes may not be made based on information not filed in the docket. Dockets are required to be established in each EPA regional office.

Congress authorized to be appropriated "such sums as may be necessary" for TSCA Title IV.

In addition to amending TSCA, Title X of the Housing and Community Development Act of 1992 authorized grants to states for risk assessments and lead-based paint removal and immobilization in private housing for low-income residents; establishing state training, certification, or accreditation programs for inspectors and abatement contractors; and research at the Department of Housing and Urban Development (HUD). Authorization for appropriations for these grants expired September 30, 1994, but appropriations have continued. Title X directed HUD to establish guidelines for federally supported work involving risk assessments, inspections, interim controls, and abatement of lead-based paint hazards. In addition, the National Institute for Occupational Safety and Health (NIOSH) was provided $10 million for training people who remove or immobilize paint.

TITLE V (REDUCING RISKS IN SCHOOLS)

At the end of 2007, the 110th Congress added a fifth title to TSCA, subtitled Healthy High-Performance Schools. Enacted as Title IV, Subtitle E (section 461) of P.L. 110-140, the Energy Independence and Security Act of 2007, TSCA Title V authorizes EPA to establish a state grant program to provide technical assistance for EPA programs to schools and develop and implement state school environmental health programs. State programs must include standards for school building design, construction, and renovation, and identify ongoing school building environmental problems and recommended solutions. Environmental problems specifically mentioned in the law include "contaminants, hazardous substances, and pollutant emissions." EPA's authority to provide grants expires five years after the date of enactment.

Title V requires the EPA Administrator, in consultation with the Secretary of Education and the Secretary of Health and Human Services, to issue voluntary guidelines within 18 months of Title V enactment for selecting sites for schools (presumably new schools). The guidelines are to account for the "special vulnerability of children to hazardous substances or pollution exposures in any case in which the potential for contamination at a potential school site exists," modes of transportation available to students and staff, efficient use of energy, and potential use of a school at the site as an emergency shelter.

Title V also requires the EPA Administrator, in consultation with the Secretary of Education and the Secretary of Health and Human Services, to issue voluntary guidelines within two years of enactment for developing and implementing state environmental health programs for schools. These guidelines must take into account the findings of federal initiatives established under "relevant federal law with respect to school facilities," including initiatives related to water and energy conservation authorized by sections 431 through 441, and work related to high-performance green buildings authorized by section 492 of P.L. 110-140. In particular, the guidelines must take into account "environmental problems, contaminants, hazardous substances, and pollutant emissions"; natural day lighting; ventilation; heating and cooling; moisture control and mold; maintenance, cleaning, and pest control; acoustics; and "other issues relating to the health, comfort, productivity, and performance of occupants of the school facilities." In addition, Title V requires that the guidelines provide "technical assistance on siting, design, management, and operation of school facilities"; collaborate with children's environmental health centers in school environmental investigations"; assist states and the public to better understand and improve the environmental health of children; and take into account "the special vulnerability of children in low-income and minority communities to exposures from contaminants, hazardous substances, and pollutant emissions."

Several provisions in Title V refer to entities established under other sections of the Energy Independence and Security Act of 2007 (P.L. 110-140). For example, Title V contains directives for the Federal Director of the Office of Federal High-Performance Green Buildings in the General Services Administration, which was created by section 436(a). In addition, there is reference to the national high-performance green building clearinghouse established in section 423(1) "to carry out public outreach to inform individuals and entities of the information and services [related to high-performance green buildings] available governmentwide." Title V requires the Federal Director to ensure, "to the maximum extent practicable," that the public clearinghouse "receives and makes available information on the exposure of children to environmental hazards in school facilities." The EPA Administrator is directed to prepare an annual report to Congress on activities carried out under Title V authority, and this report also must be made available to the public through the clearinghouse.

For the purposes of carrying out the provisions of Title V, Congress authorized appropriations of $1.5 million annually through 2013.

TITLE VI (LIMITING FORMALDEHYDE EMISSIONS)

In July 2010, Congress enacted the Formaldehyde Standards for Composite Wood Products Act (P.L. 111-199), adding a new Title VI to TSCA. The new title mandates specific formaldehyde emission standards for hardwood plywood, medium-density fiberboard, and particleboard that is sold, supplied, offered for sale, or manufactured in the United States. The standards are phased in over 2 years from enactment and are based on the voluntary national formaldehyde emissions standards established by ASTM International (formerly known as the American Society for Testing and Materials), method ASTM E-1333-96 (2002).

The standards apply to plywood, particleboard, and medium-density fiberboard in the form of an unfinished panel or incorporated into a finished good. Certain products are excluded, including many forms of lumber and panels used for outdoor applications, such as structural plywood, prefabricated wood I-joists, most windows, antiques or other previously owned goods, and composite wood products used inside automobiles, trucks, rail cars, boats, and aircraft.

EPA is required to promulgate regulations ensuring compliance with the emission standards and must include provisions relating to labeling, chain of custody requirements, sell-through provisions; ultra low-emitting formaldehyde resins, finished goods, third-party testing and certification; auditing and reporting of third-party certifiers; recordkeeping; enforcement, laminated products; and exceptions for products and components containing "de minimis amounts" of composite wood products. The new law prohibits stockpiling of products manufactured before the effective date of the Act for sale after that date. Also prohibited is any requirement for labeling products manufactured prior to the "designated date of manufacture."

P.L. 111-199 requires an annual report to Congress on the status of implementation and the extent to which relevant industries have achieved compliance. Finally, the Act directs the Secretary of Housing and Urban Development to update regulations concerning formaldehyde emissions from composite wood in manufactured homes (24 Code of Federal Regulations 3280.308) to ensure that the standards established by TSCA Title VI are implemented.

Table 2. Major *U.S. Code* Sections, Toxic Substances Control Act (codified as 15 U.S.C. 2601-2692)

15 U.S.C.	Section Title	Toxic Substances Control Act (as amended)
Subchapter I	Control of Toxic Substances	
2601	Findings, policy and intent	sec. 2
2602	Definitions	sec. 3
2603	Testing of chemical substances and mixtures	sec. 4
2604	Manufacturing and processing notices	sec. 5
2605	Regulation of hazardous chemical substances and mixtures	sec. 6
2606	Imminent hazards	sec. 7
2607	Reporting and retention of information	sec. 8
2608	Relationship to other federal laws	sec. 9
2609	Research, development, collection, dissemination, and utilization of data	sec. 10
2610	Inspections and subpoenas	sec. 11
2611	Exports	sec. 12
2612	Entry into customs territory of the United States	sec. 13
2613	Disclosure of data	sec. 14
2614	Prohibited acts	sec. 15
2615	Penalties	sec. 16
2616	Specific enforcement and seizure	sec. 17
2617	Preemption	sec. 18
2618	Judicial	sec. 19
2619	Citizens' civil actions	sec. 20
2620	Citizens' petitions	sec. 21
2621	National defense waiver	sec. 22
2622	Employee protection	sec. 23
2623	Employment effects	sec. 24
2624	Studies	sec. 25
2625	Administration	sec. 26
2627	Development and evaluation of test methods	sec. 27
2628	Authorization of appropriations	sec. 28
2629	Annual report	sec. 29
Subchapter II	Asbestos Hazard Emergency Response	
2641	Congressional findings and purpose	sec. 201
2642	Definitions	sec. 202
2643	EPA regulations	sec. 203
2644	Requirements if EPA fails to promulgate regulations	sec. 204
2645	Submission to state Governor	sec. 205
2646	Contractor and laboratory accreditation	sec. 206

Table 2. (Continued)

15 U.S.C.	Section Title	Toxic Substances Control Act (as amended)
2647	Enforcement	sec. 207
2648	Emergency authority	sec. 208
2649	State and federal law	sec. 209
2650	Asbestos contractors and local educational agencies	sec. 210
2651	Public protection	sec. 211
2652	Asbestos ombudsman	sec. 212
2653	EPA study of asbestos-containing material in public buildings	sec. 213
2654	Transition rules	sec. 214
2655	Worker protection	sec. 215
Subchapter III	Indoor Radon Abatement	
2661	National goal	sec. 301
2662	Definitions	sec. 302
2663	EPA's citizen guide	sec. 303
2664	Model construction standards and techniques	sec. 304
2665	Technical assistance to states for radon programs	sec. 305
2666	Grant Assistance to states for radon programs	sec. 306
2667	Radon in schools	sec. 307
2668	Regional radon training centers	sec. 308
2669	Study of radon in federal buildings	sec. 309
2670	Regulations	sec. 310
2671	Additional authorizations	sec. 311
Subchapter IV	Lead Exposure Reduction	
2681	Definitions	sec. 401
2682	Lead-based paint activities training and certification	sec. 402
2683	Identification of dangerous levels of lead	sec. 403
2684	Authorized state programs	sec. 404
2685	Lead abatement and measurement	sec. 405
2686	Lead hazard information pamphlet	sec. 406
2687	Regulations	sec. 407
2688	Control of lead-based paint at federal facilities	sec. 408
2689	Prohibited acts	sec. 409
2690	Relationship to other federal law	sec. 410
2691	General provisions relating to administrative proceedings	sec. 411
2692	Authorization of appropriations	sec. 412
Subchapter V	Healthy High-Performance Schools	
2695	Grants for healthy school environments	sec. 501
2695[a]	Model guidelines for siting of school facilities	sec. 502

15 U.S.C.	Section Title	Toxic Substances Control Act (as amended)
2695[b]	Public outreach	sec. 503
2695[c]	Environmental health program	sec. 504
2695[d]	Authorization of appropriations	sec. 505
Subchapter VI	Formaldehyde Standards for Composite Wood Products	
2697	Formaldehyde Standards	sec. 601

Note: This table shows only the major code sections. For more detail and to determine when a section was added, the reader should consult the official printed version of the *U.S. Code*.

SELECTED REFERENCES

Bergeson, Lynn L. *TSCA: Toxic Substances Control Act*. Basic Practice Series. Chicago, IL: Section of Environment, Energy, and Resources, American Bar Association, 2000. 151 p.

Bergeson, Lynn L., Lisa M. Campbell, and Lisa Rothenberg. TSCA and the Future of Chemical Regulation, *EPA Administrative Law Reporter*, 2000, v. 15, n. 4, 23 p.

In: Toxic Substances Control Act
Editors: Shannon M. McDonnery and Cindy L. Elroy
ISBN: 978-1-62100-783-8

Chapter 2

THE TOXIC SUBSTANCES CONTROL ACT (TSCA): IMPLEMENTATION AND NEW CHALLENGES*

Linda-Jo Schierow

SUMMARY

The basic structure of the Toxic Substances Control Act (TSCA) of 1976 has never been amended, but recent legal, scientific, and technological changes are prompting some policy makers to reexamine the law. The Kid Safe Chemicals Act (H.R. 6100/S. 3040 in the 110th Congress) would have reshaped risk assessment and management of industrial chemicals in U.S. commerce. TSCA currently regulates potential risks based on three policies: (1) Chemical manufacturers are responsible for testing chemicals to determine their potential effects on health and the environment; (2) EPA should regulate chemicals that present an unreasonable risk to health or the environment; and (3) EPA's implementation of the law should not create unnecessary economic barriers to technological innovation. Few have expressed concern about the last TSCA purpose, but TSCA's progress in achieving the first two goals has been debated: where some see success, others see failure, and both groups point to EPA's history of implementation and voluntary initiatives in support of their views. EPA has compiled an inventory of roughly 82,000 chemicals that have been produced in, or imported into, the United States at some time since 1976. The agency has promulgated regulations to restrict production or use of five chemicals under TSCA.

Recently, many states and localities have acted to regulate chemicals not regulated under TSCA using state or local authority. A few states are considering broad new laws to regulate chemicals more generally. Some large chemical manufacturers, processors, and distributors object to the emerging legal patchwork. The U.S. Congress also has considered, and in several cases enacted, legislation restricting use of specific chemicals. For example, in the 110th Congress, S. 742 and H.R. 6903 would have banned many asbestos-containing materials from U.S. commerce. Multinational companies also are faced with a variety of national laws restricting international commerce in chemicals.

---

* This is an edited, reformatted and augmented version of a Congressional Research Service publication, CRS Report for Congress, RL34118, from www.crs.gov, dated July 28, 2009.

International cooperation to harmonize regulations, and to eliminate certain persistent pollutants, has led to several international agreements that aim to ease the legal confusion, but amendments to TSCA would be required if the United States were to fully implement the agreements. New laws in other nations also have provided alternative models for chemical regulation, which some would prefer to TSCA. Others defend the current U.S. approach, arguing that TSCA is based on sound, risk-based science.

Recent progress in science and technology also pose challenges to EPA implementation of TSCA. Scientists now know that the timing and duration of exposure to a chemical can determine its effects, as can the age, gender, and heritable traits of people who are exposed. Biotechnology and nanotechnology have created genetically modified organisms and nanomaterials, respectively, which EPA must categorize as "existing" or "new" and manage as "chemical substances" under TSCA.

Faced with these challenges to TSCA, some analysts, and many in the regulated community, nevertheless believe that TSCA has performed as intended, and they support TSCA in its current form. They praise TSCA as a flexible, efficient, and effective limit to over-regulation. Other legal commentators, analysts, and some policy makers want to amend TSCA which, they contend, has not accomplished the tasks laid out for it by Congress, and is unlikely to do better in the future.

INTRODUCTION

The useful properties of thousands of chemicals provide a wide range of benefits to American consumers and bolster the U.S. economy. However, experiences with certain chemicals—for example, DDT, leaded gasoline, and asbestos—have shown that adverse effects sometimes occur when there is insufficient information about potential toxicity and widespread human or wildlife exposure. Various statutes have been enacted to gather information about chemicals produced, sold, and used in the United States and to control associated risks. This report focuses on the Toxic Substances Control Act of 1976 (TSCA). Recent legal, scientific, and technological developments are prompting legislators to reexamine TSCA; it has been the subject of a hearing and several legislative proposals in the 111th Congress.[1] This is a change from the situation that prevailed in most of the previous 30 years since it was enacted; during that time, most legislators demonstrated little interest in amending the law, despite the long-standing concerns of a few Members. The basic TSCA Title I provisions concerning chemical regulation have never been amended.[2] Companion bills in the 110th Congress, H.R. 6100 and S. 3040, would have amended TSCA to significantly reshape U.S. chemical assessment and management.

This report provides an overview of basic TSCA provisions, briefly examines the history of TSCA implementation by the U.S. Environmental Protection Agency (EPA), and describes the legal, scientific, and technological developments that are being used to provide support to calls for TSCA reform.[3]

TSCA OVERVIEW

Federal legislation to regulate U.S. commerce in chemical substances was originally proposed in 1971 by the President's Council on Environmental Quality (CEQ). Its report, "Toxic Substances," defined a need for comprehensive legislation to identify and control chemicals whose manufacture, processing, distribution, use, and/or disposal was potentially dangerous, and not adequately regulated under other environmental statutes. The House and Senate each passed bills in both the 92nd and 93rd Congresses (in 1972 and 1973, respectively), but controversies over the scope of chemical screening prior to commercial production and distribution, level of costs, and the relationship to other regulatory laws stalled final action. Episodes of environmental contamination—including contamination of the Hudson River and other waterways by polychlorinated biphenyls (PCBs), the threat of stratospheric ozone depletion from chlorofluorocarbon (CFC) emissions, and contamination of agricultural produce by polybrominated biphenyls (PBBs) in the state of Michigan—together with more exact estimates of the costs of imposing toxic substances controls, opened the way for final passage of the legislation. President Ford signed TSCA into law on October 11, 1976.

Title I contains the original, general provisions of TSCA, which are the subject of this report.

Policies, Intent, and Scope

TSCA established three general federal policies with respect to chemical substances and mixtures in U.S. commerce, "... that—

- [A]dequate data should be developed with respect to the effect of chemical substances and mixtures on health and the environment and that the development of such data should be the responsibility of those who manufacture and those who process such chemical substances and mixtures;
- [A]dequate authority should exist to regulate chemical substances and mixtures which present an unreasonable risk of injury to health or the environment, and to take action with respect to chemical substances and mixtures which are imminent hazards; and
- [A]uthority over chemical substances and mixtures should be exercised in such a manner as not to impede unduly or create unnecessary economic barriers to technological innovation while fulfilling the primary purpose of this act to assure that such innovation and commerce in such chemical substances and mixtures do not present an unreasonable risk of injury to health or the environment."[4]

In addition, Congress expressed its intent in TSCA, Section2(c):

> It is the intent of Congress that the Administrator shall carry out this Act in a reasonable and prudent manner, and that the Administrator shall consider the environmental, economic, and social impact of any action the Administrator takes or proposes to take under this Act.

The scope of TSCA is very broad, covering all "chemical substances," as defined in Section 3(2).

> ... the term "chemical substance" means any organic or inorganic substance of a particular molecular identity, including—
>
> (i) any combination of such substances occurring in whole or in part as a result of a chemical reaction or occurring in nature, and
>
> (ii) any element or uncombined radical.

The law excludes from this definition substances that are otherwise regulated, such as mixtures, pesticides, tobacco, nuclear material, substances subject to certain taxes (e.g., alcohol), and food, drugs, cosmetics, and devices regulated under the Federal Food, Drug, and Cosmetic Act.

Chemical Testing

To attain these policy goals, TSCA Section 4 directs EPA to require chemical manufacturers and processors to conduct tests for existing chemicals if: (1) the manufacture, distribution, processing, use, or disposal of the chemical "may present an unreasonable risk" of injury to health or the environment; or (2) the chemical is produced in very large volume and there is a potential for a substantial quantity to be released into the environment or for substantial or significant human exposure. Under either condition, EPA must issue a rule requiring tests (known as a test rule) if: (a) existing data are insufficient, and (b) testing is necessary to develop the data.[5]

Because there were roughly 61,000 chemicals covered by TSCA and in U.S. commerce at the time EPA was to begin developing test rules, Congress established a special interagency committee to help EPA determine which chemicals should be considered first, and to coordinate testing needs and efforts among government agencies.[6] At least every six months the Interagency Testing Committee (ITC) must consider candidate chemicals for inclusion on a list of substances that the ITC recommends to EPA for development and promulgation of test rules.[7] TSCA directs the ITC to "designate" a subset of chemicals for EPA action within 12 months. In response to a new listing on this Priority Testing List of chemicals designated for testing, EPA is required to publish a *Federal Register* notice within 12 months either to propose a test rule, or to provide reasons for not doing so.[8] The Priority Testing List can contain no more than 50 designated chemicals at any time.

EPA also is authorized under TSCA Section 8 to collect *existing* information about chemicals to help evaluate the potential risks of exposure. Section 8(a) allows EPA to issue rules requiring record keeping and reports by manufacturers and importers for specified chemicals. Required elements of such reports may include the chemical identity, molecular structure, and names; categories of use; amount manufactured or processed and expected to be manufactured or processed; description of any byproducts; existing environmental and health effect data; number of individuals exposed occupationally and duration of exposure; and the manner of its disposal.

TSCA Section 8(c) requires chemical manufacturers, processors, and distributors to maintain records of "significant adverse reactions to health or the environment ... alleged to have been caused by the substance or mixture." All records must be maintained for five years, and records of employee allegations must be kept for 30 years.

Under Section 8(d), EPA must require that manufacturers submit lists of unpublished health and safety studies known to have been conducted, and copies of such studies.

Finally, Section 8(e) requires that any commercial chemical manufacturer, processor, or distributor who has information that "reasonably supports the conclusion that such substance or mixture presents a substantial risk of injury to health or the environment" must immediately inform EPA.

Other data may be collected through federal research programs. TSCA Section 10 directs EPA to conduct and coordinate among federal agencies research, development, and monitoring that is necessary to the purposes of the act. In addition, TSCA Section 27 authorizes research and development of test methods for chemicals by the Public Health Service in cooperation with EPA.

Pre-Manufacture Notices and Significant New Use Notices

EPA is required to prevent future risks through pre-manufacture screening and regulatory tracking of new chemical products. Section 5 of TSCA requires manufacturers, importers, and processors to notify EPA at least 90 days prior to producing or otherwise introducing a new chemical product into the United States. At the same time, those submitting a Pre-Manufacture Notice (PMN) also must submit any information or test data that are known to, reasonably ascertainable by, or in possession of the notifier, and that might be useful to EPA in evaluating the chemical's potential adverse effects on human health or the environment. Exemptions from these requirements are provided or allowed upon application under certain circumstances.[9]

For existing chemicals, a similar notification procedure may be required, if the Administrator has determined by rule that new uses of a particular chemical may produce significant changes in human and environmental exposures and therefore require notification. The 90-day notice required by a Significant New Use Rule (SNUR) provides EPA with the opportunity to evaluate the chemical use and, if necessary, to prohibit or limit such activity before it occurs, to prevent unreasonable risk of injury to human health or the environment.

EPA has 90 days after notification (or up to 180 days if it extends the period for good cause) to evaluate the potential risk posed by the chemical that is the subject of a PMN or SNUR. If EPA determines that there is a reasonable basis to conclude that the substance presents or will present an unreasonable risk, the Administrator *must* promulgate requirements to protect adequately against such risk.

EPA may determine that the proposed activity related to a chemical may present an unreasonable risk based on the available scientific evidence with respect to potential for exposure and adverse effects, or, when no data exist to document such effects, on what is known about the effects of chemicals with similar chemical structures. The latter method, known as structure-activity relationship analysis, often is used to screen new chemicals.

If data are inadequate to make an informed judgment about inherent hazard and potential for exposure, and (1) manufacture, processing, distribution in commerce, use, or disposal may present an unreasonable risk, *or* (2) a chemical is to be produced in substantial quantities, and the potential for environmental release or human exposure is substantial or significant, EPA may issue a proposed order to prohibit or limit such activities until sufficient data are submitted.

Although the legislative history of TSCA includes a presumption that testing of new products would take place before they were widely used, either as the chemical was developed, or as its markets grew, TSCA forbids promulgation of blanket testing requirements for all new chemicals. This prohibition arose due to concern that uniform testing requirements might stifle innovation in the chemical industry. Thus, EPA must decide which chemicals, or categories of chemicals, warrant the costs of testing.

Regulatory Controls for Hazardous Chemicals

TSCA Section 6 requires EPA to control unreasonable risks from existing chemicals when they become known. Under TSCA Section 4(f), if EPA receives test data in response to a test rule or in connection with a PMN or SNUR, or any other information that indicates "there may be a reasonable basis to conclude that a chemical substance or mixture presents or will present a significant risk of serious or widespread harm to human beings from cancer, gene mutations, or birth defects," within 180 days of receiving such information EPA is required to initiate action to prevent or reduce that risk, or to publish a finding that such risk is not unreasonable. The decision to publish a finding (and not to initiate rulemaking) is subject to judicial review.

The law directs EPA to regulate manufacturing, processing, distribution in commerce, use, or disposal under TSCA, if a chemical poses an unreasonable risk of injury to health or the environment, and the risk cannot be reduced to a sufficient degree under another federal law administered by EPA. (Alternatively, TSCA Section 9 allows EPA to refer cases of chemical risk to other federal agencies that have the authority to prevent or reduce the risk.) TSCA Section 6 provides various regulatory alternatives. EPA has authority to:

- prohibit or limit the amount of production or distribution of a substance in commerce;
- prohibit or limit the production or distribution of a substance for a particular use;
- limit the volume or concentration of the chemical produced;
- prohibit or regulate the manner or method of commercial use;
- require warning labels and/or instructions on containers or products;
- require notification of the risk of injury to distributors and, to the extent possible, consumers;
- require record-keeping by producers;
- specify disposal methods; and
- require replacement or repurchase of products already distributed.

EPA also may impose any of these requirements in combination or for a specific geographical region. However, EPA is required by TSCA to regulate only "to the extent necessary to protect adequately" against a risk, and to use the "least burdensome" regulatory approach in controlling unreasonable risks.

Chemical Production Inventory

Section 8(b) of TSCA requires EPA to gather and disseminate information about chemical production, use, and possible adverse effects to human health and the environment. It directs EPA to develop and maintain an inventory of all chemicals, or categories of chemicals, manufactured or processed for commercial purposes in the United States.

To aid EPA in its duties under TSCA, the agency was granted considerable authority to collect information from industries. EPA may require maintenance of records and reporting of: chemical identities, names, and molecular structures; categories of use; amounts manufactured and processed for each category of use; descriptions of byproducts resulting from manufacture, processing, use, and disposal; environmental and health effects; number of individuals exposed; number of employees exposed and the duration of exposure; and manner or method of chemical disposal.

TSCA provides broad protection of proprietary confidential information about chemicals in commerce. Disclosure by EPA employees of such information generally is not permitted, except to other federal employees, or when necessary to protect health or the environment. However, data from health and safety studies of chemicals is not protected from disclosure, unless it would reveal a chemical process or chemical proportion in a mixture. Wrongful disclosure of confidential data by federal employees may result in criminal penalties.

Role of the States

All of the mandates in Title I are federal: there is no provision for authorizing state programs to implement basic Title I provisions. Neither does TSCA provide special access for state officials to confidential business information that is reported to EPA.

TSCA Section 18(a) does not allow a state or local law to remain in effect if it restricts the use of a chemical for which EPA has promulgated a rule or order under Section 5 or 6, if the federal rule is intended to protect against a risk of injury to health or the environment. State or local law is permitted only if it is identical to the federal requirement, adopted under another federal law, or prohibits the use of such substance or mixture within the relevant jurisdiction (except use in manufacture or processing of other substances). TSCA Section 18(b) allows states or localities to petition EPA to issue a rule exempting a state or local law, if compliance would not cause a violation of federal law, it provides a significantly higher degree of protection from such risk than the federal requirements, and does not unduly burden interstate commerce.

Judicial Review

TSCA Section 19 authorizes any person to file a petition for judicial review of specified rules within 60 days of issuance under TSCA. The court is directed to set aside specified rules if they are not supported by "substantial evidence" in the rulemaking record taken as a whole.

IMPLEMENTATION

EPA efforts to implement TSCA include (1) developing and collecting data relevant to risk assessment of chemicals under TSCA Sections 4 and 8, and (2) regulating chemicals that pose an unreasonable risk under TSCA Sections 5 or 6 in a manner that does not unduly oppress innovation and commerce. This section summarizes available information relevant to EPA performance under TSCA so that readers might have an objective basis for evaluating statements of opinion regarding its effectiveness.

Chemical Inventory

TSCA directs EPA to establish requirements that would distinguish between chemicals already in U.S. commerce and chemicals that would enter commerce after enactment of TSCA. The first version of the inventory of existing chemicals was compiled under TSCA Section 8(b) between 1978 and 1979. It identified approximately 62,000 chemicals[10] that manufacturers and importers reported had been produced in, or imported into, the United States for commercial purposes after January 1, 1975.[11] This included naturally occurring as well as synthetic chemicals.

EPA has added new chemicals to the TSCA inventory whenever manufacturers have submitted a Notice of Commencement (NOC) indicating that a chemical not on the current inventory (for which a PMN was submitted) was about to be manufactured and enter commerce.[12] As of November 2008, roughly 22,000 new chemical substances had entered U.S. commerce and been added to the inventory.[13] A few chemicals have been removed from the inventory, generally because they were reported in error and were not being produced commercially. (EPA does not list chemicals if they are only produced in small quantities for purposes of experimentation or research.) As of November 2008, EPA estimated that there were 84,000 chemical substances on the inventory, meaning that they had, at least for a while, been in U.S. commerce after 1976.[14] Included in this number were roughly 50,000 organic substances that are not polymers, 30,000 polymers, and 3,000 inorganic chemical substances.[15,16]

Table 1. Numbers of Chemicals in U.S. Commerce

Original inventory in 1979	62,000
Added since 1979	22,000
Inventory in 2008	84,000
Reported in 2006 inventory update	9,000

Note: Some chemicals on the 2008 Inventory may no longer be in commerce. Also, chemicals need only be reported for an inventory update if a facility produced or imported more than 10,000 pounds during the previous year (2005).

Beginning in 1986 and every four years thereafter, EPA collected information about the volume of chemicals produced and the locations of plants where chemicals were produced or imported in amounts greater than 10,000 pounds (5 tons) per year. In recent years, roughly 2,500 facilities (1,000 companies) submitted inventory update reports for about 9,000 chemicals.17 [18] The most recent inventory update was conducted in 2006. The next update will be done in 2011, because EPA amended the general rule governing inventory updates (issued under TSCA Section 8(a), changing the frequency of future updates to once every five years.[19] EPA also amended the inventory update rule to require reporting for inorganic chemicals (for which reporting has not been required in recent years), and to raise the threshold for chemical production volume that triggers reporting.[20] The new rule requires reports from roughly 3,000 facilities that produce more than 25,000 pounds, as opposed to the old level of 10,000 pounds, of chemical per year.[21] In addition, information about the current uses and exposures of chemicals will be required from facilities that produced or imported more than 300,000 pounds of a chemical per year.[22] The scope of the TSCA inventory is defined in the Code of Federal Regulations.[23]

EPA also is developing a reset of the chemical inventory.[24] Proposed in 2008, the reset would be based on reporting by those who manufacture or process chemicals and would aim to identify which of the 84,000 chemicals currently on the inventory are still being manufactured, imported, or processed in the United States. A reset inventory would include only those chemicals for which the regulated community reported activity. EPA noted several potential benefits of an inventory reset.

> [I]t would provide EPA and the public with a better understanding of the chemical substances that are actually in commerce in the United States. Another benefit is that it would provide the Agency with the opportunity to review under TSCA [s]ection 5 any chemical substances removed from the TSCA Inventory, but for which persons subsequently intended to commence manufacture or import.[25]

The public comment period on this proposal ended January 23, 2009. Relevant information is available in the public regulatory docket.[26]

Review and Management of New Chemicals

All chemicals not on the TSCA chemical inventory are, by definition, "new" and subject to the Pre-Manufacture Notice (PMN) provisions of Section 5. However, EPA rules under Section 5(h)(4) establish exemptions from providing a PMN for a new chemical produced or imported at 10,000 kilograms (roughly 22,000 pounds) or less annually; if the chemical releases to the environment, and human exposure is very low; or for certain polymers meeting specific requirements.[27] EPA has received approximately 44,000 PMNs since 1976, between 1,000 and 2,000 annually.[28] EPA protects from public disclosure the identities of as many as 90% of these new chemicals due to formal assertions by manufacturers that the information is confidential business information.[29]

Roughly 33% of PMN submissions include test data on the chemical properties. Only about 15% of submissions include data on health effects.[30] Due to the paucity of data for most new chemicals, EPA has developed quantitative structure-activity relationship (QSAR) models and rules-based expert systems to estimate physical-chemical properties, environmental fate, ecotoxicity, and human health effects for numerous classes of industrial chemicals in the absence of measured data. [31] The QSAR models are based on experimentally measured data collected from public sources and confidential submissions provided to the Agency. The underlying methodology for the predictive systems generally describes relationships between molecular structures and chemical properties (structure-activity relationships (SARs)) that impact the various endpoints of interest. Additionally, the EPA's Office of Pollution Prevention and Toxics (OPPT) has published category statements for 55 classes of chemicals with shared chemical and toxicological properties, based on experience gained through the New Chemicals Program.[32] When a new substance is identified as being a member of a category, the chemical is evaluated in the context of the potential health or environmental concerns historically associated with that category. It is important to note that substances which fall into these classes are not necessarily the chemical substances of greatest concern to the Agency, but rather include chemicals for which sufficient history has been accumulated so that the category serves as a source of guidance to both identify initial hazard concerns and potential risk as appropriate, and to formulate appropriate testing recommendations.

As of September 30, 2005, EPA reported it had taken 3,899 regulatory or voluntary actions to gather data or restrict use of roughly 10% of all PMNs.[33] EPA issued 1,320 Consent Orders under Section 5(e), subjected 575 new chemicals to SNUR requirements without an accompanying 5(e) order,[34] took four actions to protect against unreasonable risks under Section 5(f), and received information gathered through voluntary testing for at least 300 chemicals. In addition, 1,705 PMNs were "withdrawn often in face of action."

EPA also has acted proactively to encourage the development of chemicals that are likely to be less hazardous. To that end, the agency has shared a set of its models, known as the P2 Framework, with chemical manufacturers so that they may avoid designing or developing chemicals that are likely to raise concerns and prompt requests for additional data.[35] For example, one of the models in the set, EPI SuiteTM evaluates chemical structures and estimates the melting and boiling points, vapor pressure, and other physical and chemical characteristics of new chemicals. Another model, the Cancer Expert System, which is registered under the trademark OncoLogicTM, analyzes chemical structures to determine the likelihood that they might cause cancer.[36] By using EPA's models, some manufacturers have been able to design "greener" products that do not require investments in extensive toxicity tests.

Review and Management of Chemicals on the Original Inventory

Data Collection and Risk Assessment Authorized by TSCA

The TSCA Interagency Testing Committee (ITC), which was established under TSCA Section 4(e) to assist EPA in setting priorities among chemicals, has reviewed more than 40,000 chemicals and submitted 63 reports to EPA.[37] The committee has selected for reporting or testing about 4,500 chemicals for which it had concerns about toxicity or exposure and for which there were few or no data on ecological effects, environmental fate, or health effects.[38] These substances were added to a Priority Chemicals List. In response to ITC recommendations, EPA must promulgate rules adding these chemicals to a list in the Code of Federal Regulations for which reporting is required under the TSCA 8(a) PAIR rule and TSCA Section 8(d), the Health and Safety Data Reporting rule. The ITC has reviewed more than 10,200 studies submitted in response to 8(d) rules.

In addition, the ITC may "designate" up to 50 substances per year for testing under TSCA §4(e). The ITC reviewed roughly 2,000 to 6,000 chemicals before 1999 for possible addition to the Priority Testing List, and 1,000 to 2,000 were in fact added to the Priority Testing List.[39]

EPA has addressed its responsibilities for screening and managing the 61,000 "existing" chemicals (on the original inventory) by categorizing them according to relative risk, based primarily on the information reported by manufacturers between 1975 and 1979.[40] Many chemicals have been assigned a low priority for evaluation and management, because they are thought to pose no risk or a relatively small risk of harm, generally because they are produced in quantities less than 10,000 pounds per year, per site, or because they are polymers. EPA has not required reporting for such chemicals under the TSCA 8(a) inventory update rule. As a result, it is not known whether many of them still are produced and distributed within the United States.

EPA has estimated that roughly 15,000 organic and inorganic chemicals are produced at significant volumes (more than 10,000 pounds per year) and are not polymers that are generally of less concern.[41] Of these, about 3,000 were produced in volumes of one million pounds or more annually, across all U.S. companies.[42] These are known as High Production Volume (HPV) chemicals. HPV chemicals generally have received greater EPA scrutiny, because of the presumption that they have a relatively high potential for human and environmental exposure. Many of these HPV substances are considered likely to be benign. Others have risks that, while considerable, are well understood. (Chlorine gas and hydrogen peroxide are examples.) For most HPV chemicals, however, basic information about chemical properties is lacking.

When EPA becomes concerned that a chemical may pose an unreasonable risk, the agency first gathers data that is already available by using record keeping and reporting rules. For example, under TSCA Section 8(a), in addition to the inventory update rule, EPA has promulgated Preliminary Assessment Information Reporting (PAIR) rules.[43] They direct manufacturers to report within 90 days on the quantities of specified chemicals produced and released, and the extent of worker exposure. Such information is useful for determining whether exposure is sufficient to pose an unreasonable risk. Through September 2006, EPA had issued 33 PAIR rules, requiring reporting for about 1,200 chemicals.[44]

In addition, under the authority of TSCA Section 8(c), EPA has promulgated rules requiring manufacturers, processors, and distributors of chemicals to keep records of allegations of significant adverse reactions to chemical exposure.[45] Through 2006, EPA had issued two reporting rules to collect such records for two chemicals and two chemical categories.[46]

EPA rules under TSCA Section 8(d) require manufacturers to submit lists and copies of unpublished health and safety studies.[47] As of September 2006, EPA had issued 51 reporting rules for 1,200 chemicals.[48] In response, EPA received more than 50,000 studies.[49]

Under TSCA Section 8(e), which requires submission of any information that "reasonably supports the conclusion that such substance or mixture presents a substantial risk of injury to health or the environment," EPA has received and reviewed more than 16,500 initial notices and 7,750 supplemental or follow-up notices since 1977. These notices contained data concerning serious adverse health effects, ecotoxicological effects, and exposures.[50] EPA receives roughly 200 new 8(e) submissions and 100 supplemental submissions each year.[51] EPA has established lists of these studies and made the studies themselves available to the public,[52] and the databases have been updated as recently as March 2009.[53] However, the value of the studies, or the lists of studies, is greatly reduced by the confidentiality claims of the submitters: in most cases, the identity of the chemical is concealed.

To track testing, production, uses, and regulations of all TSCA inventory chemicals (the so-called "existing chemicals"), EPA began using a "Master Testing List" (MTL) in 1990. The MTL presents a consolidated listing of OPPT's priorities for testing, as well as those brought forward to OPPT by other EPA Program Offices, other Federal agencies, the ITC, and international organizations such as the Organization for Economic Cooperation and Development (OECD). However, EPA's online Master Testing List is from 1996, and has not been updated.[54]

When reporting rules fail to generate data that EPA believes are needed to assess risks, EPA has used its authority under TSCA Section 4 to require data generation (or submission, if data are in company files). EPA has issued test rules under Section 4 for approximately 254 existing chemicals: 60 chemicals using Enforceable Consent Agreements (ECAs), 24 chemicals under negotiated testing agreements, and about 170 chemicals covered by final test rules.[55]

EPA Assistant Administrators for OPPTS sometimes have criticized TSCA provisions concerning data collection. For example, former Assistant Administrator Lynn Goldman testified in 1994 that "Our available tools for gathering testing data about these chemicals are cumbersome."[56] She later explained that under the provisions of TSCA Section 4, "It's almost as if ... we have to, first, prove that chemicals are risky before we can have the testing done to show whether or not the chemicals are risky."[57] This situation results in high transaction costs due to legal challenges when test rules are promulgated: the regulated community generally can argue that there is insufficient evidence supporting the agency's determination that a rule is needed.[58] Goldman testified:

> For example, in July 1993 we promulgated a TSCA section 4 multi-chemical toxicity end point test rule covering 10 chemicals. In October 1993, however, we were sued by the Chemical Manufacturers Association [now the American Chemistry Council]. Settlement was only reached earlier this month [May 1994]. We also promulgated a final TSCA section 4 test rule on October of 1993 on four chemicals, and were sued by the manufacturers for two of those four chemicals. Settlement negotiations are still underway for those.[59]

In a recent report on federal requirements for toxicity testing, the National Research Council agreed with Dr. Goldman and noted that,

> TSCA authorizes EPA to review existing chemicals, but toxicity and exposure information on them is typically so incomplete that it does not support the review process. EPA can require testing if it determines that a chemical meets a specific set of criteria; however, in vitro and whole-animal tests are rarely required. Thus, the basis for establishing priorities and requiring testing for industrial chemicals in the united States has not progressed much over the last 20 years.[60]

Not all administrators of the program share Dr. Goldman's opinion, however. Assistant Administrator James Gulliford testified before the Senate Committee on Environment and Public Works in August 2006:

> TSCA provides the agency with the necessary authority to ensure that new chemicals are adequately reviewed, that EPA can require reporting or development of information needed to assess existing chemicals, and that those chemicals that pose an unreasonable risk can be effectively controlled. Using TSCA as the foundation for our efforts, EPA has, over the decades, developed a wide array of regulatory and voluntary approaches and tools to assist us in our goal to protect both human health and the environment. Using the strengths of both regulatory and partnership approaches we have ensured effective, timely chemical management decisions.[61]

Some of those voluntary approaches and tools are described below.

Voluntary Initiatives to Gather Data

EPA also obtains data about chemical properties through various voluntary programs, some aimed at particular chemical groups (such as certain fluorinated compounds),[62] and others aimed at entire categories of chemicals. Several High Production Volume (HPV) testing programs are examples of the latter type.[63] The regulated community considers the flexibility of TSCA that permits such voluntary programs to be one of the TSCA's greatest strengths.[64]

EPA efforts to develop toxicity data on HPV chemicals date back to the late 1980s. At that time, the Organization for Economic Cooperation and Development (OECD), an intergovernmental organization consisting of 29 developed countries, including the United States, began developing a voluntary program to develop basic toxicity information for chemicals produced in volumes greater than 2.2 million pounds per year in at least one member country or in the European Union.[65] As of 2004, the OECD had listed 4,843 such HPV chemicals. In 1990, OECD countries agreed to generate and gather data sufficient to allow an informed judgment with respect to the hazard potential of certain of these high production volume chemicals. The necessary data elements are referred to as the Screening Information Data Set, or SIDS. A SIDS has been, or is being, compiled for approximately 600 of these substances.[66]

EPA's HPV Challenge Program began in 1998, when Vice President Gore and EPA Administrator Browner called on the chemical industry to produce health and environmental effects data for approximately 2,782 chemicals produced in, or imported to, the United States in amounts greater than one million pounds per year, according to reports filed under the 1990 TSCA Inventory Update Rule. That challenge was prompted by studies conducted during the late 1990s that documented a lack of basic health and safety data for most chemicals in U.S. commerce.[67] According to the original program goals, all basic data were to be submitted by the end of 2004 and made public by the end of 2005. EPA is making all the data it receives as a result of the HPV program available to the general public, consistent with a recommendation of the National Pollution and Prevention Toxics Advisory Committee (NPPTAC). According to the EPA website on the HPV program, EPA has received "340 submissions, representing almost 900 chemical substances."[68] HPV data may be viewed online at http://www.epa.gov/HPV/whatsnew.htm.

Environmental Defense (now and previously known as Environmental Defense Fund), an advocacy group that helped to design the program, has issued three reports on the status of the HPV program to date.[69] According to Richard Denison, senior scientist with Environmental Defense who has been tracking the HPV chemicals, through July 2007, chemical manufacturers had committed to providing EPA information on roughly 1,300 chemicals produced in high volumes.[70] Data sets still were incomplete for 536 of the HPV chemicals on the original list, as of July 2007, according to Denison. Furthermore, he said that no manufacturer had committed to providing information for about 265 chemicals on that list.[71] The latest EDF information on the program may be found on the Internet.[72]

More than 500 chemicals not on the original list later qualified as HPV chemicals; 231 of these were sponsored by manufacturers through an Extended HPV Program, according to Denison.[73] On the other hand, about 327 of the chemicals on the original list were no longer produced in such high volumes, according to reports filed in response to inventory update rules in 1998 and 2002.[74,75] EPA planned a final report on the HPV Challenge Program in 2008, but no report has been identified.

The U.S. HPV Challenge Program is similar to an international program organized by chemical trade groups known as the International Council of Chemical Associations (ICCA). The ICCA initiative aims to test and assess an additional 734 chemicals produced in volumes greater than 22 million pounds annually.

Another, much smaller, U.S. initiative is the Voluntary Children's Chemical Evaluation Program (VCCEP). It aims to provide detailed information about risks to children potentially posed by a small group of 23 chemicals. Manufacturers have volunteered to conduct basic tests for 20 of these chemicals.[76]

The American Chemistry Council has noted that through the HPV program (and related OECD program), the chemical industry has developed and submitted to EPA data for "more than 95% of all chemicals in commerce today, by volume," and the public has electronic access to these data through EPA's High Production Volume website (http://www.epa.gov/hpv). The HPV program collected information for about 2,000 chemicals.[77]

Despite the noteworthy progress being made through these voluntary programs, which is greater than under any previous TSCA initiative, most existing chemicals still lack toxicity data relevant to hazard assessment.78 [79] Data also are lacking on production volume and use, which are critical for determining the potential for human and environmental exposure and for risk assessments that would permit priority setting for EPA action.[80] Moreover, with respect to new chemicals, roughly two-thirds of PMN submissions do not include test data on chemical properties, and almost 85% of PMN submissions provide no data on health effects.[81]

Some lawyers argue that TSCA acts as a disincentive to data production, and therefore to data submission, by punishing any failure to report information about adverse health impacts, but not requiring testing to determine whether such impacts might occur.[82]

Risk Management

EPA has used its Section 6 authority on eight occasions to restrict manufacture or use of six chemicals.[83] Two of these regulations were later superseded by regulations under other environmental laws.[84] Four chemicals remain regulated to some extent under TSCA Section 6: metalworking fluids, hexavalent chromium use to treat water in comfort cooling systems (that is, cooling towers dedicated exclusively to heating, ventilation, and air conditioning or refrigeration systems), PCBs, and new uses of asbestos.[85] Regulation of PCBs and elemental mercury exports is required explicitly by TSCA Section 6.

According to Ed Brooks, of EPA's Chemical Control Division, EPA used its Section 6 authority sparingly because "With respect to the unreasonable risk issue, ... the Agency came to view Section 6 rulemaking as an inherently large and complex undertaking that offered little prospect of resulting in success."[86]

In four instances, EPA referred chemicals for regulation to another federal agency. In 1983 and 1984, EPA referred six chemicals to the Occupational Safety and Health Administration under TSCA Section 9(a).[87] In 1990, EPA sent a 9(a) report to the Food and Drug Administration (FDA) on dioxins and furans in wood and paper products.[88] In testimony before the Senate Committee on Environment and Public Works, Subcommittee on Toxic Substances, Research and Development, Lynn R. Goldman, then Assistant Administrator of EPA's Office of Pesticides, Prevention, and Toxic Substances, testified that "the formal referral mechanism [of Section 9] has proven burdensome to EPA and cumbersome as a mechanism for obtaining prompt consideration by applicable agencies."[89]

Impact of a 1991 Decision by the Fifth Circuit Court on Section 6 Rulemaking[90]

In 1991, the U.S. Court of Appeals for the Fifth Circuit vacated and remanded an EPA rule promulgated under Section 6 that prohibited the manufacture, importation, processing, and distribution of asbestos in almost all products.[91] The substantive heart of the *Corrosion Proof* decision was its conclusion that EPA had insufficiently justified its ban. The ruling is described in more detail in the Appendix to this report.

With very limited exception, legal commentators have viewed TSCA section 6, particularly as construed in *Corrosion Proof Fittings*, as imposing high evidentiary hurdles on EPA regulators, so that little regulation under its authority may be expected.[92] As explained by Robert B. Haemer, *Corrosion Proof Fittings* "may have done the most damage to EPA's ability to regulate chemical substances." He continues:

> The fact that the court found ten years of rulemaking and a 45,000 page record inadequate to support a ban on asbestos makes it appear that EPA management has good reason to avoid rulemaking altogether. Requiring EPA to use the balancing approach recommended by the Corrosion Proof court would result in the agency making tough policy choices that cannot be resolved solely by science The time and effort required to flawlessly follow rulemaking procedures affects [sic] EPA's decisions about whether to pursue section 6 rulemakings, especially considering that more procedure may not necessarily produce better administrative decisions. It is even more difficult for EPA to surmount an overly restrictive interpretation of reasonable risk.... [93]
>
> The court's remand of the asbestos rule in Corrosion Proof Fittings indicates that TSCA's failure is tied to its structure, not the lack of need for the statute itself. The balancing of risks in the face of a very high hurdle of scientific uncertainty under TSCA leaves EPA almost paralyzed to take action to regulate toxic substances.[94]

A 1993 study by the Carnegie Commission on Science, Technology, and Government, *Risk and the Environment: Improving Regulatory Decision Making*, concluded, "Regardless of whether the statute, the courts, the agency, or others should be faulted in this case, it is unsettling that EPA could not satisfy TSCA's requirements for promulgating a single rule after a decade's effort."[95]

The only favorable comment by a legal scholar regarding TSCA and *Corrosion Proof Fittings*, as revealed by CRS research, was the following statement by the EPA Assistant Administrator for Enforcement and Compliance Assurance during the George W. Bush Administration—

Recent Events and Trends

Few legislators have expressed much interest in TSCA during its 30-year history: Congress has held few oversight hearings on its implementation, and the basic TSCA provisions in Title I have never been amended.[97] However, recent legal, scientific, and technological developments appear to have increased legislative interest and are discussed below. Recent Congressional and Administrative initiatives that address the purported weaknesses of TSCA also are summarized.

State Laws and Local Ordinances

Many states and localities have enacted laws restricting the sale or use of various chemicals[98] or categories of substances that are federally managed under TSCA. For example, numerous state and even local governments have enacted laws regulating bioengineered organisms, although EPA treats such organisms as "new chemical substances" (see below).[99] Those promoting revisions to TSCA argue that state laws and local ordinances restricting chemicals are evidence that TSCA is not effective in controlling chemicals in the marketplace, and that citizens have lost confidence in the ability of the act to adequately protect public health and the environment.[100] Some California legislators have been modeling proposals based on the laws of other nations. For example, a law recently enacted in California that restricts formaldehyde emissions from certain wood products is similar to a law in the European Union. Other bills in the California Assembly or Senate have specifically referenced Canadian or Dutch law.[101]

A number of California's legislative proposals derive from a University of California (Berkeley) report commissioned in January 2004 by Members of the California legislature.[102] That report concluded that the cause of the chemical challenges facing California is the failure of TSCA to provide an effective vehicle to motivate chemical producers to generate and distribute adequate information on the toxicity of their products. This "information deficit," the report continues, makes it "difficult for businesses and consumers to choose safer chemicals" and has "undermined the efficient operation of the market." As a result, the market is driven by the function and price of chemicals more than by their toxic properties, according to the report's principal author.[103] The report also suggested that the process is self-sustaining: because the market is driven by knowledge of what chemicals can do and what they cost, the report claims that new graduates with PhDs in chemistry from major universities can lack even a rudimentary understanding of toxicology.[104] The solution for California, the report concludes, is for it to take a leadership role in chemicals policy.[105]

As the number of state and local restrictions on chemicals increases, compliance becomes more difficult and costly for chemical manufacturers and distributors who operate in multiple states.[106] The emerging legal patchwork may also be less firmly based on sound science. For these reasons, some large chemical makers might lean toward TSCA reform to preempt state and local regulatory action. TSCA currently does not prevent state and local regulation of chemicals, unless they are already regulated under the act.[107]

International Agreements on Chemicals

Globalization of commerce in chemicals also is forcing some reconsideration of TSCA. International commerce in chemicals has grown significantly during the 30 years of TSCA's existence, and most of the largest chemical manufacturers, processors, and distributors now operate internationally. This means that they must adjust their business practices to accommodate the expectations of diverse governments, labor forces, and customers. Proliferating and sometimes conflicting obligations with respect to the chemical industry have prompted some multinational firms to advocate for international harmonization of regulations.[108]

The Executive Branch, working through the State Department and EPA, has sought to smooth the way for American businesses abroad (at the same time that it reduces its own burden for data collection and chemical risk assessments), through informal agreements and formal treaties. Business interests and other non-governmental organizations often have participated in negotiations. Domestic implementation of such agreements, however, is constrained by U.S. environmental statutes.

Between 1998 and 2001, the United States signed two international treaties and one executive agreement to ban or strictly regulate certain toxic chemicals that persist and bioaccumulate in the environment. The agreements apply to all production, import, export, use, and disposal of the listed chemicals. But TSCA Section 12(a) explicitly excludes chemicals intended solely for export from regulation under TSCA, deferring to the authority of the importing nations to impose any necessary restrictions on chemical imports or uses. To implement the international agreements, TSCA would have to be amended to permit regulation of chemical production for export, at least in the case of the chemicals specified in the treaties.

Although there is broad U.S. support for all three international agreements, stakeholders and policy makers have not been able to agree on implementing legislation targeted specifically to the necessary TSCA changes. Legislators appear preoccupied by the larger issues that surround TSCA specifically (discussed in the following section of this report) and chemical regulation more generally. Until these larger issues are resolved, implementing legislation seems unlikely to be enacted. Meanwhile, multinational chemical company representatives and international environmental protection groups can be expected to continue pushing for legislative action.[109]

New Chemical Laws in Other Nations

Recent legislation in the European Union (EU) addressed many of the broader questions about how chemicals should be regulated. The legislation

- is based on the EU version of the precautionary principle;[110]
- requires data production and reporting for most chemicals in commerce;
- shifts responsibility for demonstrating a chemical's safety from regulators to chemical makers and processors;
- reverses the default status for certain chemicals without data from safe to unsafe; and
- requires reduced use of specified toxic chemicals when safer substitutes are available.

Adopted in December 2006, the EU law for the Registration, Evaluation, Authorization, and Restriction of Chemicals, known as REACH, is heralded by some as a model for other countries that are striving to develop sustainable economies based on the precautionary principle. Others are concerned about the potential negative effect of REACH on the European economy and international commerce.

U.S. chemical exporters, and even manufacturers whose products contain certain chemicals, are required to meet REACH requirements, which are to be phased in over 11 years. Many U.S. environmentalists hope that REACH implementation in the EU will demonstrate the feasibility of its approach to chemical regulation, and show the way to TSCA reform. Some argue further that failing to amend TSCA in the near term will reduce (or further reduce) U.S. stature as a leader in global environmental policy.[111]

Others reject the approach taken by REACH and defend TSCA, arguing that the U.S. approach continues to provide the leading example of chemical regulation based on sound, risk-based science.[112] As stated in an American Chemistry Council (ACC) factsheet:

> The United States chemical management regulatory system is based on the use of credible scientific information and embodies several layers of precaution that are protective of human health and the environment.[113]

Moreover, the trilateral Montebello Agreement reportedly is seen by some as an American alternative to REACH that will focus resources efficiently on chemicals of greatest concern.[114]

Implementation of REACH will provide the world with evidence regarding the pros and cons of its approach to chemicals policy. These lessons will probably influence the debate about future U.S. chemical policy generally, and TSCA in particular. In addition, REACH is forcing multinational firms to produce toxicity and exposure data in order to market their products in Europe. Once reported to the EU, those data might become public or might be provided to EPA.[115] For comparisons of REACH and TSCA, see Government Accountability Office report GAO-07-825, *Chemical Regulation: Comparison of U.S. and Recently Enacted European Union Approaches to Protect against the Risks of Toxic Chemicals*, or Richard Denison's 2007 report *Not That Innocent.*[116] Denison's report also compares REACH and TSCA to the Canadian Environmental Protection Act of 1999.

Scientific Developments and Issues

Toxicology

Toxicology is the study of how chemicals adversely affect the health of individuals. It is an ancient area of study, but its modern form emerged only recently, largely during the 1960s and 1970s. The first textbook of toxicology was published in 1972.[117] Since that time, the science has grown and developed rapidly. The Presidential/Congressional Commission on Risk Assessment and Risk Management, which was established by Congress in the Clean Air Act Amendments of 1990, recommended in 1997 that TSCA "be updated to reflect advances in toxicology and regulation" since TSCA was enacted.[118]

TSCA reflects the concerns of the early days of toxicology, and the knowledge and methods of that first toxicology book. At the time TSCA became law, concerns focused on acute effects, birth defects, or cancer due to accidental poisoning incidents, pharmaceutical drugs, or occupational exposures. Thus, TSCA addresses individual chemicals and does not account for the variety of metabolic processes leading to toxicity, vast individual differences in sensitivity and vulnerability to toxic effects (and consequently, the inherent difficulty of proving that an individual case or group of cases of disease resulted from a particular exposure), or for effects on neurological development, reproduction, the immune system, or endocrine systems.

During the 1990s, Congress directed EPA to conduct its risk assessment taking into account potential:

- vulnerability and sensitivity of developing human embryos and children, as well as other major identifiable subgroups of consumers, to toxic chemicals;[119]
- ability of chemicals to disrupt the functioning of endocrine systems;[120]
- exposure from a variety of sources and environmental media (for example, drinking water as well as workplace air); [121] and
- cumulative exposure from different chemicals that have similar effects on the body.[122]

Although such factors are not excluded as considerations under TSCA, public health advocates have argued that they do not influence decisions enough, given the uncertainties of the toxicology and the need to balance risks and benefits under TSCA.[123]

Computational Toxicology

The most recent innovation with respect to toxicology emerged in the late 1990s and is developing rapidly: computational toxicology.[124] Computational toxicology refers to computer-assisted techniques for estimating risks to human health or the environment based on mathematical models that link scientific knowledge about various chemicals, environmental media (air, water, land, etc.), and the biology of human and other potentially affected organisms. Computational toxicology is particularly valuable for comparing and analyzing large amounts of very detailed biological data, for example on the molecular structure of the human genome and the functions of its parts. This has allowed scientists to identify genetic variations that may make some individuals more or less vulnerable to damage from exposure to certain chemicals. For more information about these emerging techniques, see the interim report by the National Research Council's Committee on Toxicity Testing and Assessment of Environmental Agents.[125]

Computational toxicology also is expected to improve the scientific basis for EPA's decisions about whether to require data collection or to regulate particular chemicals for which data are lacking. Data can be easily and relatively quickly collected on the identities of proteins produced within living cells as they respond to different chemicals or other stressors.[126] Such data indicating biological effects of exposure are generated using rapid, so-called "high-throughput" biochemical tests and recorded in vast databases. The databases then are analyzed for patterns, which may be used to inform models intended to predict the environmental and toxicity characteristics of chemicals not yet tested. By matching this information on the biological response to toxic substances with genomic information, scientists can identify genetic variations more or less susceptible to toxic effects of exposure. A recent report calls for amendments to TSCA that would require such tests, with the aim of more rapidly developing these tools for toxicity assessment.[127]

As mentioned previously, EPA already relies heavily on its quantitative structure-activity relationship (QSAR) models for setting priorities and conducting screening-level risk assessments. These models quantitatively correlate what is known about particular molecular substructures and the biological activity or chemical reactivity of the chemicals in which such structures have been found. The correlations then are used to predict the activity or reactivity of other chemicals with similar structures but for which data are lacking.

If these models become even more reliable predictors of chemical properties, the question may arise whether QSAR is a sufficient basis for an unreasonable risk determination.[128] EPA may make this decision on its own authority, but Congress also might wish to weigh in on that decision. One former EPA Assistant Administrator has argued that the empirical basis for SAR is weak, and that "SAR has allowed both EPA and the chemical industry to defend the TSCA program and to claim that it adequately protects the public."[129] The empirical basis for SAR is expected to strengthen over time, however, and many scientists see SAR positively, as a potentially powerful tool that, in the long term, may reduce costs for the regulated community and reduce the need to require some animal-based toxicity tests.

Exposure Data

When TSCA was enacted, risk assessment was a primitive tool based on simple toxicological models, usually of a single incident of exposure to a single chemical, followed (usually relatively quickly) by an obvious health effect. Multiple, low-level, episodic, or chronic exposures to multiple chemicals were thought to be too complex to model. Today EPA routinely models longterm, low-level exposure through multiple pathways, and sometimes looks at cumulative exposure to different chemicals with similar modes of action.[130] Such complex exposure assessment was mandated by the Food Quality Protection Act of 1996 and is conducted routinely for pesticides.

Research also has determined that the timing of an exposure can be important, especially to a developing fetus or a young child. Thus, if there are data indicating that exposure to a chemical is likely to adversely affect fetal or infant development, rat or mouse experiments may be conducted in which exposure is restricted to particular periods, for example, before or after mating, during the gestation period, or soon after birth.[131]

TSCA does not prevent consideration of aggregate or cumulative exposure or of its timing, but neither does it require them. TSCA also does not provide guidance with respect to the use of such information in regulatory decisions. For example, if an unreasonable risk results from exposure to two or more chemicals, it is not clear whether TSCA authorizes EPA to control the individual chemicals contributing to the risk.[132] Amendments to TSCA might address such issues.

Technological Developments and Issues

Advances in science and technology also are raising some concerns about TSCA, particularly with respect to whether and how EPA's procedures for identifying and managing unreasonable risks might be applied to new forms of chemical substances like genetically modified organisms or nanoparticles.

Genetically Modified Organisms

Soon after TSCA was enacted, entrepreneurs began applying new technologies for cutting, copying, and pasting pieces of genetic material obtained from one organism into another. The resulting genetically modified organisms (GMOs) are useful for various purposes. For example, some could produce specialty enzymes for use by industry or proteins that control plant pests, while others could break down pollutants in the environment. These products of recombined DNA could not have occurred as a result of normal reproduction, but instead required significant human intervention.

Public concerns about the possible human health or environmental effects of GMO products led federal agencies to adopt in 1986 a "Coordinated Framework for Regulation of Biotechnology." The Framework established a federal policy in favor of regulating GMOs that are not naturally occurring and combine genetic material from different genera,[133] or that are capable of causing disease (that is, "pathogens"). In accord with the policy, federal agencies regulate GMOs according to their properties and intended uses under existing statutory authority.[134] For example, EPA regulates GMOs that produce or contain pesticides under the Federal Insecticide, Fungicide, and Rodenticide Act.

EPA regulates GMOs that are not pesticides as new chemical substances under TSCA, unless they are outside the TSCA definition of a chemical substance.135 [136] (For example, a GMO that is food or that produces pharmaceuticals would be regulated by the Food and Drug Administration under the Federal Food, Drug, and Cosmetic Act.) EPA also oversees significant new commercial uses of existing microbes under TSCA Section 5.[137] EPA policy with respect to bioengineered organisms is based on its 1986 interpretation of what constitutes a "new" microorganism, as explained in an EPA Fact Sheet:

> New microorganisms are those microorganisms formed by combining genetic material from organisms in different genera (intergeneric). A genus (pl. genera) is a level in a classification system based on the relatedness of organisms. EPA believes that intergeneric microorganisms have a sufficiently high likelihood of expressing new traits or new combinations of traits to be termed "new" and warrant review.[138]

Some have criticized this interpretation and the resulting regulatory arrangement. For example, a critic noted in 1988, "The first difficulty is that the TSCA gives the EPA authority to regulate 'chemical substances,' and there is some question as to whether living microorganisms developed for deliberate release fall within this definition."[139] A 2004 report by the Pew Initiative on Food and Biotechnology raised the same point.[140] The definition of "chemical substances" subject to TSCA is described above, in the subsection "Policies, Intent, and Scope." Nevertheless, EPA includes microorganisms that are not intergeneric on the inventory of existing "chemical substances" and requires PMNs for intergeneric microorganisms.[141] At least eight microorganism PMNs have been received by OPPT, according to EPA.[142] OPPT has reviewed bacteria for degradation of hazardous wastes, enhanced nitrogen fixation in plants, and for closed system production of enzymes.[143]

Other critics of the current federal Framework believe that the policy (if not the underlying statutes) is dated, particularly in light of the recent use of biotechnology to engineer large animals for various purposes.[144] They raise the question, are cloned mammals or the substances they produce also "new chemical substances" under TSCA? Investment in developing markets for such bioengineered livestock and products reportedly is suffering from a lack of clear federal rules.[145]

On the other hand, many support the current regulatory framework, arguing that the dangers of genetically modified organisms are adequately controlled.[146] Although they admit that there is a possibility that a dangerous new microbe might be created inadvertently, they maintain that the risk is small, and, "Now that genetically altered bacteria have been handled for more than 20 years without disaster, earlier anxieties about mutant germs have diminished."[147]

Nanotechnology

More recently, scientists and engineers have begun to examine, design, and manipulate materials at the molecular level, or nanoscale.[148] At this scale, particles have chemical, physical, and biological properties that vary, depending on particle size and shape, even when particles are made of the same elements. Recent work in biochemistry, physical chemistry, and materials science has advanced to the point that a rapid increase in commercial applications of nanomaterials is expected. Many patents for commercial applications of nanotechnology already are pending, and hundreds of products are being marketed, including many cosmetics, sunscreen, tennis balls, food additives, clothes washers, and odor-free clothing.

While the potential economic gains and beneficial uses for nanotechnology are exciting prospects, the potential risks associated with nanoparticles are a concern for some scientists, policy makers, and industrial trade, consumer, and environmental groups.[149] There is scientific evidence that some nanoparticles may be hazardous. For example, certain nanoparticles are known to be toxic to microbes,[150] and EPA has reported studies that have found nanoparticles generally (but not always) are more toxic than larger particles of identical chemical composition.[151] Yet, such studies are rare, and nanoparticles are diverse, so that one study with one kind of particle may not be informative with respect to the properties of other kinds of particles. Research into the inherent properties and behaviors of various nanoparticles in living organisms or ecosystems is only beginning.[152]

According to EPA, despite the scientific uncertainties surrounding nanoparticles, "EPA has the obligation and mandate to protect human health and safeguard the environment by better understanding and addressing potential risks from exposure to these nanoscale materials and products containing nanoscale materials."[153] Different stakeholders have different views about which TSCA provisions they would like to see used for nanomaterials.

Some environmental groups have argued that all products of nanotechnology are new and should be subject to PMN requirements.[154] Others would prohibit uses of nanomaterials that were untested or unsafe, require a "full lifecycle environmental, health, and safety impact assessments and robust testing prior to commercialization of a nanotechnology-based product," and ensure "full and meaningful participation" by the public and workers.[155] One analyst has suggested that EPA regulation should focus on the specific products of nanotechnology, rather than on more generic nanomaterials.[156] Another view is that the relevant TSCA authority for regulating nanomaterials depends on each material's properties: If the nanomaterial has unique properties that would not be predictable based on the properties of larger forms of the same chemical, then it might be considered "new."[157]

On January 23, 2008, EPA released a document outlining its approach to determining whether a chemical is "new" to the TSCA inventory.[158]

> Certain nanoscale substances that will be manufactured or imported for commercial purposes are expected to be new chemical substances and therefore subject to TSCA new chemical reporting requirements, as are any other new chemical substances ... EPA does not expect, however, that all nanoscale substances will qualify as new chemicals under TSCA. EPA thus intends to determine whether nanoscale substances are new or existing chemical substances based on the case-by-case approach that the Agency has historically applied in determining the Inventory status of chemical substances ... A chemical substance with a molecular identity that is not identical to any chemical substance on the TSCA Inventory is considered to be a new chemical substance (i.e. not on the Inventory); a chemical substance that has the same molecular identity as a substance listed on the Inventory is considered to be an existing chemical substance.[159]

On October 31, 2008, EPA published in the *Federal Register* its determination that carbon nanotubes are distinct from graphite and other forms of carbon and may be new molecular forms requiring submission of PMNs.[160] According to EPA, it has received and reviewed "numerous new chemical notices under TSCA for nanoscale materials," and steps have been take to control or limit exposures by limiting uses, requiring use of personal protective equipment by those who might be exposed to the materials during manufacture or processing, and limiting environmental releases.[161] In addition, EPA has required some testing to generate health and environmental effects data.

EPA does not intend to use particle size in its determination of a chemical's identity.

> Although a nanoscale substance that has the same molecular identity as a non-nanoscale substance listed on the Inventory differs in particle size and may differ in certain physical and/or chemical properties resulting from the difference in particle size, EPA considers the two forms to be the same chemical substance because they have the same molecular identity.[162]

Rather, EPA states that it intends to take size and physical or chemical properties into account when assessing risk of existing chemicals.[163] However, EPA has taken no action to date that would require manufacturers to notify the Agency if new nanoscale uses are proposed for existing chemical substances. The question that arises then is whether EPA would be notified about the existence of commercial nanoscale applications of existing chemicals, and have the opportunity to evaluate them for hazard potential prior to entry to the U.S. market.

It is clear, however, that EPA has been working to become informed about existing and new nanotechnologies, and conferring with stakeholders, as well as counterpart agencies in other nations, about how best to address nanomaterials. The agency has gathered data about nanotechnologies through a voluntary stewardship program known as the Nanoscale Materials Stewardship Program (NMSP). Formally announced October 18, 2006, the program was launched January 28, 2008.[164] Stakeholders were asked to respond within six months. As of August 22, 2008, EPA reported that 22 organizations had submitted information and 10 more had promised to submit information for the basic program. Three organizations agreed to participate in the "in-depth" part of the program.[165]

J. Clarence Davies, who was EPA Assistant Administrator for Policy, Planning and Evaluation during the administration of President George Herbert Walker Bush, and who helped author the original legislative proposal that became TSCA, recently evaluated the law as a means of regulating nanotechnology. His report concluded that the law "is extremely deficient in many respects and needs to be amended."[166]

In the absence of federal regulation, at least one city has acted to regulate nanotechnology. Berkeley, California issued an ordinance December 13, 2006, which requires facilities that handle engineered nanoscale materials to disclose information to the city about the amounts of materials they handle, uses of such material, and benefits and toxicity of the materials.[167] If toxicity and exposure data are unavailable, nanomaterials will be considered by the city to be "toxic" and therefore subject to the same requirements for risk management as other toxic chemicals.[168]

LEGISLATIVE AND ADMINISTRATIVE INITIATIVES

Legislation

The House Committee on Energy and Commerce, Subcommittee on Commerce, Trade, and Consumer Protection held a hearing February 26, 2009, titled "Revisiting the Toxic Substances Control Act of 1976." Witnesses represented diverse perspectives, but all agreed that TSCA should be reviewed, and most supported at least some targeted amendments. Differences were apparent in views with respect to the value of REACH and other laws as models for TSCA reform and the extent to which the basic elements of TSCA Title I should be changed.

Kid Safe Chemicals Act

Companion bills in the 110th Congress, H.R. 6100 and S. 3040, would have amended TSCA, adding a new title to the end of the act, to significantly reshape U.S. chemical assessment and management. Known as the Kid-Safe Chemicals Act of 2008, H.R. 6100/S. 3040 aimed to "eliminate the exposure of all children, workers, consumers, and sensitive subgroups to harmful chemicals distributed in commerce by calendar year 2020." To that end, the bill would have established a safety standard for chemicals in commerce that—

> (A) provides a reasonable certainty that no harm will be caused by aggregate exposure of a fetus, infant, child, worker, or member of other sensitive subgroup to the chemical substance; and

(B) is requisite to protect the public welfare from any known or anticipated adverse effects associated with the chemical substance.

Chemical manufacturers would have been required to submit to EPA: 1) a statement that each chemical they manufacture or import meets the safety standard, or that there are insufficient data to determine whether that is the case, and 2) "all reasonably available information" regarding chemical properties, uses, production volume, exposure, and fate. Based on all available information, EPA then would have been required to categorize all chemicals in commerce based on criteria relating to human exposure, known health effects, and persistence in the environment, and to identify at least 300 high-priority chemicals. The bills would have directed EPA to evaluate manufacturers' safety and data statements for those 300 chemicals within four and a half years of enactment of the Kid-Safe Chemicals Act. H.R. 6100/S. 3040 would have required EPA to evaluate statements within 15 years for all chemicals in commerce as of the date of enactment.

No new chemical would have been permitted to enter U.S. commerce unless EPA had found that the manufacturer had demonstrated conformance with the safety standard. If manufacturers failed to submit required statements or data for a chemical, or if the EPA Administrator determined that a chemical failed to meet the safety standard, then manufacture, importation, and distribution of that chemical in the United States would have been prohibited. EPA would have been authorized to prohibit or permit specific uses.

H.R. 6100/S. 3040 would have established an incentive for manufacturers to conduct studies to determine the level of risk posed by their chemicals by changing the regulatory default status for chemicals lacking toxicity and exposure data from generally permitted to generally banned. EPA would no longer have had to prove that an unreasonable risk may exist in order to require data to be developed. Manufacturers who failed to produce and submit required safety data would have lost the right to market their chemicals in the United States. The bill's requirements for proving safety before marketing, together with its establishment of new programs to inform the public about chemical hazards and uses, and to fund development of "safer" or "greener" chemicals and processes, would have been likely to reduce use over time of the more toxic chemicals in commerce. Reduced use of toxic chemicals has long been a goal of environmental groups.

H.R. 6100/S. 3040 had the strong support of environmental and public health advocacy groups,[169] but was opposed or supported only with reservations by trade groups representing the chemical industry.[170]

Other Proposals

The 110th Congress amended TSCA to address concerns about exports of elemental mercury (H.R. 6) and the quality of elementary and secondary school environments (S. 1534).[171] Other proposals would have amended TSCA to ban asbestos in most products (H.R. 6903, S. 742), eliminate chlorine manufacture using mercury cells (H.R. 5580, S. 1818), or ban manufacture, processing, possession, and distribution in commerce of sodium fluoroacetate (H.R. 4775). H.R. 3085 and companion bill S. 1811 would have amended TSCA to establish a new grant program aimed at reducing exposure of young children to lead-based paint in commercial child-care facilities. H.R. 3643 would have established a Coordinated Environmental Public Health Network to facilitate efforts by local, state, and federal public health agencies to monitor disease rates and environmental hazards.

The 111th Congress is again considering proposals (H.R. 2190 and S. 1428) to reduce exposure to mercury, in part through a TSCA ban on chlorine manufacture using mercury cells. H.R. 2420 would use TSCA to restrict use of lead, mercury, hexavalent chromium, polybrominated biphenyls (PBB), polybrominated diphenyl ethers (PBDE), and cadmium in manufacturing of certain electronic products.

EPA's Initiatives

In August 2007, EPA announced that the United States, Mexico, and Canada had reached an agreement at Montebello, Quebec, at the Security and Prosperity Partnership of North America (SPP) Leaders' Summit.[172,173] The three countries committed to coordinate efforts to assess and manage risks of approximately 9,000 chemicals produced or imported in quantities greater than 25,000 pounds per year. The EPA commitments under the SPP are being fulfilled by the Chemical Assessment and Management Program (ChAMP). EPA will apply the results of EPA's work on roughly 2,000 HPV chemicals and extend its efforts to about 7,000 moderate production volume (MPV) chemicals, relying in part on work completed by Canada's Chemical Management Program. That program was announced by the Canadian government on December 8, 2006,[174] but Canada has been screening and categorizing all 23,000 chemicals on its Domestic Substances List, its equivalent of the TSCA Inventory, since 1999.[175] The Canadian approach to prioritizing chemicals for review, assessment, and management has resulted in new data reporting requirements for the chemicals of highest priority.[176] "EPA plans to use the Canadian results as a starting point for U.S. efforts to assess the hazards, and if data are adequate the risks, of moderate-volume chemicals, using available data and estimation approaches to prepare initial scientific assessments."[177] No new U.S. data will be collected. However, EPA plans to summarize available data and make it available to the public. The first risk-based characterizations for HPV chemicals have been posted online.[178] As of July 2009, EPA had developed and posted risk-based prioritizations for 220 HPV chemicals.[179]

CONCLUSION

It is widely agreed that the regulation of chemicals in U.S. commerce should be based on sound science, cost-benefit analysis, and relative risks, that stakeholders should be involved in developing and evaluating risk-reduction measures, and that chemicals posing unreasonable risks to the environment or public health should be adequately controlled. Congress enacted the Toxic Substances Control Act in 1976 to generate scientific information needed for chemical risk assessment, and to regulate chemicals in a way that would balance public health and environmental risks with economic costs and benefits.

Analysts and policy makers currently are evaluating TSCA performance over the past 30 years and considering how the law is likely to perform in the future. Some analysts, and most in the regulated community, believe that generally TSCA has performed as intended, and they support TSCA in its current form, although most admit it needs minor adjustments. They praise TSCA as a flexible, efficient, and effective limit to over-regulation. Other policy analysts and legal commentators want to amend TSCA, because they think that it has not accomplished the tasks laid out for it by Congress and is unlikely to do better in the future, especially given recent and emerging changes in science and technology.[180] Some would like TSCA amendments that would reduce risk from exposure to existing and emerging chemical hazards through greater restriction of chemical uses.

The available evidence indicates that EPA has had limited success using TSCA to gather information about new chemicals, but has demonstrated creativity and expertise in making use of available information to categorize such chemicals based on hazard potential, thereby reducing risks potentially associated with exposure to chemicals entering U.S. commerce. The agency has had some success in gathering information about existing chemicals, but has regulated only a handful. Based on a lack of expressed concern by stakeholders and the competitive strength of the U.S. chemical industry, EPA also appears to have avoided imposing a regulatory burden that unduly oppresses innovation and commerce.

Whether the amount of chemical regulation in the United States adequately controls unreasonable risks is a key policy question. However, it is clear that a few chemicals posed risks that Congress found unreasonable and TSCA (Title I) failed to control: Congress amended TSCA on four occasions to control risks associated with asbestos, lead, elemental mercury, and radon. Some remain dissatisfied with TSCA. For example, in the 110th Congress, S. 742, as reported by the Senate Committee on Environment and Public Works, and H.R. 6903 would have banned many asbestos-containing materials. Numerous states also have acted to control risks from chemicals that are not regulated under TSCA. In addition, many nations have joined together to regulate persistent, organic, pollutants and persistent, bioaccumulative toxic substances in ways that the United States cannot under the current provisions of TSCA.[181] The European Union adopted a new law, REACH, that takes a different approach to the regulation of chemicals, eliminating the distinction between new and existing chemicals and requiring manufacturers to identify hazards and manage risks for all uses of their chemicals. Multinational companies, therefore, may have to comply with multiple, possibly redundant or conflicting regulations.

Even if one concludes that TSCA has performed successfully in the past, it may be reasonable to question the adequacy of a 1976 chemical law in the light of 30 years of scientific and technological advances. In particular, nanotechnology and GMO advances pose new challenges that many feel require clarified and possibly augmented authority under TSCA, to protect human health and the environment.

Appendix. A Key Court Case

In 1991, the U.S. Court of Appeals for the Fifth Circuit vacated and remanded an EPA rule promulgated under Section 6 that prohibited the manufacture, importation, processing, and distribution of asbestos in almost all products.[182] The substantive heart of the *Corrosion Proof* decision was its conclusion that EPA had insufficiently justified its ban. This conclusion was based on two grounds. First, the court said that EPA failed to give adequate weight to Section 6(a) insistence that the regulatory approach chosen by EPA be the "least burdensome" to achieve the agency-determined acceptable level of (non-zero) risk. EPA's burden was especially difficult here, because the court noted that in imposing an asbestos ban, EPA chose the *most* burdensome of the options afforded by Section 6(a). By analyzing only two scenarios—the ban and no TSCA regulation at all—the court held that EPA failed to show, as TSCA requires, that there was not some *intermediate* regulation that would achieve the acceptable risk level. "[T]he proper course for the EPA to follow is to consider each regulatory option, beginning with the least burdensome, and the costs and benefits of regulation under each option."[183] Only such an exercise assures that the agency has not skipped a less-burdensome alternative.

Second, the court said EPA also must present a stronger case for a ban of products for which substitutes are not now available (as describes some of the asbestos products covered by the ban here), than of products for which substitutes are available. This it did not do. As to asbestos products for which substitutes *are* now available, EPA declined to consider the harm from a probable substitute's increased use, even where it is a known carcinogen, the court added. Thus, EPA cannot assure that its ban will increase workplace safety, depriving the ban of a reasonable basis. To be sure, EPA need not seek out and test every possible substitute, but where interested parties introduce evidence showing the toxicity or decreased safety of probable substitutes, EPA must consider the comparative toxic costs of each—that is, whether its chosen section 6(a) option is increasing workplace safety at all.

As another facet of this insufficient evidence issue, the court determined that EPA failed to consider adequately the *costs* imposed by its ban. Under section 6(a), EPA may regulate only to address "unreasonable risk"—that is, whether "the severity of the injury that may result from the product, factored by the likelihood of the injury, offsets the harm the regulation itself imposes upon manufacturers and consumers."[184] The high costs imposed on industry by the asbestos ban, compared to the small number of lives predicted to be saved, suggested to the court that EPA could not have given the former serious consideration.

Finally, the court examined *both* the failure to examine intermediate options (first ground above) and the insufficiency of evidence (second ground above) as these issues affected specific asbestos products covered by the ban, spelling out the deficiencies in greater detail. For example, in the case of friction products, EPA failed to study the effects of non-asbestos brakes on automotive safety, despite evidence that non-asbestos brakes could increase the number of highway fatalities.

End Notes

[1] 15 U.S.C. 2601-2692.

[2] Title I also contains provisions requiring regulation of PCBs and prohibiting certain activities with respect to elemental mercury (P.L. 110-414). Four titles have been added to TSCA to address other concerns—asbestos in 1986 (Title II, P.L. 99-519), radon in 1988 (Title III, P.L. 100-551), lead in 1992 (Title IV, P.L. 102-550), and, in 2007, school environments (Title V, P.L. 110-140).

[3] For more detailed information about the provisions of TSCA Title I, particularly those that address polychlorinated biphenyls (PCBs) or elemental mercury, or for information about Titles II, III, IV, or V, which concern asbestos, radon, lead, and school environments, respectively, see CRS Report RL31905, *The Toxic Substances Control Act (TSCA): A Summary of the Act and Its Major Requirements*, by Linda-Jo Schierow.

[4] TSCA, Section2(b).

[5] EPA interpretation of these requirements has been assisted by at least two court rulings. More information about the judicial decisions and EPA procedure may be found on the agency's website, "TSCA Section 4 Test Rules," at http://www.epa.gov/oppt/chemtest/pubs/sct4rule.html.

[6] The potential chemical universe (the universe of chemicals that could be synthesized and those that exist but which have not yet been identified) has been described as "unimaginably immense" (Christian Daughton,

2005, "'Emerging' Chemicals as Pollutants in the Environment: a 21st Century Perspective," *Renewable Resources Journal*, v. 23, n. 4, p. 9). The known universe of chemicals is a small fraction of that potential chemical universe: As of February 16, 2007, the Chemical Abstract Service had indexed more than 30 million organic and inorganic chemicals, 12 million of which it classified as "in commerce" worldwide, although it is not clear how this number was determined, and it is much larger than would be expected based on the numbers in national inventories. Roughly 245,000 chemicals were regulated or inventoried, http://www.cas.org/expertise

[7] TSCA Section 4(e).

[8] Interagency Testing Committee homepage, http://www.epa.gov/opptintr/itc/.

[9] Exemptions are authorized at TSCA §5(h), §5(i), and §12. For EPA interpretations of these authorities, see 40 CFR §§720.30, 720,36, and 720.38 and 723.

[10] U.S. EPA, 2008, "Background Discussion Piece: EPA's TSCA Inventory Reset," http://www.epa.gov/CHAMP/pubs/ hpv/INV_Reset_112508.pdf.

[11] 42 *Federal Register* 64572.

[12] Although a NOC technically means the chemical has entered commerce, in fact it may or may not ever be marketed, according to EPA (Charles Auer, personal communication, August 5, 2007).

[13] EPA, Inventory Reset.

[14] The American Chemistry Council (ACC), a trade group for chemical manufacturers, has a fact sheet, "TSCA Myth vs. Fact," on their website that takes issue with statements claiming that there are some 80,000 chemicals in commerce. The ACC argues that many chemicals on the original inventory are no longer "in commerce." http://www.americanchemistry.com/s_acc/bin.asp?SID=1&DID=3384&CID=433&VID=115&DOC

[15] U.S. EPA, 2007, *Overview: Office of Pollution Prevention and Toxics Programs*, p. 6, http://www.epa.gov/oppt/pubs/oppt101c2.pdf.

[16] A polymer is a compound, usually large, composed of numerous copies of a much simpler compound (known as the monomer) which form long chains. Many polymers are not toxic, and therefore are of limited concern to EPA. Criteria for determining whether a polymer is eligible for exemption from PMN requirements may be found at 40 CFR 723.250.

[17] ACC, "Questions and Answers About Chemical Testing and Regulations," July 11, 2005, http://www.americanchemistry.com/s_acc/bin.asp?CID=435&DID=1497&DOC

[18] 68 *Federal Register* 884, January 7, 2003.

[19] 70 *Federal Register* 75059-75070, December 19, 2005.

[20] 68 *Federal Register* 847-906, January 7, 2003.

[21] EPA, Office of Pollution Prevention and Toxics. "Economic Analysis for the Amended Inventory Update Final Rule," August 2002, p. 3-11. This document is available through the EPA docket (EPA-HQ-OPPT-2002-0054) for the rule, at http://www.regulations.

[22] Ibid.

[23] 40 CFR 710.4.

[24] EPA, Inventory Reset.

[25] EPA, Inventory Reset, p. 3.

[26] Regulatory dockets may be accessed through http://www.regulations. The inventory reset docket identification number is EPA-HQ-OPPT-2008-0785.

[27] 40 CFR 723.50.

[28] EPA Overview, p. 10. The EPA report states that the total number of PMNs is 36,600, but that is the same as the number that appeared in the 2003 version of this report. Adding 1,500 notices per year through 2008 results in the 44,000 estimate, which also corresponds to the other EPA statement that roughly half of PMN chemicals enter commerce, or some 22,000 chemicals.

[29] Ibid., p. 10. That percentage drops to 65% for new chemicals that actually enter commerce.

[30] Ibid., p. 8.

[31] Ibid.

[32] Kelly Mayo, EPA OPPT, personal communication, Feb. 25, 2009.

[33] EPA Overview, p. 10.

[34] Because consent orders only bind the PMN submitter, EPA sometimes issues a Significant New Use Rule under Section 5(e) to ensure that other producers or processors must adhere to the same restrictions that were imposed on the PMN submitter. According to EPA (Overview, p. 11), 734 Consent Orders for PMN chemicals were accompanied by SNURs through September 30, 2005.

[35] EPA, "Sustainable futures—Voluntary pilot project under the TSCA new chemicals program; Notice," December 11, 2002, 67 *Federal Register* 76285-86286.

[36] EPA Overview, Appendix B-50.

[37] Reports are available online at http://tsca-itc.syrres.com/Reports/.

[38] John D. Walker, Director, TSCA Interagency Testing Committee, personal communication, October 6, 1999 (CRS requested updated information from EPA but it was not provided); ITC website, "Frequently Asked Questions," http://www.epa.gov/opptintr/itc/pubs/faq.htm.

[39] Walker, personal communication (Updated information was requested but not provided.)

[40] U.S. Congress, Senate, Committee on Environment and Public Works, Subcommittee on Toxic Substances, Research and Development, Hearing, July 13, 1994, "Reauthorization of the Toxic Substances Control Act," S. Hrg. 103-776, statement of Lynn R. Goldman (Washington, DC: U.S. Govt. Print. Off.) p. 136.

[41] EPA Overview, p. 15.

[42] The estimated number of such chemicals, roughly 3,000, has not changed since the late 1970s, but chemical identities have changed: some chemicals produced in high volumes at that time no longer are produced at such high levels, while others are being produced at high volumes now that were not then. Moreover, some chemicals qualify intermittently as high-production volume, being produced in greater volumes in some years and lesser volumes in others.

[43] 40 CFR 712.

[44] EPA Overview, p. 16. For chemicals subject to 8(a) reporting rules, see 40 CFR 704, 710, and 712.

[45] 40 CFR 717.

[46] EPA Overview, p. 16.

[47] 40 CFR 716.

[48] EPA Overview, p. 16.

[49] Ibid.

[50] EPA, Interagency Testing Committee, Substantial Risk Information, TSCA Section 8(e), http://www.epa.gov/oppt/ itc/pubs/sect8e.htm.

[51] EPA Overview, p. 17. The apparent inconsistency between EPA's annual and total numbers is a result of the voluntary Compliance Audit Program (CAP) which allowed manufacturers to file overdue notices and pay pre-set penalties of up to one million dollars. CAP began in 1991 (56 FR 4128, February 1), ended on May 15, 1996 (68 FR 33131, June 3, 2003), and brought in as many as 10,000 notices, http://www.epa.gov/opptintr/tsca8e/pubs/ basicinformation.htm.

[52] EPA, Toxic Substances Control Act Section 8(e) Notices, http://www.epa.gov/oppt/tsca8e/pubs/ 8eandfyisubmissions.html.

[53] EPA, 8(e) and FYI Submissions Received March 2009, http://www.epa.gov/oppt/tsca8e/pubs/8emonthlyreports/ 2009/8emar2009.html.

[54] EPA, 1996 Master Testing List, http://www.epa.gov/opptintr/chemtest/pubs/mtl.html; Greg Schweer, (Chief of the Chemical Information and Testing Branch in OPPT), personal communication, July 27, 2007.

[55] Although the EPA Overview states on page 15 that test data have been generated for about 200 chemicals, that number was not updated from the 2003 draft. It omits the 51 chemicals addressed in test rules published March 16, 2006 (71 *FR* 13707-13735) and April 26, 2004 (69 *FR* 22402-22441). http://www.epa.gov/opptintr/chemtest/pubs/ 4final.html.

[56] U.S. Congress, Senate, Committee on Environment and Public Works, Subcommittee on Toxic Substances, Research and Development, Hearing, May 17, 1994, "Reauthorization of the Toxic Substances Control Act," S. Hrg. 103-776, statement of Lynn R. Goldman (Washington, DC: U.S. Govt. Print. Off.) p. 6.

[57] Ibid., p. 8.

[58] As explained in an earlier section, the provisions of Section 4 authorize test rules only if EPA determines that a chemical "may present an unreasonable risk," or that there is a potential for a substantial quantity to be released into the environment or for substantial or significant human exposure.

[59] U.S. Congress, Senate, Committee on Environment and Public Works, Subcommittee on Toxic Substances, Research and Development, Hearing, May 17, 1994, "Reauthorization of the Toxic Substances Control Act," S. Hrg. 103-776, statement of Lynn R. Goldman. (Washington, DC: U.S. Govt. Print. Off.), p. 6.

[60] National Research Council, *Toxicity Testing for Assessment of Environmental Agents: Interim Report*, (Washington, DC: The National Academies Press, 2006), pp. 100, 112.

[61] U.S. Congress, Senate, Committee on Environment and Public Works, Hearing, August 2, 2006, "Oversight on the Toxic Substances Control Act and the Chemicals Management Program at EPA," submitted testimony of James B. Gulliford.

[62] EPA Overview, p. 17.

[63] Overview, pp. 30-33.

[64] Kathleen M. Roberts (Senior Director, Regulatory and Technical Affairs, American Chemistry Council), personal correspondence, September 5, 2007.

[65] Organisation for Economic Co-operation and Development. "Description of OECD work on investigation of high production volume chemicals," http://www.oecd.org/document/21/0,2340,en_2649_201185_ 1939669_1_1_1_1,00.html.

[66] EPA, "OECD SIDS voluntary testing program for international high production volume chemicals," http://www.epa.gov/oppt/chemtest/pubs/oecdsids.html.

[67] David Roe, William Pease, Karen Florini, and Ellen Silbergeld. *Toxic Ignorance.* (Washington, DC: Environmental Defense Fund, 1997); EPA, Office of Pollution Prevention and Toxics, *Chemical Hazard Data Availability Study,* (Washington, DC: EPA, 1998).

[68] EPA, High Production Volume Information System (HPVIS), http://www.epa.gov/hpv/hpvis/index.html.

[69] Richard A. Denison and Karen Florini. *Facing the Challenge: A Status Report on the U.S. HPV Challenge Program.* (Washington, DC: Environmental Defense, 2003). Richard A. Denison, *Orphan Chemicals in the HPV Challenge: A Status Report.* (Washington, DC: Environmental Defense, 2004). Richard A. Denison, *High Hopes, Low Marks: A Final Report Card on the High Production Volume Chemical Challenge.* (Washington, DC: Environmental Defense, 2007).

[70] Denison 2007, p. 11-12.

[71] Ibid., p. 11.

[72] Environmental Defense, "Welcome to the HPV Chemical Tracker," 2008, http://www.edf.org/documents/2734_WelcomeTracker.htm?redirect=hpvtracker.

[73] Denison, p. 23.

[74] Ibid., p. 11.

[75] Jim Willis, "High Production Volume (HPV) Challenge Program – Future Directions," presentation to the First U.S. Conference on Characterizing Chemicals in Commerce: Using Data on High Production Volume (HPV) Chemicals, Austin, Texas, December 13, 2006.

[76] EPA Overview, p. 34.

[77] The basic screening data being collected includes data for four health-related endpoints (acute toxicity, chronic toxicity, mutagenicity, and reproductive effects/developmental toxicity), ecological effects, and environmental fate endpoints.

[78] EPA 1998.

[79] Physicians' Committee for Responsible Medicine, "The Availability of HPV Chemical Data," http://www.pcrm.org/resch/anexp/hpv_report.html; James W. Conrad, Jr., "Open Secrets: The Widespread Availability of Information about the Health and Environmental Effects of Chemicals," *Law & Contemporary Problems,* v. 69 (Summer 2006.) pp. 141-165.

[80] EPA, Office of Pollution Prevention and Toxics, "Economic analysis for the amended inventory update final rule," August 2002, pp. 2-8.

[81] EPA Overview, p. 8.

[82] Wendy E. Wagner, "Commons ignorance: The failure of environmental law to produce needed information on health and the environment," *Duke Law Journal*, v. 53 (2004), pp. 1619-1745; David W. Case, "The EPA's HPV Challenge Program: A toxic tort liability trap?" *Washington & Lee Law Review*, v. 62 (2005), pp. 147-206.

[83] EPA Overview, p. 20. EPA also devotes significant resources to so-called "national program chemicals," which include dioxin, mercury, and the chemicals addressed explicitly by TSCA Section 6(e) and Titles II through IV, PCBs, asbestos, radon, and lead, respectively. With respect to these chemicals, EPA coordinates federal activities as well as international efforts to reduce risks.

[84] EPA Overview, p. 20.

[85] EPA Overview, p. 20. Also see 40 CFR Parts 747, 749, 761, and 763, respectively.

[86] Ed Brooks, "Evolution of Risk Management of Existing Chemicals Under TSCA," In: *TSCA at Twenty, Chemicals in the Environment: Public Access Information*, Issue 4 (Fall 1996), EPA 749-R-96-001, EPA, Washington, DC.

[87] The chemicals were 4,4-Methylenedianiline (48 *FR* 42898, September 20, 1983), 1,3-Butadiene (48 *FR* 20524, May 15, 1984), and four glycol ethers (51 *FR* 18488, May 20, 1986).

[88] 55 *FR* 53047, December 26, 1990.

[89] U.S. Congress, Senate, Committee on Environment and Public Works, Subcomittee on Toxic Substances, Research and Development, Hearing, July 13, 1994, "Reauthorization of the Toxic Substances Control Act," S. Hrg. 103-776, statement of Lynn R. Goldman, (Washington, DC: U.S. Govt. Print. Off.), p. 140.

[90] This section of the report was written chiefly by Robert Meltz, Legislative Attorney, CRS American Law Division.

[91] *Corrosion Proof Fittings v. EPA*, 947 F.2d 1201 (5th Cir. 1991).

[92] See, for example, Thomas O. McGarrity, *Professor Sunstein's Fuzzy Math*, 90 Geo. L. J. 2341, 2376 (2002); Thomas Sullivan (ed.), ENVIRONMENTAL LAW HANDBOOK 573 (16th ed.) (2001); Robert B. Haemer, *Reform of the Toxic Substances Control Act: Achieving Balance in the Regulation of Toxic Substances*, 6 Envtl. Lawyer 99, 115 (1999); and Joyce Merritt, Comment, *Standard of Review Under the Toxic Substances Control Act:* Corrosion Proof Fittings v. EPA, 8 J. Nat. Res. & Envtl. L. 167, 176 (1992/1993).

[93] Robert B. Haemer, "Reform of the Toxic Substances Control Act: Achieving balance in the regulation of toxic substances," *Environmental Lawyer*, v. 6, n. 99 (1999), pp. 118-119.

[94] Id. at 126. Contrary to the criticisms of those who would rewrite toxic substance control statutes, or restrict the scope of judicial review under these statutes, *Corrosion Proof Fittings* illustrates the importance of the substantive protections accorded private parties under the current toxic substances regulatory statutes. ... *Corrosion Proof Fittings* is a case study in how judicial review can prevent inefficient and wasteful regulation of toxic substances.[96]

[95] Carnegie Commission on Science, Technology, and Government, *Risk and the Environment: Improving Regulatory Decision Making.* (New York: Carnegie Commission on Science, Technology, and Government, 1993).

[96] Granta Nakayama, "Corrosion Proof Fittings v. EPA: No Death Penalty for Asbestos Under TSCA," *George Mason Independent Law Review*, v. 1 (1992), pp. 99-101.

[97] However, the 110th Congress amended Title I when it enacted P.L. 110-414, which prohibits certain activities with respect to elemental mercury.

[98] A general compendium of information about state chemical policies is provided electronically by the University of Massachusetts, Lowell, at http://www.chemicalspolicy.org/usstatelevel.shtml. Restrictions include a total ban on decabrominated diphenyl ether in Washington and restrictions on formaldehyde emissions from certain wood products by the California Air Resources Board. ("Washington State Passes PBDE Ban. Policy News," April 27, 2007, *Environmental Science & Technology*, v. 41, n. 9, p. 2655; Carolyn Whetzel, "California Adopts Emission Standards For Formaldehyde From Wood Products," *Daily Environment Reporter*, May 2, 2007, p. A-2, http://www.arb.ca.gov/regact/2007/compwood07/compwood07.htm.)

[99] National Conference of State Legislatures, "Agriculture: Biotechnology Statutes Chart," http://www.ncsl.org/programs/agri/biotchlg.htm.

[100] Daryl Ditz, "Cloudy Skies, Chance of Sun: A Forecast for U.S. Reform of Chemicals Policy," (Washington, DC: Center for International Environmental Law, 2006); Traci Watson, "States and cities move to curb toxic substances the EPA hasn't," *USA Today*, May 5, 2007, http://www.usatoday.com/news/washington/2007-05-07-epachemicals_N.htm?csp=34.

[101] Jordan Rau, "Legislature Targets Toxic Risks in Products," *Los Angeles Times*, May 30, 2005; California Senate bill SB 973, Chemicals of Concern, introduced February 23, 2007, http://www.leginfo.ca.gov/pub/07-08/bill/sen/sb_0951- 1000/sb_973_bill_20070223_introduced.html.

[102] Michael P. Wilson, *Green Chemistry in California: A Framework for Leadership in Chemicals Policy and Innovation*, (Berkeley: California Policy Research Center, University of California, 2006), http://coeh.berkeley.edu/ greenchemistry/.

[103] Ibid.

[104] "Stakeholders mull need for strategy to address emerging chemical issues," special report, April 30, 2007, *Daily Environment Report,* p. B-1.

[105] Michael P. Wilson, Testimony before the California Senate Environmental Quality Committee, June 28, 2006, Sacramento, CA.

[106] Pat Phibbs-Rizzuto, "State efforts to restrict chemicals rising, speakers at global chemical conference say," *Daily Environment Report*, March 12, 2007, p. A-4.

[107] TSCA Section 18 preempts state and local actions that establish or continue in effect requirements applicable to a chemical substance or mixture that is regulated federally under TSCA Section 5 or 6, unless a state requirement is identical to the federal requirement, implements another federal law, or prohibits use of the

substance or mixture within the state. Section 18 allows a state to ask EPA to allow a state requirement that provides a significantly higher degree of protection from risk than does the federal requirement.

108 American Electronics Association, "AeA International Environment Overview, Issues Summary," http://aeanet.org/ GovernmentAffairs/gamb_EnvOverview.asp.

109 For more information about these international agreements, see CRS Report RS22379, *Persistent Organic Pollutants (POPs): Fact Sheet on Three International Agreements*, by Linda-Jo Schierow.

110 Generally, the European Commission describes the precautionary principle as a risk management strategy used when "there are reasonable grounds for concern that potential hazards may affect the environment or human, animal or plant health, and when at the same time the available data preclude a detailed risk evaluation." In applying the precautionary principle, the EU strives to achieve a high level of protection by taking protective action before all relevant scientific knowledge is available. The EU definition of the precautionary principle is being refined over time by case law and through the diverse contexts in which it is employed. For a thorough discussion of the precautionary principle see the Communication from the Commission of the European Communities which was issued in the year 2000. http://ec.europa eu/dgs/health consumer/library/pub/pub07_en.pdf.

111 Meghan Purvis, "EU: Burden of proof shifted to chemical maker," The Forum: Who's Ahead In Environmental Protection: The United States or the European Union? *The Environmental Forum*, (March/April, 2006), p. 50.

112 ACC, Registration, Evaluation, and Authorization of Chemicals, http://www.americanchemistry.com/s_acc/ secjolicyissues.asp?CID=621&DID=2217.

113 ACC, TSCA Fact Sheet, August 2, 2006, http://www.americanchemistry.com/s_acc/bin.asp?SID=1&DID=2766& CID=433&VID=115&DOC=File.PDF.

114 Pat Rizzuto, "Canadian, U.S. Trade Associations Praise Trilateral Agreement on Chemical Reviews," *Daily Environment Report*, August 22, 2007, p. A-2.

115 For more information about REACH, see CRS Report RS22673, *Chemical Regulation in the European Union: Registration, Evaluation, and Authorization of Chemicals*, by Linda-Jo Schierow.

116 Denison, 2007.

117 Louis J. Casarett and John Doull (Eds.), *Toxicology: The Basic Science of Poisons*. (New York: Macmillan, 1975).

118 Commission on Risk Assessment and Risk Management, *Risk Assessment and Risk Management in Regulatory Decision-Making,* Final Report, Vol. 2 (1997), p. 126.

119 Food Quality Protection Act of 1976, P.L. 104-170, Section 405, which amended the Federal Food, Drug, and Cosmetic Act, Section 408(b)(2)(C) and (D).

120 Food Quality Protection Act of 1976, P.L. 104-170, Section 405, which amended the Federal Food, Drug, and Cosmetic Act, Section 408 by adding subsection (p). Safe Drinking Water Act, 42 USC Sections 300F-300j-26.

121 Food Quality Protection Act of 1976, P.L. 104-170, Section 405, which amended the Federal Food, Drug, and Cosmetic Act, Section 408(b)(2)(D).

122 Ibid.

123 Children's Environmental Health Network, "In Support of Child-Safe U.S. Chemical Policies: Statement of Principles," (April 2005), http://www.cehn.org/cehn/chemicals Child%20Safe%20Chemicals%20Statement%20of%20Principles.htm.

124 Computational toxicology also is referred to as *in silico* toxicology, as opposed to *in vitro* toxicology, which refers to toxicology based on experiments using tissues grown in laboratory glassware, or *in vivo* toxicology, referring to toxicology based on observation of living organisms.

125 Committee on Toxicity Testing and Assessment of Environmental Agents, National Research Council, *Toxicity Testing for Assessment of Environmental Agents: Interim Report*, (Washington, DC: The National Academies Press, 2006), pp. 194-221.

126 The application of computers to analyze biological information is known as bioinformatics. When the biological information being studied is the proteins being manufactured within the cells of a particular tissue at a particular time, the field of study is known as proteomics. When the focus is on the function of various portions of a genome (human or otherwise), the field is called genomics. When the focus is on how genomes are affected by exposure to toxic substances, the field is called toxicogenomics.

127 Reut Snir, *Applying Toxicogenomics Data in Chemical Regulation*. Foresight and Governance Project, Woodrow Wilson International Center for Scholars, Washington, DC (2007), 29 pp.

128 No one has argued to date that QSAR is suitable for any purpose other than screening.

[129] J. Clarence Davies, *EPA and Nanotechnology: Oversight for the 21st Century*, Woodrow Wilson International Center for Scholars, Project on Emerging Nanotechnologies, Washington, DC (2007), p. 18, http://www.nanotechproject.org.

[130] For a description of modern techniques for toxicity testing, see Chapter 2 in Toxicity Testing for Assessment of Environmental Agents: Interim Report, by the Committee on Toxicity Testing and Assessment of Environmental Agents, National Research Council, published in 2006 by the National Academies Press in Washington, DC.

[131] Ibid.

[132] However, there may be a precedent for EPA action based on potential effects due to combinations of chemicals. According to EPA, metal working fluids were regulated because they could combine with nitrates or nitrites to form carcinogenic nitrosamines (Charles Auer, personal communication, August 5, 2007).

[133] That is, the covered organism has genetic material from two organisms that would not be joined in nature because they are not of the same species. "Genera" is plural for genus, "a level in a classification system based on the relatedness of organisms" as defined in the EPA fact sheet at http://www.epa.gov/oppt/biotech/pubs/pdf/fs-002.pdf.

[134] David T. Kingsbury, Regulation of Biotechnology: A. Perspective on the US 'Coordinated Framework,' Chapter 14. In: *SCOPE 44 Introduction of Genetically Designed Organisms into the Environment*, H.A. Mooney & G. Bernardi eds., (U.K.: Wiley, 1990.), http://www.icsu-scope

[135] Rules for products of biotechnology may be found in the Code of Federal Regulations, Title 40, Part 725. The rules also are posted online at http://www.epa.gov/biotech_rule/.

[136] U.S. Congress, House of Representatives, Committee on Agriculture, Subcommittee on Conservation, Credit, and Research, Hearing, June 17, 2003, testimony of Stephen Johnson, Assistant Administrator, Office of Prevention, Pesticides, and Toxic Substances, U.S. EPA.

[137] Ibid.

[138] EPA, "Microbial products of biotechnology: Final regulations under the Toxic Substances Control Act summary," http://www.epa.gov/biotech_rule/pubs/fs-001.htm.

[139] Gary Marchant, "Modified Rules for Modified Bugs: Balancing Safety and Efficiency in the Regulation of Deliberate Release of Genetically Engineered Microorganisms." *Harvard Journal of Law and Technology*, v. 1, (Spring 1988), pp. 163-208.

[140] Pew Initiative on Food and Biotechnology, "Issues in the Regulation of Genetically Engineered Plants and Animals," Executive Summary (2004), p. 9, http://pewagbiotech.org/research/regulation/.

[141] 40 CRF §725.3.

[142] EPA Overview, p. 12.

[143] EPA Overview, Appendix, p. B-11.

[144] Pew Initiative on Food and Biotechnology, pp. 6-7.

[145] Andrew Pollack, "Without U.S. rules, biotech food lacks investors," *New York Times*, July 30, 2007, http://www.nytimes.com/2007/07/30/washington/30animal.html?_r=1&scp=2&sq=July%2030, %202007&st =cse.

[146] U.S. Congress, House of Representatives, Committee on Agriculture, Subcommittee on Conservation, Credit, and Research, Hearing, June 17, 2003, testimony of Stephen Johnson, Assistant Administrator, Office of Prevention, Pesticides, and Toxic Substances, U.S. EPA.

[147] Eric S. Grace, *Biotechnology Unzipped: Promises and Realities*, Revised 2nd edition. (Washington DC: Joseph Henry Press, 2006), p. 216.

[148] A nanometer is one-billionth of a meter, which is about 1/75,000 of a human hair or the width of ten hydrogen atoms in a line. A bacterium is a few hundred nanometers across. Nanoscience may be defined as the study of the fundamental principles of molecules and other structures with at least one dimension roughly between 1 and 100 nanometers. For a more detailed explanation of nanotechnology, see *Nanotechnology: A Gentle Introduction to the Next Big Idea*, by Mark and Daniel Ratner (Upper Saddle River, NJ: Prentice Hall, 2003). For standard terminology relevant to nanotechnology, see ASTM Standard E 2456—06 at http://www.astm.org.

[149] Environmental Defense and American Chemistry Council, Nanotechnology Panel Joint Statement of Principles, Comments on EPA's Notice of a Public Meeting on Nanoscale Materials, 70 *Federal Register* 24574, June 23, 2005, http://www.environmentaldefense.org/documents/4857_ACC-ED_nanotech.pdf.

[150] Silver, for example, is toxic, and some product manufacturers have made antibacterial claims for their products containing nanosilver. In addition, research has demonstrated the toxicity of C_{60} fullerenes to bacteria in water

under laboratory conditions (J. D. Fortner, D. Y. Lyon, C. M. Sayes, et al. "C60 in water: Nanocrystal formation and microbial response," *Environmental Science & Technology*, v. 39, (2005), pp. 4307-4316.)

[151] Science Policy Council, U.S. Environmental Protection Agency's Nanotechnology White Paper, EPA 100/B-07/001, (Washington, DC: U.S. Environmental Protection Agency, 2007), p. 54.

[152] Naturally occurring nanoparticles exist, and some (for example particles in exhaust from diesel fuel) have been studied for years.

[153] EPA Fact Sheet for Nanotechnology under the Toxic Substances Control Act, http://www.epa.gov/oppt/nano/nanofacts.htm#usf.

[154] John Balbus, Richard Denison, Karen Florini, and Scott Walsh. "Getting Nanotechnology Right the First Time," *Issues in Science and Technology*, (Summer 2005), pp. 65-71.

[155] Natural Resources Defense Council, "Health facts: Nanotechnology's invisible threat: Small science, big consequences," (December 2006), http://www.nrdc.org/health

[156] Davies, p. 23.

[157] Pat Rizzuto, "EPA Reviews 15 New Nanoscale Chemicals," *Daily Environment Report*, v. 158, (August 16, 2006), p. A-7.

[158] EPA, TSCA Inventory Status of Nanoscale Substances – General Approach (2008), http://www.epa.gov/oppt/nano/ nmsp-inventorypaper2008.pdf.

[159] Ibid., p. 3. The document elaborates: "EPA views molecular identity as being based on such structural and compositional features as the types and number of atoms in the molecule, the types and number of chemical bonds, the connectivity of the atoms in the molecule, and the spatial arrangement of the atoms within the molecule. EPA considers chemical substances that differ in any of these structural and compositional features to have different molecular identities."

[160] 73 Federal Register 64946-64947, Oct. 31, 2008.

[161] EPA, "Nanotechnology under the Toxic Substances Control Act," http://www.epa.gov/oppt/nano/.

[162] Ibid.

[163] Ibid.

[164] EPA, Nanotechnology under the Toxic Substances Control Act, http://www.epa.gov/oppt/nano/#stewardship.

[165] EPA, Nanoscale Materials Stewardship Program.

[166] Davies, p. 5.

[167] Pat Phibbs-Rizzuto, "Toxic substances makers, users of nanomaterials in Berkeley must provide certain data to city by June," *Daily Environment Report*, v. 86, May 4, 2007, p. A-3.

[168] For more information about engineered nanomaterials and some challenges associated with regulating nanotechnology, see CRS Report RL34332, *Engineered Nanoscale Materials and Derivative Products: Regulatory Challenges*, by Linda-Jo Schierow, or CRS Report RL34511, *Nanotechnology: A Policy Primer*, by John F. Sargent Jr.

[169] For example, see the Environmental Working Group blog on the Kid-Safe Chemicals Act (in the 110th Congress, H.R. 6100/S. 3040) at http://www.ewg.org/kid-safe-chemicals

[170] For example, see the May 21, 2008, press release of the American Chemistry Council, http://www.americanchemistry.com/newsroom.

[171] For more information about these provisions, see CRS Report RL31905, *The Toxic Substances Control Act (TSCA): A Summary of the Act and Its Major Requirements*, by Linda-Jo Schierow.

[172] EPA, EPA Newsroom, "U.S., Canada and Mexico Take Lead to Manage Industrial Chemicals," August 21, 2007, http://yosemite.epa.gov/opa/admpress.nsf/d0cf6618525a9efb85257359003fb69d/77660c0da9fe643e8525733e0065d48b!OpenDocument.

[173] Regulatory Cooperation in the Area of Chemicals, 2007 Joint Statement: Prime Minister Harper, President Bush and President Calderón, North American Leaders' Summit, August 21, 2007, Security and Prosperity Partnership of North America, http://www.spp.gov/pdf/spp_reg_coop_chemicals

[174] Government of Canada, "Chemical Substances," http://www.chemicalsubstanceschimiques.gc.ca/en/.

[175] Environment Canada, "Existing Substances Evaluation, CEPA Registry, Domestic Substances List Categorization and Screening Program," http://www.ec.gc.ca/substances/ese/eng/dsl/dslprog.cfm.

[176] Richard A. Denison, *Not That Innocent*. (Washington, DC: Environmental Defense, 2007), p. IV-3.

[177] EPA, Press release, August 21, 2007.

[178] EPA, "HPV Chemical Hazard Characterizations," http://iaspub.epa.gov/oppthpv/ hpv_hc_characterization .get_report.

[179] EPA, "Risk-Based Prioritization (RBP) Decisions Summary," http://www.epa.gov/champ/pubs/hpv/2009-RBPDecisions.pdf.

[180] Wilson. *Green Chemistry*, p. 16.

[181] However, the United States does regulate these chemicals. For more on these international agreements and issues related to them, see CRS Report RS22379, *Persistent Organic Pollutants (POPs): Fact Sheet on Three International Agreements*, by Linda-Jo Schierow.

[182] *Corrosion Proof Fittings v. EPA*, 947 F.2d 1201 (5th Cir. 1991).

[183] Id. at 1217.

[184] Id. at 1222.

In: Toxic Substances Control Act ISBN: 978-1-62100-783-8
Editors: Shannon M. McDonnery and Cindy L. Elroy

Chapter 3

PROPOSED REFORM OF THE TOXIC SUBSTANCES CONTROL ACT (TSCA) IN THE 112TH CONGRESS: S. 847 COMPARED WITH CURRENT LAW*

Linda-Jo Schierow

SUMMARY

Thirty-five years of experience implementing and enforcing the Toxic Substances Control Act (TSCA) have demonstrated the strengths and weaknesses of the law and led many to propose legislative changes to TSCA's core provisions. Stakeholders appear to agree that TSCA needs to be updated, although there is disagreement about the extent and nature of any proposed revisions. S. 847 in the 112th Congress legislation would amend core provisions of TSCA Title I. This report compares key provisions of S. 847, as introduced, with current law (15 U.S.C. 2601 *et seq.*).

Generally, S. 847 would increase the amount of information about chemical toxicity and usage that chemical manufacturers and processors would be required to submit to the U.S. Environmental Protection Agency (EPA), and would facilitate EPA regulation of toxic chemicals. The bill directs EPA to establish, by rule, varied or tiered minimum data set requirements for different chemical substances or categories of substances. Data would be required from chemical manufacturers and processors for all chemicals within 5 years of the date of enactment of S. 847, earlier for high-priority chemicals. All chemicals already in commerce are to be placed on a list and prioritized by EPA into three groups based on the need for risk management. A chemical must be included in the highest priority class if it "is, or is degraded and metabolized into, a persistent, bioaccumulative, and toxic substance with the potential for widespread exposure to humans or other organisms." EPA is required to determine whether chemicals in the top two priority classes, as well as all new chemicals, meet a stringent new safety standard, given the imposition of any needed restrictions on manufacture, processing, distribution, use, or disposal. The bill would prohibit any activities with respect to an evaluated chemical substance that the EPA had not specifically allowed in the safety standard determination.

---

* This is an edited, reformatted and augmented version of a Congressional Research Service publication, CRS Report for Congress, R41937, from www.crs.gov, dated July 25, 2011.

In contrast, current law authorizes data collection from manufacturers only if exposure is expected to be substantial or if EPA determines that a chemical may pose an unreasonable risk. TSCA as currently written allows all chemicals to enter and remain in commerce unless EPA can show that a chemical poses "an unreasonable risk of injury to health or the environment." EPA then must regulate to control unreasonable risk, but only to the extent necessary using the "least burdensome" means of available control. This TSCA standard has been interpreted to require cost-benefit balancing.

S. 847 also would add new sections to TSCA. Of particular significance is a section authorizing actions that would allow U.S. implementation of three international agreements, which the United States has signed but not yet ratified. Other new sections would provide authority for EPA to support research in so-called "green" engineering and chemistry, promote alternatives to toxicity testing on animals, encourage research on children's environmental health, and require biomonitoring of pregnant women and infants. A "hot spots" provision would require EPA to identify locations where residents are disproportionately exposed to pollution and to develop strategies for reducing their risks. Key provisions of S. 847 are compared with current law in Tables 1 through 6.

INTRODUCTION

In 1976, President Gerald R. Ford signed the Toxic Substances Control Act (15 U.S.C. 2601 *et seq.*; TSCA), giving the U.S. Environmental Protection Agency (EPA) authority to regulate production and use of industrial chemicals not otherwise regulated in U.S. commerce.[1] Thirty-five years of experience with TSCA implementation and enforcement have demonstrated the strengths and weaknesses of the law and led many to propose legislative changes to TSCA's core provisions in Title I. [2] Based on hearing testimony, stakeholders generally agree that TSCA needs to be updated, although there is disagreement about the extent and nature of any proposed revisions.[3] Democrats introduced legislation to amend TSCA Title I in the 111th Congress (S. 3209 and H.R. 5820), but Congress did not vote on either bill. On April 14, 2011, Senator Frank Lautenberg introduced similar, but not identical, legislation (S. 847) in the 112th Congress. To date, no other legislation has been introduced that would amend core provisions of TSCA Title I. Therefore, this report compares key provisions of S. 847, as introduced, with provisions of TSCA Title I (15 U.S.C. 2601 *et seq.*) that would be affected if S. 847 becomes law. These provisions are summarized in Tables 1 through 5. New provisions that would be added to the end of TSCA Title I by S. 847—for example, those related to reduced use of animals for toxicity testing—are summarized in Table 6.

EFFECTS OF THE PROPOSED LEGISLATION ON CURRENT LAW

S. 847 would not affect Titles II through VI of TSCA, nor would it change the basic organization of TSCA Title I. For example, provisions related to testing would still be in Section 4, requirements for notifying EPA when a new chemical or new use is proposed would still be in Section 5, and regulatory authorities would remain in Section 6. Also unaffected would be changes to TSCA Title I that were enacted during the 110th Congress, such as a provision that bans exports of elemental mercury.[4] However, S. 847 would amend or delete most of the original Title I provisions and would make substantial additions to current law. Some key changes are summarized below.

Minimum Data Set Requirements

S. 847, as introduced, directs the EPA Administrator to establish varied or tiered minimum data set requirements for different chemical substances or categories of substances. Manufacturers would be given a specified period of time to produce and submit data meeting the minimum data requirements for chemicals that are already in commerce and for any new chemicals that they propose to manufacture. Data sets would have to be submitted within 5 years of the date of enactment of S. 847.

Current law does not routinely require submission of data for chemicals, but EPA has the authority to require data submission if it promulgates a rule based on a finding that a chemical "may present an unreasonable risk of injury to health or the environment" and the agency demonstrates a data need.

Prioritization of Chemicals

S. 847 directs the EPA Administrator to prioritize all chemicals already in commerce for evaluation and risk management by establishing a list that "contains the names of the chemical substances that ... warrant placement within 1 of 3 priority classes ... and identifies the priority class to which each listed chemical substance or category of chemical substance has been assigned by the Administrator." Priority class 1 chemicals would be defined as those "... that the Administrator determines require immediate risk management." The Administrator would be required to place between 20 and 30 chemicals in this category, and the data set for a high-priority chemical would have to be submitted within 18 months of its placement on the priority class 1 list. Priority class 2 chemicals would be defined as those "that the Administrator determines require safety standard determinations ... based on any more-than-theoretical concern, that there is uncertainty as to whether a chemical substance would satisfy the safety standard." Priority class 3 chemicals would be defined as those "that the Administrator determines require no immediate action."

Chemicals are not prioritized under current law.

Safety Standard and Burden of Proof

The Senate bill would establish a health-based safety standard for chemical use that protects vulnerable populations: manufacturers would be required to produce scientific data demonstrating "there is a reasonable certainty that no harm will result to human health or the environment from aggregate exposure to the chemical substance." S. 847 would prohibit manufacture, processing, and distribution of any chemical substance for any use that had not been included in the safety determination issued for that chemical. Moreover, an exemption from a prohibition would be allowed for a particular use only if: it were "in the paramount interest of national security"; lack of the chemical use "would cause significant disruption in the national economy"; the use were essential or critical and there were no safer feasible alternative; or the chemical use, relative to alternatives, provided a benefit to health, the environment, or public safety.

In contrast, current law allows manufacture of and commerce in a chemical unless EPA promulgates a rule including a finding that a chemical presents or will present an "unreasonable risk" to human health or the environment. If EPA demonstrates that a risk associated with a chemical is unreasonable (relative to the benefits provided by the chemical and the estimated risks and benefits of any alternatives), the Agency is required to regulate, but only to the extent necessary to reduce that risk to a reasonable level and using "the least burdensome" restriction.

EPA Authority to Manage Risks

S. 847 would expedite regulatory action, relative to the process under current law, by authorizing EPA in some cases to issue administrative orders instead of rules (which must be promulgated under current law), exempting certain EPA decisions from judicial review, and removing certain TSCA requirements that are in addition to requirements specified in the Administrative Procedure Act (5 U.S.C. 553) for notice and comment rulemaking.

The scope of EPA oversight also would be expanded by S. 847. As introduced, the bill includes language that allows EPA to define various distinct forms of substances that are the same in terms of molecular identity but differ in structure and function, such as manufactured nanoscale forms of carbon and silver. The introduced bill also broadens the scope of environmental risks that EPA may manage to include risks found in the indoor environment; currently, TSCA applies only to chemicals in the ambient environment. S. 847 also would appear to more clearly authorize EPA control of risks posed by articles containing a substance.

The proposed amendments to TSCA would increase public access to information about EPA's decisions, as well as to some information about chemicals that currently is treated as confidential business information.

S. 847 would authorize EPA activities not currently authorized under TSCA to allow implementation of three international agreements pertaining to persistent organic pollutants and other hazardous chemicals. For example, the proposal would authorize EPA to regulate chemicals manufactured solely for export. The authority provided by the bill would be specific to three international agreements, rather than more generally authorizing regulatory activity to implement any ratified international agreement concerning chemicals. The bill would prohibit production and use of chemicals when it was inconsistent with U.S. obligations under any of the three international agreements after they had entered into force for the United States.

State Preemption

The effect of TSCA on state and local chemical laws would be modified by S. 847, as introduced. Current law, TSCA Section 18, generally does not preempt state laws. However, if EPA requires testing of a chemical under section 4, no state may require testing of the same substance for similar purposes. Similarly, if EPA prescribes a rule or order under section 5 or 6, no state or political subdivision may have a requirement for the same substance to protect against the same risk unless the state or local requirement is identical to the federal requirement, is adopted under authority of another federal law, or generally prohibits the use of the substance in the state or political subdivision. TSCA authorizes states and political subdivisions to petition EPA, and authorizes EPA to grant petitions, by rule, to exempt a law in effect in a state or political subdivision under certain circumstances. A petition may be granted if compliance with the requirement would not cause activities involving the substance to be in violation of the EPA requirement, and the state or local requirement provides a significantly higher degree of protection from the risk than the EPA requirement does, but does not "unduly burden interstate commerce." S. 847 would simplify this section of TSCA. An amended TSCA would not preempt laws relating to a chemical substance, mixture, or article unless compliance with both federal and the state or local law were impossible.

Miscellaneous Provisions

Several new provisions are included in S. 847. One provision, for example, would require definition and listing of localities with populations that are "disproportionately exposed" to toxic chemicals. EPA would be directed to develop an action plan to reduce exposure in such "hot spots."

EPA would be required to establish a program to create market incentives for the development of safer alternatives to existing chemical substances that reduce or avoid the use and generation of hazardous substances. The program would be required to expedite review of a new chemical substance if an alternatives analysis indicated it was a safer alternative, and to recognize a substance or product determined by EPA to be a safer alternative.

Another provision would direct the EPA Administrator to coordinate with the Secretary of Health and Human Services to conduct a biomonitoring study to determine whether a chemical that research had indicated may be present in human biological substances and that may have adverse effects on human development in fact was present in pregnant women and infants. If the chemical were found to be present, manufacturers and processors would have to disclose to EPA, commercial customers, consumers, and the general public all known uses of the chemical and all articles in which the chemical was expected to be present.

Children's environmental health also is addressed by the bill. It would establish a children's environmental health research program at EPA and an advisory committee to provide independent advice relating to implementation of TSCA and protection of children's health.

S. 847, as introduced, also establishes at least four research centers to encourage the development of safer alternatives to existing hazardous chemical substances. "Green chemistry and engineering" also would be promoted through grants.

Finally, S. 847 would direct EPA to minimize use of animals in toxicity testing. An advisory committee would be established to publish a list of testing methods that reduce use of animals. This provision aims to expedite development of so-called "alternative testing methods," which have been under development for many years, but remain a minor component of toxicity testing programs.

Tables 1 through 6 summarize these and other selected provisions of S. 847.

Table 1. Titles and Definitions in Selected Provisions of TSCA (15 U.S.C. 2601 et seq.) and the Safe Chemicals Act (S. 847), as Introduced

Provision	15 U.S.C. 2601 et seq.	S. 847
Title	Toxic Substances Control Act (TSCA)	Safe Chemicals Act of 2011 (SCA)
Revised definitions	TSCA definitions are in alphabetical order in section 3 (15 U.S.C. 2602).	S. 847 section 4 would amend definitions in TSCA section 3.
Chemical substance	"[A]ny organic or inorganic substance of a particular molecular identity, including - (i) any combination of such substances occurring in whole or in part as a result of a chemical reaction or occurring in nature and (ii) any element or uncombined radical." The term does not include any mixture, pesticide, tobacco, nuclear material, firearms, shells or cartridges for firearms, food, food additive, drug, cosmetic, or devices regulated by other specified federal laws. [TSCA 3(2)]	Proposed TSCA 3(5) is the same as 15 U.S.C. 2602(2), but also authorizes EPA to determine that "a variant of a chemical substance is a new chemical substance," notwithstanding molecular identity.
Distribute in commerce / Distribution in commerce	"[T]o sell, or the sale of the substance, mixture, or article in commerce; to introduce or deliver for introduction into commerce, or the introduction or delivery for introduction into commerce of, the substance, mixture, or article; or to hold, or the holding of, the substance, mixture, or article after its introduction into commerce." [TSCA 3(4)]	Would amend the TSCA 3(8) definition to include "to export or offer for export the substance, mixture, or article."
Environment	"[I]ncludes water, air, and land and the interrelationship which exists among and between water, air, and land and all living things." [TSCA 3(5)]	Would amend the TSCA 3(10) definition to include "ambient" and "indoor air."
New chemical substance	"[A]ny chemical substance which is not included in the chemical substance list compiled and published under section 2607(b) of this title, [corresponding to TSCA section 6(b)]." [TSCA 3(9)]	Proposed TSCA 3(15) revises the definition, eliminating reference to listing under 15 U.S.C. 2607(b) and instead referring to any chemical substance that does not have a submitted declaration under Proposed TSCA section 8(a).

Standards for the development of test data	A "prescription of (A) the - (i) health and environmental effects, and (ii) information relating to toxicity, persistence, and other characteristics which affect health and the environment, for which test data for a chemical substance or mixture are to be developed and any analysis that is to be performed on such data, and (B) to the extent necessary to assure that data respecting such effects and characteristics are reliable and adequate (i) the manner in which such data are to be developed, (ii) the specification of any test protocol or methodology to be employed in the development of such data, and (iii) such other requirements as are necessary to provide such assurance." [TSCA 3(12)]	This definition would be eliminated.
New definitions		
Aggregate exposure	No comparable definition.	Total exposure to a chemical substance regardless of the source of exposure, including activities involved in the manufacture, processing, distribution, use, or disposal of chemicals; contamination of food, air, water, soil, and house dust from current or prior uses or activity; accidental releases; permitted sources of pollution; nonpoint sources of pollution;
		documented background levels from natural and anthropogenic sources; and a mixture or article containing that chemical substance. The term would include exposure from a chemical substance that is not considered a chemical substance under TSCA solely because of its use as, or in, food, cosmetics, or medical devices. [Proposed TSCA 3(2)]
Bioaccumulative	No comparable definition.	As determined by the EPA
		Administrator, the ability to significantly accumulate in biota, or highly likely to accumulate in biota. [Proposed TSCA 3(3)]
Chemical identity	No comparable definition.	Each common and trade name, the most current internationally standardized name, the Chemical Abstracts Service registration number, and the molecular structure of a chemical substance, and for a mixture, the chemical identities and proportions of the components. [Proposed TSCA 3(4)]

Table 1. (Continued)

Provision	15 U.S.C. 2601 et seq.	S. 847
Cumulative exposure	No comparable definition.	The sum of aggregate exposure to each chemical substance that is known or suspected to contribute "appreciably to the risk of the same or a similar adverse effect." [Proposed TSCA 3(7)]
End consumer	No comparable definition.	An "individual or other entity that purchases and uses or consumes a chemical substance (or mixture or article containing that chemical substance)." [Proposed TSCA 3(9)]
Federal agency	No comparable definition.	"[A]ny department, agency, or other independent agency or establishment of the Federal Government including any Government corporation, and the Government Printing Office." [Proposed TSCA 3(11]
Persistent	No comparable definition.	Determined by the EPA Administrator to significantly persist in one or more environmental media. [Proposed TSCA 3(16)]
Person	No comparable definition.	An "individual, trust, firm, joint stock company, corporation (including a government corporation), partnership, association, State, municipality, commission, political subdivision of a State, or any interstate body." Includes "each Federal agency and any officer, agent, or employee of a Federal agency." [Proposed TSCA 3(17)]
Special substance characteristics	No comparable definition.	Defines "special substance characteristic" to mean "such physical, chemical, or biological characteristic, other than molecular identity, that the Administrator determines, by order or rule, may significantly affect the risks posed by substances exhibiting that characteristic."
		Allows consideration of size, shape, reactivity, and any other properties that may significantly affect risks posed. [Proposed TSCA 3(20)]

Toxic	No comparable definition.	Satisfies one of the following conditions: has a toxicological property meeting criteria for Category 1 or 2 for any toxicity endpoint established by the Globally Harmonized System for the Classification and Labeling of Hazardous Substances; "causes an adverse effect that has been demonstrated in humans or other exposed organisms"; or "the weight of evidence … demonstrates the potential for an adverse effect in humans or other exposed organisms." [Proposed TSCA 3(22)]
Toxicological property	No comparable definition.	"[A]ctual or potential toxicity or other adverse effects of a chemical substance or mixture, including actual or potential effects of exposure" on mortality, morbidity, reproduction, growth and development, the immune system, the endocrine system, brain or nervous system, other organ systems, or "any other biological functions in humans or nonhuman organisms." [Proposed TSCA 3(23)]
Vulnerable human population	No comparable definition.	A "human population that is subject to a disproportionate exposure to, or the potential for a disproportionate adverse effect from exposure to, a chemical substance or mixture …" and includes those who work with chemical substances and mixtures, individuals with preexisting medical conditions, the elderly, pregnant women, infants, children, adolescents, and "members of any other appropriate population identified by the Administrator." [Proposed TSCA 3(25)]

Table 2. Testing in Selected Provisions of TSCA (15 U.S.C. 2601 et seq.) and the Safe Chemicals Act (S. 847), as Introduced

Provision	15 U.S.C. 2601 et seq.	S. 847
Testing authorities and requirements	TSCA 4(a) [15 U.S.C. 2603(a)] directs the EPA Administrator to promulgate a rule requiring that testing be conducted on a substance or mixture to develop health and environmental effects data if: (1) the manufacture, processing, distribution, use, or disposal of the chemical "may present an unreasonable risk of injury to health or the environment," or (2) the chemical is produced in very large volume and there is a potential for a substantial quantity to be released into the environment or for substantial or significant human exposure. In either case, EPA also must find that (a) existing data are insufficient to resolve the question of safety, and (b) testing is necessary to develop the data.	S. 847, section 5, amends TSCA 4. Proposed TSCA 4(a) directs the EPA Administrator within one year of enactment of S. 847 to promulgate a rule establishing varied or tiered minimum data sets for different chemical substances or categories of substances. Data sets must encourage and facilitate use of alternative testing methods and strategies in accordance with section 30 and must include "the minimum amount of information necessary" for the conduct of a screening-level risk assessment of the substance or category of substances. The rule must require submission to EPA of such data by each manufacturer and processor of a new chemical substance and each manufacturer and processor of an existing chemical. Also requires updates of minimum data set submissions.
		Proposed TSCA 4(b) authorizes EPA to require, by rule or order, testing and submission of test results by a specified date "as necessary for making any determination or carrying out any provision" of TSCA. Authorizes EPA to require submission of a sample of any chemical for the purpose of conducting tests and making a determination or carrying out any provision of the act.
Provision	15 U.S.C. 2601 et seq.	S. 847
Test rule requirements	TSCA 4(b) [15 U.S.C. 2603(b)] requires EPA in any test rule to identify the chemical substance or mixture for which testing is required, specify standards for the development of test data, and specify the period during which test results must be submitted.	Proposed TSCA 4(c) is similar to 15 U.S.C. 2603(b), but is applicable to EPA orders as well as rules.

Deadlines for initial data submission	No comparable provision.	Proposed TSCA 4(a) requires submission to EPA of the minimum data set for an existing chemical within 18 months of the date that EPA assigns the chemical to a priority class under section 6(a) or 5 years of the date of enactment of the SCA, whichever is earlier. Submission of the minimum data set is required for a new chemical at the time notice is provided to EPA [under revised TSCA section 5(a)] that a new chemical will be manufactured.
Persons required to submit data	TSCA 4(b) [15 U.S.C. 2603(b)] requires manufacturers and processors to conduct tests in response to a rule issued by EPA, but allows EPA to permit such persons to designate one person or a qualified third party to conduct such tests and submit data on their behalf.	Proposed TSCA 4(c) directs EPA to specify in any rule or order persons required to conduct tests and submit data, but allows designation of a single data provider, as is allowed under current law. In the event that a single data provider is designated, all parties remain individually liable for testing requirements
Failure to submit data	No comparable provision.	Proposed TSCA 4(a)(3) and 4(b)(3) authorize EPA to, by order, take any regulatory action authorized under section 6(c) if a manufacturer or processor fails to submit required data or a required chemical sample.
Data exemption	TSCA 4(c) [15 U.S.C. 2603(c)] allows manufacturers and processors to request an exemption, and directs EPA to grant an exemption if data would be duplicative. Provides for reimbursement by the exempted persons to manufacturers and processors who collected and submitted data. EPA is required to order a manufacturer or processor who is exempt to reimburse the entity that submitted data. Such an order is a final agency action for the purpose of judicial review.	Proposed TSCA 4(d) would have the same effect as TSCA, except exemptions could apply to orders as well as rules, and the bill does not provide that the EPA Administrator's order to reimburse is a final agency action for the purpose of judicial review.
Cessation of manufacture or processing	No comparable provision.	Proposed TSCA 4(b)(4) explicitly exempts from requirements any manufacturer or processor who has submitted a declaration of cessation of manufacture or processing of a chemical substance.

Table 2. (Continued)

Provision	15 U.S.C. 2601 et seq.	S. 847
Contents of minimum data set	No comparable provision.	Proposed TSCA 4(a) directs EPA to include in the minimum data set information on characteristics, toxicological properties, exposure, and use of a chemical substance, information that the EPA anticipates will be necessary for the conduct of a screening-level risk assessment of the chemical. Allows EPA to provide for varied or tiered testing for different chemicals or categories of chemicals.
Prescribed data needs	TSCA 4(b) [15 U.S.C. 2603(b)] authorizes EPA to prescribe data development standards for effects which may present an unreasonable risk of injury to health or the environment and for characteristics of chemical substances and mixtures which may present such a risk, as well as for methodologies including epidemiological studies, serial or hierarchical tests, in vitro tests, and whole animal tests.	Proposed TSCA 4(c) authorizes EPA to prescribe data development standards for health and environmental information, including information pertaining to: any effect that may be considered in a safety standard determination; exposure, including presence in human tissues and fluids; and any characteristic of a chemical that may present an adverse effect. Also authorizes EPA to prescribe biomonitoring studies, in addition to methodologies already permitted under 15 U.S.C. 2603(b).
Petition for standards for development of test data	TSCA 4(g) [15 U.S.C. 2603(g)] authorizes manufacturers to petition EPA to prescribe standards for the development of test data for a new chemical.	This provision would be eliminated.
Alternatives to animal testing	No comparable provision.a	Requires that animal tests are consistent with provisions of Proposed TSCA section 30, promoting alternatives to animal testing.
Review and revision of data needs	TSCA 4(b) [15 U.S.C. 2603(b)]requires annual review and revision, if necessary, of standards for the development of data.	Proposed TSCA 4(c)(3)(C) changes the interval between required reviews and revisions, if necessary, from one to 3 years.

Rulemaking process	TSCA 4(b) [15 U.S.C. 2603(b)] directs EPA to issue test rules pursuant to 5 U.S.C. 553 (Administrative Procedure Act, procedures for informal notice and comment rulemaking). In addition, persons must be given an opportunity for oral presentation of data, views, or arguments and to make written submissions; a transcript must be made of oral presentations; and the EPA Administrator must publish findings required by TSCA 4(a)(1)(A) or (B).	Proposed TSCA 4(c) omits TSCA requirements for rulemaking that go beyond the notice and comment requirements of 5 U.S.C. 553. Proposed TSCA 4(b) authorizes EPA to issue orders in lieu of rules.
Public notice of receipt of data	TSCA 4(d) [15 U.S.C. 2603(d)] requires that EPA provide public notice of receipt of data and make data available for examination by any person (subject to section 14).	Proposed TSCA 4(e) is similar to 15 U.S.C. 2603(d) in requiring public notice of the receipt of data, but applies also to data submitted in accord with an EPA order, and requires that data be made "available on a publicly accessible Internet site."
Interagency testing committee (ITC)	TSCA 4(e) [15 U.S.C. 2603(e)] establishes the ITC to advise the EPA Administrator regarding chemicals that should receive priority consideration for promulgation of a test rule [under subsection (a)].	Proposed TSCA 6(a)(5) establishes the Interagency Prioritization and Testing Committee, which is similar to the ITC in composition.
Committee recommendations for testing	TSCA 4(e) [15 U.S.C. 2603(e)] directs the ITC to establish a prioritized list of chemicals for the EPA Administrator to consider testing and to designate up to 50 chemicals on the list as the highest priority. In selecting chemicals, the committee is authorized to consider all relevant factors, including "the extent to which the substance or mixture is closely related to a chemical substance or mixture which is known to present an unreasonable risk of injury to health or the environment." Priority attention is to be given to chemicals "known to cause or contribute to or which are suspected of causing or contributing to cancer, gene mutations, or birth defects."	Proposed TSCA 6(a)(5) changes the directive to the interagency committee with respect to the basis for recommendations for issuance of test rules or orders. The committee is directed to make recommendations for issuance of test rules or orders based on "all factors relevant to risk." The committee also is to make recommendations for prioritization of chemical substances for risk assessment and management using the criteria established for each priority class under proposed TSCA 6(a)(2)(B), 6(a)(3)(B), and 6(a)(4)(B).

Table 2. (Continued)

Provision	15 U.S.C. 2601 et seq.	S. 847
		Recommendations are to be updated annually, if necessary. The EPA Administrator is directed to provide reasonable opportunity to any interested person to file written comments on the recommendations. The Administrator is required to consider any comments received and to make them available to the public.
Prohibition of judicial review for committee recommendations	No comparable provision.	Proposed TSCA 6(a)(5) protects from judicial review recommendations by the Interagency Prioritization and Testing Committee.
Required agency actions	TSCA 4(f) [15 U.S.C. 2603(f)] requires the EPA Administrator to respond within 180 days to new information indicating "that there may be a reasonable basis to conclude that a chemical substance or mixture presents or will present a significant risk of serious or widespread harm to human beings from cancer, gene mutations, or birth defects." Requires EPA to "initiate appropriate action under section 5, 6, or 7 to prevent or reduce to a sufficient extent such risk or publish in the Federal Register a finding that such risk is not unreasonable." A finding that a risk is not unreasonable is a final agency action for purposes of judicial review.	This provision would be eliminated, but proposed TSCA 6(a)(2) directs the Administrator to assign a chemical substance to priority class 1 if "the chemical substance is, or is degraded and metabolized into, a persistent, bioaccumulative, and toxic substance with the potential for widespread exposure to humans or other organisms." "As soon as practicable, but not later than 18 months after the date on which a chemical substance is assigned to priority class 1," EPA must impose conditions on its manufacturing, processing, use, distribution in commerce, and disposal that are determined to be necessary to achieve "the greatest practicable reductions in human or environmental exposure" to the chemical substance. Proposed TSCA 6(a)(2)(E) directs EPA to promptly revise the priority 1 list of chemicals whenever the addition or removal of a chemical substance from the list is warranted.

Requests from other federal agencies	No comparable provision.	Proposed TSCA 4(f) authorizes any federal agency to request that EPA seek information unavailable to that other agency which it has determined would assist it in carrying out its duties or exercising its authority. Requires EPA within 60 days to collect and provide such information to the requesting agency, collect information under TSCA 8, issue a rule or order to develop the data, or publish in the Federal Register the reason for not taking any of these actions.
Certification of data submitted	No comparable provision.	Proposed TSCA 4(g) requires that each submission of information under a rule or order be accompanied by a certification of the accuracy, reliability, and completeness (to the extent reasonably ascertainable) of the information provided. Such certification must be signed by a responsible official of the manufacturer or processor.

[a] However, EPA has stated that it "is committed to examining alternative test methods that reduce the number of animals needed for testing, reduce pain and suffering of test animals, and whenever possible, replace animals in testing with validated in vitro (non-animal) test systems. EPA has released guidance on this issue ..." (U.S. EPA, "Fact Sheet on Animal Welfare," April 2001, EPA 745-F-99-003, http://www. epa.gov/ HPV/pubs/general/anfacs.pdf).

Table 3. Notices in Selected Provisions of TSCA (15 U.S.C. 2601 et seq.) and the Safe Chemicals Act (S. 847), as Introduced

Provision	15 U.S.C. 2601 et seq.	S. 847
Notices concerning new chemicals or uses	TSCA 5(a)(1) [15 U.S.C. 2604(a)(1)] prohibits manufacture of a new chemical and prohibits manufacture or processing of any chemical for a use which is a significant new use unless notice is submitted to EPA 90 days prior to such manufacture or processing.	Proposed TSCA 5(a)(1)-(3) treats new chemicals in a similar manner to current law, but also requires notice prior to processing for a new chemical. For an existing chemical that has met the safety standard, requires notice prior to manufacture or processing for a new use, at new production volume, or in a manner other than specified in the safety determination.
		No notice is required for an existing chemical for which EPA has not yet made a safety determination, when manufacture or process would be for a new use or at a significantly increased volume, but in such cases, proposed TSCA 5(a)(2) requires submission of a new or updated declaration as required under proposed TSCA 8(a).
New use determination	TSCA 5(a)(2) [15 U.S.C. 2604(a)(2)] directs EPA to designate a significant new use of an existing chemical by promulgating a rule after considering "all relevant factors, including – (A) the projected volume of manufacturing and processing of a chemical substance, (B) the extent to which a use changes the type or form of exposure of human beings or the environment to a chemical substance, (C) the extent to which a use increases the magnitude and duration of exposure of human beings or the environment to a chemical substance, and (D) the reasonably anticipated manner and methods of manufacturing, processing, distribution in commerce, and disposal of a chemical substance."	Prior to a safety standard determination for an existing chemical, proposed TSCA 5(a) designates a use to be a new use if at the time of enactment of S. 847 that use was not ongoing, or if manufacture or processing of the substance would be at a significantly increased volume. After a safety standard determination has been made for an existing chemical, a new use is any use, production volume, or manner other than those the EPA Administrator specified in the safety standard determination.
Special substance characteristics	No comparable provision.	Proposed TSCA 5(a)(6) directs the EPA Administrator to determine by order or rule that a variant of a chemical substance exhibiting one or more "special substance characteristics" [such as size or reactivity, as defined in proposed TSCA 3(20)] is a new use or a new chemical substance.

Notice content	TSCA 5(d) [15 U.S.C. 2604(d)] requires that notices contain the information required by TSCA 8(a)(2)(A)-(D), (F), and (G). [See "Reporting and record keeping" below.]	Proposed TSCA 5(c) requires a notice to include the declaration made under proposed TSCA 8(a)(2), the minimum data set established under TSCA 4(a), and a statement that the chemical will meet the applicable safety standard.
Certification	No comparable provision.	Proposed TSCA 5(e) requires that each submission of information under a rule or order be accompanied by a certification of the accuracy, reliability, and completeness (to the extent reasonably ascertainable) of the information provided. Such certification must be signed by a responsible official of the manufacturer or processor.
Submission of test data with notice	TSCA 5(b) [15 U.S.C. 2604(b)] requires persons who propose to manufacture a new chemical or to manufacture or process a chemical for a significant new use to submit with such notice any test data that are required by rule under TSCA 4(a). If no test data are required under TSCA 4(a), but the chemical has been listed under TSCA 5(b)(4), indicating that the EPA Administrator has determined that it "presents or may present an unreasonable risk," manufacturers and processors must submit data showing that manufacture, processing, distribution in commerce, use, and disposal (in the case of a new chemical or mixture), or the new use (in the case of a significant new use), "will not present an unreasonable risk of injury to health or the environment."	At the time a manufacturer or processor notifies EPA that it plans to manufacture or process a chemical substance that is new, proposed TSCA 5(b) requires submission of: any data required for that chemical substance under a section 4(b) test rule or order; the section 8(a) declaration; and the minimum data set established under proposed section 4(a). When providing notice to EPA regarding a new use of a chemical for which the EPA Administrator previously has made the safety determination, manufacturers must provide an update for the minimum data set. With respect to a new use of a chemical which has not been evaluated for safety, manufacturers must submit to EPA a new or updated declaration under proposed TSCA 8(a).
Public availability of data	TSCA 5(b)(3) [15 U.S.C. 2604(b)(3)] directs EPA to make such data publicly available, subject to protections for confidential business information in section 14.	Proposed TSCA 5(b)(2) requires EPA to make data available on a publicly accessible Internet site, subject to proposed TSCA 14.
EPA's response to notice	No comparable provision, but EPA has 90 days to decide whether the chemical or chemical use may present an unreasonable risk of injury to health or the environment.	Proposed TSCA 5(a)(4) requires EPA to determine within 180 days after receiving notice and data whether it has been established that the chemical substance or mixture meets the safety standard under proposed TSCA section 6(b).
Extension of the notice period	TSCA 5(c) [15 U.S.C. 2604(c)] authorizes EPA to extend the period between notice and manufacture for additional periods of up to a total of 90 days "for good cause."	Authorizes EPA to extend the determination deadline for periods not to exceed one year.

Table 3. (Continued)

Provision	15 U.S.C. 2601 et seq.	S. 847
Publication of notice	TSCA 5(d) [15 U.S.C. 2604(d)(1)] requires notice to be available for examination by interested persons, subject to disclosure restrictions at TSCA 14 [15 U.S.C. 2613]. [See "Disclosure of data" section below.] Directs EPA to publish a notice identifying the chemical, listing the intended uses, and describing the nature of tests performed and data that were developed pursuant to a rule.	Proposed TSCA 5(b)(3)-(4) is similar to current law [TSCA 5(d)(1)], but specifies that EPA must make notices available on a publicly accessible Internet site and requires disclosure of the availability of the minimum data set. In addition, requires EPA to make available on the internet monthly a list of chemical substances for which notice has been received. [Also, see "Disclosure of data" section below.]
"Manufacture" and "process"	TSCA 5(i) [15 U.S.C. 2604(i)] defines "manufacture" and "process" as used in TSCA section 5 to mean manufacturing and processing for commercial purposes.	Proposed TSCA 5(f) provides the same definition as current law.
Safety determination for new chemical or new use	No specific provision, but TSCA requires an EPA finding that manufacture, processing, distribution in commerce, use, and disposal of a chemical "may present an unreasonable risk of injury to health or the environment," when the agency issues a test rule under TSCA 4(a). Similarly, EPA must find that a chemical substance "presents an unreasonable risk" before EPA can issue a rule to ensure that risks are adequately regulated.	Proposed TSCA 5(a) prohibits manufacture and processing of a chemical for which notice is required unless the EPA Administrator finds either: 1) that the manufacturers and processors have established that the chemical meets the safety standard under proposed TSCA 6(b), or 2) that the new chemical substance or its metabolite or degradation product is not, and is not expected to be— manufactured in a volume of more than one million pounds annually or released into the environment in a volume of more than 100,000 pounds annually; a known, probable, or suspected reproductive, developmental, neurological, or immunological toxicant, carcinogen, mutagen, or endocrine disruptor, or has other toxicological properties of concern; persistent and bioaccumulative; found in human cord blood, or otherwise found in human blood,
		fluids, or tissue, unless it is naturally present at the level commonly found in that medium; or found in food, drinking water, ambient or indoor air, residential soil, or house dust, unless it is naturally present at the level commonly found in that medium.

		With respect to a new use of a chemical for which the EPA Administrator previously has made the safety determination, manufacturers must provide evidence that permits the EPA Administrator to amend the safety determination. With respect to a new use of a chemical for which the EPA Administrator has not yet made a safety standard determination, manufacturers must provide the declaration described in proposed 8(a).
Protection against unreasonable risks	TSCA 5(f) [15 U.S.C. 2604(f)] directs EPA to control an unreasonable risk posed by a new chemical or a significant new use of a chemical in the interim between the expiration of the notification period and the effective date of a rule that is being developed to control such risk. EPA is directed to issue a proposed rule or an order. If the EPA Administrator issues a proposed rule, it is effective on the date it is issued.	This provision would be eliminated. S. 847 requires risk management prior to production and distribution.
Regulation pending development of information	TSCA 5(e) [15 U.S.C. 2604(e)] authorizes the EPA Administrator to issue a proposed order to prohibit or limit manufacture, processing, distribution in commerce, use, or disposal of a new chemical or significant new use in the event that the EPA Administrator determines that: the information available "is insufficient to permit a reasoned evaluation of the health and environmental effects" of the chemical; and either the chemical may present an unreasonable risk, or it will be produced in substantial quantities and "may reasonably be anticipated to enter the environment in substantial quantities or there is or may be significant or substantial human exposure to the substance." If EPA makes such a determination but no order is issued or objections are filed to the order, then EPA must apply to the District Court to prohibit or limit activities with respect to the chemical, unless EPA finds on the basis of the objections that the determination cannot be made.	This provision would be eliminated. Proposed TSCA 5(a) requires submission of data and a safety determination prior to production and distribution of a new chemical or of an existing chemical for a new use.

Table 3. (Continued)

Provision	15 U.S.C. 2601 et seq.	S. 847
Statement of reasons for not taking action	If EPA does not take action with respect to a chemical covered by a test rule [under TSCA 4(a)], a significant new use rule [under TSCA 5(a)(1)(B)], or listed under TSCA 5(b)(4), then TSCA 5(g) directs the EPA Administrator to publish a statement of reasons for not taking action.	This provision would be eliminated.
Exemptions from notice requirements		
General authority	TSCA 5(h)(4) [15 U.S.C. 2604(h)(4)] authorizes EPA upon application and by rule to exempt a manufacturer of a new chemical substance from notification and data requirements, if the EPA Administrator determines it will not "present an unreasonable risk of injury to health or the environment." Any such rule must be promulgated in accord with TSCA section 6(c)(2) and (3) (see below).	This provision would be eliminated.
Intermediate production chemicals	TSCA 5(h)(5) [15 U.S.C. 2604(h)(5)] authorizes exemptions upon application for production-related (temporary, so-called "intermediate") chemicals when no human or environmental exposure will occur.	Proposed TSCA 5(d)(4) is the same as current law.
Test marketing	TSCA 5(h)(1) [15 U.S.C. 2604(h)(1)] authorizes EPA to exempt any person from notification or data requirements so as to permit manufacture or processing for test marketing purposes, if the person applies for such exemption and demonstrates the chemical will not present an "unreasonable risk."	Proposed TSCA 5(d)(1) is similar to current law but a person must show that it "will not endanger human health or the environment." "Test marketing" is defined in proposed TSCA 5(f) to exclude provision of a chemical or article containing a chemical to an end consumer.

Equivalent chemicals and duplicative data	TSCA 5(h)(2) [15 U.S.C. 2604(h)(2)] allows manufacturers and processors of new chemicals or chemicals with significant new uses that are on the priority list but are not subject to a TSCA 4(b) data submission requirement to request from EPA an exemption from the TSCA 5(b) requirement that they submit data showing that manufacture, processing, distribution in commerce, use, and disposal of the chemical substance, or the significant new use, will not present an unreasonable risk. Directs EPA to grant such exemption if the chemical is equivalent to a substance for which data has been submitted and data would be duplicative. Provides for reimbursement by the exempted persons to manufacturers and processors who collected and submitted data. EPA is required to order a manufacturer or processor who is exempt to reimburse the entity that submitted data. Such an order is a final agency action for the purpose of judicial review.	Proposed TSCA 5(d)(2) allows manufacturers and processors of new chemicals or chemicals with new uses to request, and EPA to grant, full or partial exemption from data submission requirements if the chemical is equivalent to a chemical substance for which data have been submitted and submission would be duplicative of data previously submitted to EPA. Provides for reimbursement by the exempted persons to those who collected and submitted data in the same manner as current law.
Small quantities	TSCA 5(h)(3) [15 U.S.C. 2604(h)(3)] exempts from notification and data requirements manufacturing and processing of small quantities for purposes of scientific experimentation or chemical research on, or analysis of, such substances or another substance, including product development.	Proposed TSCA 5(d)(3) is the same as current law.
EPA response to exemption requests	TSCA 5(h)(6) [15 U.S.C. 2604(h)(6)] requires EPA to publish notices of, and request comments on, requests for exemptions that the agency receives. EPA must issue an approval or disapproval within 45 days.	Proposed TSCA 5(d)(5) is the same as current law.

Table 3. (Continued)

Provision	15 U.S.C. 2601 et seq.	S. 847
Chemicals of concern list (priority list)	TSCA 5(b)(4) [15 U.S.C. 2604(b)(4)] authorizes EPA to "by rule, compile and keep current a list of chemical substances with respect to which the EPA Administrator finds that the manufacture, processing, distribution in commerce, use, or disposal, or any combination of such activities, presents or may present an unreasonable risk of injury to health or the environment." In listing decisions the EPA Administrator is directed to consider "all relevant factors, including – (I) the effects of the chemical substance to health and the magnitude of human exposure to such substance; and (II) the effects of the chemical substance on the environment and the magnitude of environmental exposure to such substance." Any rule listing a chemical must identify "uses that the Administrator determines, by rule under subsection (a)(2), would constitute a significant new use of such substance."	This provision would be eliminated, but proposed TSCA 6(a) directs EPA by order to establish a list that "contains the names of the chemical substances that … warrant placement within 1 of 3 priority classes … and identifies the priority class to which each listed chemical substance or category of chemical substance has been assigned by the EPA Administrator." EPA must give due consideration in listing decisions to recommendations provided by the Interagency Prioritization and Testing Committee. Proposed TSCA 6(a)(6) prohibits judicial review of EPA's decisions about listing, including any EPA response to a petition to list a particular chemical substance.
	Any rulemaking under this provision must be promulgated pursuant to the procedures specified in the Administrative Procedure Act (5 U.S.C. 553) providing for notice and public comment, and must provide opportunity for oral and written presentation of data, views, or arguments. In addition, a transcript must be kept of any oral presentation and the EPA Administrator must make and publish with the rule the finding that an activity related to the chemical "presents or may present an unreasonable risk of injury to health or the environment."	
Priority class 1	No comparable provision.	Priority class 1 chemicals are those "that the Administrator determines require immediate risk management." A chemical must be assigned to priority class 1 if it "is, or is degraded and metabolized into, a persistent, bioaccumulative, and toxic substance with the potential for widespread exposure to humans or other organisms."

		Proposed TSCA 6(a)(2)(C) requires that at least 20 but no more than 30 chemicals be assigned to priority class 1 within one year of enactment of S. 847. Proposed TSCA 6(a)(2)(E) directs the EPA Administrator to revise the list whenever the EPA Administrator determines that addition or removal of a chemical substance is warranted, but a substance only may be removed "if the Administrator finds that such substance meets the safety standard under subsection (b)."
Priority class 2	No comparable provision.	Priority class 2 chemicals are those "that the Administrator determines require safety standard determinations … based on any more-than-theoretical concern, that there is uncertainty as to whether a chemical substance would satisfy the safety standard in a determination made under " proposed TSCA 6(b).
		The timing of additions to the priority class 2 list of chemicals should be "expeditious" but "shall not exceed the rate at which the Administrator reasonably anticipates completing safety determinations under subsection (b)."
		The EPA Administrator is required to first assign to priority class 2 those chemicals "that present the greater risks to human health or the environment." Proposed TSCA 6(a)(3)(C) prohibits removal of a chemical from the list until the EPA Administrator has made a safety determination for that chemical.
Priority class 3	No comparable provision.	Priority class 3 chemicals are those "that the Administrator determines require no immediate action." A chemical is to be assigned to this list if it has intrinsic properties that pose no risk of adverse effects to human health or the environment under existing, proposed, or anticipated levels of exposure or production or patterns of use. The EPA Administrator is directed to "promptly revise the list under paragraph (1) whenever the Administrator determines that the addition or removal of a chemical substance from priority class 3 is warranted."

Table 4. Restrictions in Selected Provisions of TSCA (15 U.S.C. 2601 et seq.) and the Safe Chemicals Act (S. 847), as Introduced

Provision	15 U.S.C. 2601 et seq.	S. 847
Regulation	TSCA 6(a) [15 U.S.C. 2605(a)] directs EPA by rule to apply one or more requirements "to the extent necessary to protect adequately against" an "unreasonable risk" "using the least burdensome requirements," if EPA finds that "there is a reasonable basis to conclude that the manufacture, processing, distribution in commerce, use, or disposal of a chemical substance or mixture … presents or will present an unreasonable risk of injury to health or the environment." Specifies various regulatory options. Authorizes regulations to: prohibit or limit the amount of substance manufactured, processed, or distributed in commerce, generally or for a specific use; require labeling, recordkeeping, provision of notice to distributors and to the public of unreasonable risk of injury, or replacement or repurchase of a substance; and specify methods of disposal.	S. 847 does not require rulemaking, but section 7 would authorize EPA to specify allowed uses of any substance that meets the safety standard and to impose conditions on its manufacture, processing, use, distribution in commerce, or disposal to "ensure the safety standard is met." Many of the conditions that EPA is authorized to impose are the same as the regulatory options listed in current law, but S. 847 also would authorize EPA to impose a requirement that the manufacturers and processors of a chemical substance or mixture or article containing it develop a risk reduction management plan to achieve a risk reduction specified by the EPA Administrator. The bill, as introduced, does not authorize the option of requiring manufacturers or processors to give notice of unreasonable risk of injury to distributors or the public or to replace or repurchase a substance.
	TSCA 6(c) [15 U.S.C. 2605(c)] specifies procedures for rulemaking that allow for informal hearings and requires EPA to publish a statement describing the health and environmental effects, level of exposure, benefits of the substance, and "reasonably ascertainable economic consequences of the rule, after consideration of the effect on the national economy, small business, technological innovation, the environment, and public health." Requires that EPA's decisions be based on the rulemaking record. Directs EPA to promulgate needed rules under other environmental laws, unless it is in the public interest to issue rules under TSCA.	In addition, S. 847 differs from current law in that the bill does not authorize limiting conditions to specified geographic areas, nor does it prohibit requiring a person to take an action that would be in violation of a law or requirement of a state or political subdivision. [Proposed TSCA 6(b) and (c)]

Safety standard	No comparable provision, but in general terms, the standard embedded in TSCA is that EPA should protect against "unreasonable risk," a standard that appears to require risk assessment but allows balancing of risks and benefits.	Proposed TSCA 6(b)(1)(C) directs the EPA Administrator to base a determination of whether a chemical meets its safety standard "solely on considerations of human health and the environment, including the health of vulnerable human populations."
		To the extent practicable, the EPA Administrator is required to incorporate "any available scientific information relating to the effect of cumulative exposure … on human health and the environment." For a chemical to meet the safety standard, the EPA Administrator must find that "there is a reasonable certainty that no harm will result to human health or the environment from aggregate exposure to the chemical substance."
General process for safety determinations	No comparable provision.	Proposed TSCA 6(b)(1) requires that EPA produce a risk assessment addressing health and environmental impacts in support of any determination that a manufacturer or processor of a chemical substance has met the applicable safety standard. Risk assessments must be transparent and understandable to the public and to risk managers. No risk assessment is required when EPA determines that the safety standard has not been met, and such determination is not subject to judicial review.
		Proposed TSCA 6(b)(1) also establishes that manufacturers and processors of a chemical substance are responsible for providing sufficient information for the EPA Administrator to determine whether the substance meets the applicable safety standard, and that the EPA Administrator has the responsibility of determining within 180 days of data submission whether the manufacturers and processors have met the applicable safety standard.

Table 4. (Continued)

Provision	15 U.S.C. 2601 et seq.	S. 847
Scientific standards for data assessment	No comparable provision.	Proposed TSCA 6(b)(1)(C) requires the EPA Administrator to "use the best available science" in conducting a risk assessment considering the recommendations of the National Academy of Sciences in the report entitled "Science and Decisions." Every 5 years, the EPA Administrator is required to review the methodology and may revise it "to reflect new scientific developments or understandings."
Safety of chemicals for export	No comparable provision.	Proposed TSCA directs EPA to consider risks that a chemical manufactured in whole or in part for export may pose in the United States during production and distribution in commerce, including in imported products containing the substance.
Safety determinations for existing chemicals EPA's determination Failure to submit data Failure by EPA to meet required deadline Resubmission	No comparable provision. No comparable provision. No comparable provision. No comparable provision.	Within 1 year after receipt of a data submission, EPA is directed to determine, by order, whether the manufacturers and processors of the substance have established that the substance meets the safety standard. If data are not submitted, proposed TSCA 6(b)(2) authorizes EPA to take any action authorized under subsection (c). If EPA fails to meet the deadline for a safety determination, proposed TSCA 6(b)(2) provides that manufacturers and processors are required to provide to EPA, the public, their employees, and customers written notice that a determination by EPA of the safety of the chemical is pending. Proposed TSCA 6(b)(2) provides that within 30 months of assignment of a chemical to priority class 2 under proposed TSCA 6(a), manufacturers must submit updated information for any previously submitted minimum dataset. In addition, requires that at least every 15 years, manufacturers and processors of each chemical substance submit an updated minimum dataset and indicate whether the substance and specified uses meet the safety standard.

Redetermination Petition for redetermination	No comparable provision. No comparable provision.	EPA may initiate a redetermination of whether a chemical meets the safety standard if new information raises a question in that regard, on the receipt of a renewal submission, or 15 years following the previous determination. Authorizes any person to petition the EPA Administrator for a redetermination. The Administrator must decide whether to make the requested redetermination and publish the decision and its basis in the Federal Register within 180 days.
Restrictions on substances that do not meet the safety standard	No comparable provision, but TSCA 6(a) directs EPA by rule to apply one or more requirements (such as labeling or banning particular uses) "to the extent necessary to protect adequately against" an "unreasonable risk" "using the least burdensome requirements," if the EPA Administrator finds that "there is a reasonable basis to conclude that the manufacture, processing, distribution in commerce, use, or disposal of a chemical substance or mixture, or that any combination of such activities, presents or will present an unreasonable risk of injury to health or the environment."	Proposed TSCA 6(b)(3) prohibits manufacture, processing, and distribution in commerce of a chemical substance, mixture, or article if EPA makes a safety determination and does not determine that a substance meets the safety standard. Such prohibition is effective immediately for a new chemical or after one year for any other chemical.
Use restrictions for substances meeting the safety standard	No comparable provision.	Proposed TSCA 6(b) prohibits manufacture, processing, and distribution in commerce of a chemical substance, mixture, or article for any use not specified in the safety determination if EPA determines that the chemical and its specified uses meet the safety standard.
Effective date of Section 6 rules	TSCA 6(d) [15 U.S.C. 2605(d)] directs EPA to make such rules effective "as soon as feasible," and allows EPA to make a proposed rule effective upon publication until the effective date of the final rule if there is an unreasonable risk of serious or widespread injury to health or the environment and a court has granted relief under section 7.	Proposed TSCA 6(i) directs EPA to specify a date on which a rule or order shall take effect and that such date should be "as soon as feasible."

Table 4. (Continued)

Provision	15 U.S.C. 2601 et seq.	S. 847
Quality control	TSCA 6(b) [15 U.S.C. 2605(b)] authorizes EPA to review and regulate a manufacturer's or processor's quality control procedures if there is "a reasonable basis to conclude" that the manner of manufacturing or processing "unintentionally causes a chemical … to present or which will cause it to present an unreasonable risk of injury to health or the environment." EPA also is authorized to order the manufacturer or processor to provide notice to its customers of such risk and to replace or repurchase the substance as is necessary to adequately protect health or the environment. Requires any determination that a chemical presents an unreasonable risk to be made on the record after opportunity for hearing.	Proposed TSCA 6(d) is similar to current law but applies when there is "a reasonable basis to conclude" that the manner of manufacturing or processing "may present a substantial endangerment to human health or the environment." Does not require such determination to be made on the record after opportunity for hearing.
Resale of used articles	No comparable provision.	Proposed TSCA 6(e)(3) provides that restrictions established under sections 4(a)(3), 4(b)(3), 6(b)(2)(A)(iv), 6(b)(3), 8(b)(6), or 8(c)(3) do not apply to resale of an article subject to a restriction under proposed TSCA 6(b) if the article has previously been used.
Delay of effective date of restrictions	No comparable provision.	Proposed TSCA 6(e)(4) authorizes EPA to order delay in the effective date of a restriction for 3 years for retail sales to an end consumer of a chemical substance, mixture, or article subject to a restriction under sections 4(a)(3), 4(b)(3), 6(b)(2)(A)(iv), 6(b)(3), 8(b)(6), 8(c)(3), or 29, if necessary and appropriate, if it "will not present a substantial endangerment to human health or the environment." EPA authority does not extend to any retailer who has failed to comply with an order requesting information under proposed TSCA section 8.

Exemptions from prohibitions and other restrictions	No comparable provision.	Proposed TSCA 6(e) authorizes EPA to grant, by order, exemptions (and renewals of exemptions) to restrictions proposed to be established under sections 4(a)(3), 4(b)(3), 6(b)(2)(A)(iv), 6(b)(3), 8(b)(6), 8(c)(3), and 29 for particular uses.
		Exemptions and renewals may be granted for up to 5 years, if manufacturers and processors "have established by clear and convincing evidence that the uses to be exempted meet the exemption criteria." Those criteria are: 1) that the exemption is in the paramount interest of national security; 2) lack of availability would cause significant disruption in the national economy; or 3) the use is a critical or essential use for which there is no safer feasible alternative, or the specified use compared to available alternatives provides a net benefit to human health, the environment, or public safety. The manufacturer or processor must notify customers and the public of any exemptions granted. EPA is directed to impose any condition on a granted exemption that is necessary to ensure the protection of human health and the environment.
Certification of the quality of submitted information	No comparable provision.	Proposed TSCA 6(h) requires that each submission of information under a rule or order be accompanied by a certification of the accuracy, reliability, and completeness (to the extent reasonably ascertainable) of the information provided. Such certification must be signed by a responsible official of the manufacturer or processor.
Mercury	15 U.S.C. 2605(f) prohibits federal agencies from conveying, selling, or distributing elemental mercury to any federal agency, state or local government, or private entity, except to facilitate storage at a federal agency.	Proposed TSCA 6(g) is the same as current law.

Table 4. (Continued)

Provision	15 U.S.C. 2601 et seq.	S. 847
Polychlorinated biphenyls (PCBs)	TSCA 6(e) [15 U.S.C. 2605(e)] directs EPA to prescribe methods of disposal for PCBs and to require PCBs to be marked with clear and adequate warnings and instructions regarding processing, distribution in commerce, use, or disposal. Prohibits use of any PCB other than "in a totally enclosed manner," unless EPA finds that such activity "will not present an unreasonable risk of injury to health or the environment." Prohibits manufacture, processing, and distribution in commerce. Authorizes any person to petition for an exemption and authorizes EPA to grant such exemption if EPA finds that an unreasonable risk would not result, and "good faith efforts have been made to develop a chemical substance which does not present an unreasonable risk … and which may be substituted for such [PCB]." Requires use of rulemaking procedure in TSCA 6(c).	Proposed TSCA 6(f) is similar to existing law but authorizes the EPA Administrator to act by order or rule, and to grant exemptions from the general prohibitions on manufacturing, processing, distribution in commerce, or use when such activities "will not present a substantial endangerment to health or the environment" rather than when activities "will not present an unreasonable risk."
Imminent hazards Relief	Authorizes an appropriate district court to grant relief necessary to protect health or the environment from unreasonable risk.	Similar to current law, but authorizes district court to grant relief necessary to protect health or the environment from "the risk associated with the activity involved in the civil action."
Civil actions	TSCA 7(a) [15 U.S.C. 2606(a)] authorizes EPA to begin a civil action: for seizure of "an imminently hazardous" chemical substance, mixture, or article; for relief against any person who manufactures, processes, distributes in commerce, or uses, or disposes of such chemical or article; or for both seizure and relief. Requires EPA to commence such civil action if the agency has not made a rule under TSCA 6(a) effective immediately.	Similar to current law, but authorizes EPA civil action against a person who manufactures, processes, distributes in commerce, uses, or disposes of a chemical substance or mixture, or any article containing a chemical substance or mixture, or who contributes to any of those activities, when a chemical, mixture, or article "may present an imminent and substantial endangerment to health or the environment, as determined by the Administrator."

	Requires that EPA "where appropriate, concurrently with the filing of an action … initiate a proceeding for the promulgation of a rule" under TSCA 6(a). Defines "imminently hazardous chemical substance or mixture" to mean a chemical that "presents an imminent and unreasonable risk of serious or widespread injury to health or the environment."	Does not require EPA to commence action if the agency has not made a rule effective immediately concerning the chemical. Also authorizes EPA to issue orders to protect health or the environment from a chemical substance or mixture or article containing such substance or mixture that may present an imminent and substantial endangerment to health or the environment.
		Would eliminate authority concurrently to initiate a proceeding for the promulgation of a rule under TSCA 6(a) [15 U.S.C. 2605(a)]. Also would eliminate the definition for "imminently hazardous chemical substance or mixture."

Table 5. Reporting Requirements in Selected Provisions of TSCA (15 U.S.C. 2601 et seq.) and the Safe Chemicals Act (S. 847), as Introduced

Provision	15 U.S.C. 2601 et seq.	S. 847
EPA authority to require reporting and record keeping	TSCA 8(a) [15 U.S.C. 2607(a)] authorizes EPA, to the extent necessary for the effective enforcement of the law, to promulgate rules requiring maintenance of records and submission of reports to EPA by persons who manufacture or process or who propose to manufacture or process a chemical substance. Prohibits a rule requiring maintenance of records or submission of reports with respect to changes in the proportions of the components of a mixture unless necessary for effective enforcement.	Proposed TSCA 8(b) authorizes EPA by rule or order to require any person who manufactures, processes, distributes in commerce, uses, or disposes of a chemical substance to maintain records of and report any information that would assist the EPA Administrator in administering TSCA.
Declaration	No comparable provision	Proposed TSCA 8(a) requires each manufacturer and processor of a chemical substance to submit a declaration of current manufacturing or processing for each substance, mixture, or article manufactured or processed. Each declaration must be accompanied by certification of its accuracy, reliability, and comprehensiveness.
Failure to submit declaration	No comparable provision.	EPA may by order prohibit manufacture, processing, or distribution of any substance if a manufacturer or processor violates EPA requirements for submitting or updating a declaration.
Information required to be submitted	TSCA 8(a) authorizes collection of information including: trade name or common name, chemical identity, categories of use, amount of each chemical manufactured or processed, byproducts resulting from such manufacture or processing, "all existing data concerning the environmental and health effects," number of individuals exposed, and, in the initial report, the manner of disposal.	Proposed TSCA 8(a) requires the declaration to state: the chemical identity and substance characteristics; name and location of each facility where the substance is manufactured or processed or from which it is distributed; a list and copies of health and safety studies that are reasonably ascertainable;

		and all other information not previously submitted to EPA regarding the physical, chemical, and toxicological properties of the substance, its annual production volume and known uses, exposure and fate information, and the name and location of each facility to which the substance is sent for processing, distribution, or use. Or, the declaration may say that all production, importation, processing, and export of a substance has ceased or will cease within 180 days. Declarations must be updated and submitted at least every 3 years, and immediately when new information becomes available regarding a physical, chemical, or toxicological property or use of, or exposure to, the substance.
Inventory	TSCA 8(b) [15 U.S.C. 2607(b)] directs EPA to compile, keep current, and publish an inventory of each chemical manufactured or processed in the United States. New chemicals are to be listed when manufacture or processing begins. The list should exclude chemicals produced in small quantities for purposes of scientific experimentation, analysis, or research. Authorizes EPA to list chemicals by category rather than individually.	Proposed TSCA 8(c) is the same as TSCA 8(b), except that it omits the authority in current law to list chemicals by category rather than individually.
Small quantities for research and development	TSCA 8(a)(3) [15 U.S.C. 2607(a)(3)] explicitly authorizes EPA to require reporting from small manufacturers and processors of chemical substances or mixtures subject to a rule proposed or promulgated under TSCA 4, 5(b)(4), or 6 or an order under TSCA 5(e) or with respect to which relief has been granted under TSCA 5 or 6. Reporting also may be required once under TSCA 8(b) for the original inventory (see above) from processors and manufacturers who are small	Proposed TSCA 8(b)(2) authorizes EPA to define by rule manufacture, processing, distribution in commerce, use, or disposal of a chemical substance in small quantities solely for purposes of research, and to issue a rule or order under this subsection only if EPA determines maintenance of records or submission of reports is necessary for effective enforcement of the law.

Table 5. (Continued)

Provision	15 U.S.C. 2601 et seq.	S. 847
	(as determined by the EPA Administrator after consultation with the Small Business Administration). TSCA 8(b) [15 U.S.C. 2607(b)]directs EPA to limit record keeping and reporting requirements for those who manufacture or process a chemical in small quantities solely for purposes of scientific experimentation or analysis of a chemical substance.	
Public access	No comparable provision.	Proposed TSCA 8(d) directs EPA to establish an electronic database of information relating to the toxicity and use of and exposure to chemical substances. It is required to include descriptions of "all significant decisions made by the Administrator" and significant information submitted under TSCA Title I.
Records of significant adverse reactions	TSCA 8(c) [15 U.S.C. 2607(c)] requires all manufacturers and processors to keep records of all reports of significant adverse reactions to health or the environment alleged to have resulted from exposure to a chemical substance or mixture.	Proposed TSCA 8(e) is similar to TSCA but does not apply to mixtures. For chemical substances, it also requires submission of such records to EPA.
Information from other federal agencies	No comparable provision.	Proposed TSCA 8(f) requires each federal agency and institution to submit to EPA a synopsis of the data and records in its control that may be useful to EPA in carrying out TSCA Title I. Such synopsis shall be updated and resubmitted at least once every 3 years. On request by the EPA Administrator, federal agencies are directed to submit information relating to hazard, use, exposure, or risk of a chemical substance (or mixture or article containing that chemical substance).
Health and safety studies	TSCA 8(d) [15 U.S.C. 2607(d)] directs EPA to require manufacturers, processors, and distributors to submit lists and copies of health and safety studies for each chemical manufactured or processed.	Requires submission of such studies as part of the declaration under proposed TSCA 8(a).

Substantial risk notice	TSCA 8(e) [15 U.S.C. 2607(e)] requires manufacturers, processors, and distributors who obtain information "which reasonably supports the conclusion" that a chemical substance or mixture "presents a substantial risk of injury to health or the environment" to inform EPA.	Proposed TSCA 8(g) is the same as current TSCA 8(e).
Certification	No comparable provision.	Proposed TSCA 8(h) requires that each submission of information under a rule or order be accompanied by a certification of the accuracy, reliability, and completeness (to the extent reasonably ascertainable) of the information provided. Such certification must be signed by a responsible official of the manufacturer or processor.
"Manufacture" and "process"	TSCA 8(f) [15 U.S.C. 2607(f)] defines "manufacture" and "process" to mean manufacture or process for commercial purposes.	Proposed TSCA 8(i) is the same as current TSCA 8(f).

Table 6. Other Selected Provisions of TSCA (15 U.S.C. 2601 et seq.) and the Safe Chemicals Act (S. 847), as Introduced

Provision	15 U.S.C. 2601 et seq.	S. 847
Action under laws administered by other federal agencies	If EPA has a reasonable basis to conclude that activities with respect to a chemical substance or mixture present or will present an unreasonable risk, and EPA determines that such risk may be prevented or reduced to a sufficient extent by action taken under a federal law not administered by EPA, then TSCA 9(a) [15 U.S.C. 2608(a)] directs EPA to submit to the agency which administers such law a report describing the risk and activities that present such risks. The EPA report must request that the other federal agency 1) tell EPA whether the risk may be prevented or reduced under the law the agency administers, and 2) issue an order declaring whether the activities present a risk. If EPA makes a report and the other agency either 1) issues an order declaring that the activities do not present the risk, or 2) initiates action to protect against such risk, then EPA may not take regulatory action under TSCA 6 or 7.	Proposed TSCA 9(a) is similar to current law, but does not apply to mixtures and the criterion for EPA action differs. If the EPA Administrator determines "that the manufacture, processing, distribution in commerce, use, or disposal of a chemical … does not meet a safety standard … or requires conditions or restrictions" to do so, and "that action may be taken under a Federal law not administered by the Administrator" then EPA must submit a report to the other agency describing the activities that prevent the chemical from meeting the safety standard or restrictions or conditions required to meet the safety standard. The report must request that the other agency 1) determine whether action may be taken under a Federal law administered by the agency, and if so, 2) initiate such action and provide a timetable for action, and 3) respond to EPA's report. If the other agency initiates civil action under Federal law within 90 days or a shorter timeframe specified in the report, EPA may not take action under proposed TSCA with respect to the civil action except under TSCA 7.
		If the other agency determines that action cannot be taken under its authorities; does not initiate action or complete action within the timeframe provided; or fails to respond, then EPA may, by order, initiate action to ensure compliance with a safety standard.
Occupational safety and health	TSCA 9(c) states that any EPA exercise of authority under TSCA is deemed to be exercising statutory authority to prescribe or enforce standards or regulations affecting occupational safety and health.	Same as current law. In addition, S. 847 directs EPA to ensure that any EPA actions to address workplace exposures "are consistent with the industrial hygiene hierarchy of controls."

Coordination	TSCA 9(d) directs EPA to consult and coordinate with appropriate federal agency heads to achieve "maximum enforcement" "... while imposing the least burdens of duplicative requirements" on those being regulated.	Strikes the requirement that coordination for the purpose of enforcement should impose the least burdens of duplicative requirements.
Inspections	TSCA 11 [15 U.S.C. 2610] authorizes EPA to inspect premises in which chemicals are manufactured, processed, stored, or held before or after distribution in commerce and any conveyance used to transport chemicals in commerce.	Proposed TSCA 11(a) and (b) are similar to current TSCA 11 but also apply to premises and conveyances handling articles subject to TSCA. Inspections are not limited by requiring presentation of credentials or provision of written notice.
	Limits inspections by requiring presentation of appropriate credentials and written notice to the person in charge of the premises or conveyance to be inspected on each occasion of inspection. Requires inspections to begin and end with reasonable promptness and to "be conducted at reasonable times, within reasonable limits, and in a reasonable manner." Prohibits inspection of financial, sales, pricing, personnel, or research data, unless they are described specifically in the required written notice.	Authorizes EPA to inspect any place where records relating to compliance with the law are held and to inspect and obtain samples of any chemicals, containers, or labeling. Does not prohibit inspection of any data.
Subpoenas and warrants	TSCA 11(c) [15 U.S.C. 2610(c)] authorizes EPA to require by subpoena attendance and testimony of witnesses, production of reports, documents, answers to questions, and other information. Authorizes district courts to order compliance in the event of contumacy, failure, or refusal to obey.	Proposed TSCA 11(c) authorizes EPA to require attendance, testimony, and production of documents, items, answers to questions and other information deemed necessary. In the event that "there is reason to believe that the provisions" of the law have been violated, proposed TSCA 11(d) empowers EPA to obtain and to execute warrants authorizing entry, inspection, and copying of records, or seizures of any chemical in violation.
Exports Exclusion from requirements	TSCA 12(a) [15 U.S.C. 2611(a)] excludes chemical products manufactured for export (other than elemental mercury) from TSCA requirements except for reporting and record keeping requirements in Section 8. This exclusion applies as long as the products are labeled for export only and their manufacture, processing, and distribution do not pose an unreasonable risk within the United States.	Proposed TSCA 12 would eliminate the current exclusion from requirements for chemicals manufactured, processed, or distributed in commerce solely for the purpose of export.

Table 6. (Continued)

Provision	15 U.S.C. 2601 et seq.	S. 847
	EPA may require testing to allow assessment of the risk within the United States.	
Mercury	TSCA 12(c) [15 U.S.C. 2611(c)] prohibits the export of elemental mercury (but not of coal containing mercury). Authorizes exemptions from this prohibition for essential uses.	Same as current law.
Notice of export	TSCA 12(b) [15 U.S.C. 2611(b)] requires anyone who exports or intends to export a substance that is subject to a test rule or order under section 4 or a proposed or final rule under section 5 or 6, or for which action is pending or relief has been granted under section 5 or 7, to notify EPA of such exportation or intent, and EPA must then notify the countries that will be receiving the substance that data are available or that restrictions are in place in the United States for such substance.	Proposed TSCA 12(a) is similar to current TSCA 12(b), but excludes from requirements those who "intend" to export, and applies only to exports of chemicals subject to data submission requirements under proposed TSCA 5 or 6(b), or for which action has been taken under TSCA 6 or 7. Also, S. 847 allows exporters 30 days from the date of export for providing notice to EPA, and specifies that EPA must provide notice to countries "promptly thereafter." Requires exporters to notify EPA, and EPA to notify receiving countries, of any change in the status of a chemical. EPA also must notify receiving countries that it has received new data or if there is any change in risk management action taken under section 6 or 7. Requires EPA to maintain copies of current notices provided to other governments and to make them available to the public electronically.
Imports	TSCA 13 [15 U.S.C. 2612] directs the Secretary of the Treasury to refuse entry into the United States of chemicals that fail to comply with a rule under TSCA or that are in violation of TSCA.	Proposed TSCA 13 is similar to current law but transfers authority to the Secretary of the Department of Homeland Security. In addition, a new paragraph (3) in proposed TSCA 13(a) explicitly subjects to TSCA requirements chemical substances and mixtures imported as part of an article, except "as the Administrator may provide by rule under this Act, or as the Secretary of Homeland Security may provide by rule."

Disclosure of data	TSCA 14 [15 U.S.C. 2613] provides broad protection of proprietary confidential information about chemicals in commerce. Disclosure by EPA employees of such information generally is not permitted, except to other federal employees or when relevant in any proceeding under TSCA. Disclosure of information is required when "necessary to protect health or the environment against an unreasonable risk of injury to health or the environment." Manufacturers, processors, or distributors in commerce may designate data that they believe is entitled to confidential treatment. If EPA proposes to release such data the EPA Administrator must notify the manufacturer, processor, or distributor who designated the data.	Proposed TSCA 14 requires conformance to the standards of the Freedom of Information Act (FOIA). Like current law, S. 847 prohibits disclosure of proprietary confidential information by EPA employees except to other federal agencies and EPA contractors, but it specifically directs EPA to disclose information upon request to a state, tribal, or municipal government for the purpose of administration or enforcement of a law if an agreement ensures that the recipient government will take appropriate steps to maintain the confidentiality of the information in accordance with proposed TSCA 14 and 40 CFR 350.19,
		which directs EPA to provide confidential information to states if EPA receives a written request from a governor and the state agrees to safeguard the information with procedures equivalent to those used by EPA and the governor agrees to disclose the information only to employees. Directs EPA to release information if it is necessary to protect health or the environment against "an imminent and substantial endangerment" to health or the environment. Requires those designating data as confidential to justify such claims and to certify that the information is not otherwise publicly available. The EPA Administrator is required to by order develop standards for justifying claims and necessary documentation and within one year of enactment, to identify by rule the types of information for which EPA shall not specify prospectively the term of confidentiality. Requests must be reviewed by EPA within 90 days. If approved, submitted information will be protected from disclosure for up to 5 years.

Table 6. (Continued)

Provision	15 U.S.C. 2601 et seq.	S. 847
Health and safety information	Disclosure of health and safety information is not prohibited when it relates to a chemical which has been offered for commercial distribution, or for which testing is being required under section 4, or for which notification is required under section 5, unless data disclosure would reveal a chemical process or chemical proportion in a mixture.	Proposed TSCA 14 specifies data that are not to be protected, including the health and safety data allowed to be disclosed by current law, the identity of a chemical, any safety standard determination, and information "indicating the presence of a chemical in a consumer article intended for use or reasonably expected to be used by children or to which children can otherwise be reasonably expected to be exposed."
Penalties for disclosure and inappropriate designation	TSCA 14(d) provides that knowing and willful disclosure of protected information by a federal employee may result in a fine of up to $5,000 or imprisonment for up to one year, or both.	Proposed TSCA 14(f) is the same as current TSCA 14(d).
Risk information for workers	No comparable provision.	Proposed TSCA 14(h) requires EPA to provide standards for and facilitate sharing with each certified or recognized bargaining agent information regarding chemical identity, safety standard determination, and health and safety data that pertains to substances that workers may come into contact with or otherwise be exposed to during the course of work.
Prohibited Acts	TSCA 15 [15 U.S.C. 2614] prohibits any person from failing or refusing to comply with rules, orders, or other requirements of TSCA, using for commercial purposes a chemical substance or mixture that was known to be manufactured, processed, or distributed in commerce in violation of the law, failing or refusing to establish and maintain records, submit reports, notices, or other information, or to permit access to or copying of records, or failing or refusing to permit entry or inspection.	Proposed TSCA 15 is similar to current law and prohibits all the same actions, but also prohibits manufacturing, processing, distributing in commerce, or disposing of a chemical or article or using an article that was known to have been manufactured, processed, or distributed in commerce in violation of the law. S. 847 also prohibits failing or refusing to establish and maintain "accurate and complete" records, reports, notices, information, disclosures, declarations, certifications, or other information.

		Prohibits submitting information "that is materially false, in whole or in part," or falsifying or concealing "any material fact." Prohibits taking any action prohibited by proposed TSCA.
Penalties	TSCA 16 [15 U.S.C. 2615] authorizes civil penalties, not to exceed $25,000 per violation per day, and affords the defendant an opportunity to request a hearing before an order is issued and to petition for judicial review of an order after it is issued with the U.S. Court of Appeals for the District of Columbia Circuit or for any other circuit in which the person resides or transacts business. Criminal penalties of up to $25,000 per day of violation or up to one year of imprisonment, or both, also are authorized for knowing or willful violations.	Proposed TSCA 16 increases the maximum civil penalty per violation per day to $37,500 and authorizes EPA to commence a civil action in an appropriate U.S. district court to assess penalties. Changes the court in which a person may file a petition for judicial review to eliminate jurisdiction in any federal circuit court, instead vesting jurisdiction in the appropriate district court for the district in which the person resides or transacts business.
		Removes criminal sanctions for "willfully" violating any provision of TSCA, as proposed, but increases the maximum penalty for "knowing" violations to $50,000 per day of violation or up to 5 years of imprisonment, or both. Adds a provision that any person who knowingly violates any provision of the law and "who knows at the time that he thereby places another person in imminent danger of death or serious bodily injury to any person shall upon conviction be subject to a fine of not more than $250,000 or imprisonment of not more than 15 years, or both." A person who is not an individual is subject to a fine of not more than $1,000,000.
Seizure	TSCA 17 [15 U.S.C. 2616] makes substances produced in violation of Title IV (Lead Exposure Reduction) liable to be proceeded against, by process of libel, for seizure and condemnation in any district where the substance is found.	Proposed TSCA 17 is similar to current law but S. 847 applies to "articles" rather than "products" and to any articles, substances, or mixtures, that are subject to any title of TSCA.

Table 6. (Continued)

Provision	15 U.S.C. 2601 et seq.	S. 847
Enforcement	TSCA 17 [15 U.S.C. 2616] provides jurisdiction to district courts over civil actions to restrain any violation or any person from taking any action prohibited, to compel the taking of any action required, or to direct any manufacturer or processor in violation of section 5 or 6 or of Title IV (or a rule or order under those provisions): to give notice to distributors and to others in possession of the substance, to give public notice of risk, and to replace or repurchase the substance. Authorizes civil actions brought in the U.S. district court for the judicial district wherein any violation occurred or where the defendant is found or transacts business.	Proposed TSCA 17 authorizes the EPA Administrator to commence a civil action in the appropriate district court to compel compliance of any person with any provision of TSCA or any rule or order promulgated pursuant to TSCA. Authorizes EPA to seek civil or criminal penalties, enjoin any violation, or order compliance, through an administrative proceeding, with any provision of TSCA or with any rule or order issued under it. Gives district courts jurisdiction over civil actions to seek penalties or enjoin violations in the U.S. district court for the judicial district wherein any violation occurred or where the defendant is found or transacts business. Gives jurisdiction over civil actions ordering compliance to the U.S. district court for the judicial district where the defendant is found or transacts business.
Preemption of state law	TSCA 18 [15 U.S.C. 2617] does not preempt state laws, with two exceptions: 1) when EPA requires testing of a chemical under section 4, no state may require testing of the same substance for similar purposes; and 2) if EPA prescribes a rule or order under section 5 or 6 to protect against a risk, no state or political subdivision may have a requirement for such substance to protect against such risk unless it is identical to the EPA requirement, is adopted under authority of the Clean Air Act or another federal law, or prohibits the use of such substance in such state or political subdivision (other than use in manufacture or processing of other substances or mixtures).	Proposed TSCA 18 does not preempt laws of states or political subdivisions relating to a chemical substance, mixture, or article unless compliance with both the law of the state or political subdivision and federal law is impossible.

Exemption from state or local law preemption	TSCA 18 [15 U.S.C. 2617] authorizes EPA, upon application by a state or political subdivision, by rule to exempt a law in effect in the state or political subdivision, if compliance with the requirement would not cause activities involving the substance to be in violation of the EPA requirement, and the requirement of the state or political subdivision provides a significantly higher degree of protection from the risk than the EPA requirement does and does not "unduly burden interstate commerce."	No comparable provision. (Since state laws are not preempted, there is no need for an exemption.)
Standard for judicial review	TSCA 19 [15 U.S.C. 2618] authorizes any person to file a petition with the U.S. Court of Appeals for the District of Columbia Circuit or for the circuit in which such person resides or in which the person's principal place of business is located, for judicial review of rules promulgated under TSCA sections 4(a), 5(a)(2), 5(b)(4), 6(a), 6(e), or 8 within 60 days of issuance. The appropriate district court is directed to set aside specified rules if they are not supported by "substantial evidence in the rulemaking record … taken as a whole," which is defined in TSCA 19(a)(3).	Similar to current law, but TSCA 19, as proposed, authorizes filing a petition for judicial review of any rule or order issued under TSCA, as proposed, rather than only specified rules, and would eliminate the directive in current law to the court (to set aside a rule not supported by substantial evidence in the rulemaking record taken as a whole).
Citizen suits	TSCA 20 [15 U.S.C. 2619] authorizes civil suits by any person against any person in violation of TSCA or rules or orders promulgated under specified sections of TSCA. It also authorizes suits against EPA to compel performance of nondiscretionary actions under TSCA.	Proposed TSCA 20 is similar to current law, but authorizes suits against any person in violation of rules or orders promulgated under any provision of TSCA, as proposed.
Citizen petitions	TSCA 21 [15 U.S.C. 2620] provides the public with the right to petition EPA to initiate rulemaking or repeal of specified rules. Requires the EPA Administrator to grant or deny the petition within 90 days of its filing.	Proposed TSCA 21 is similar to current law, but authorizes petitions for EPA to initiate any action authorized under the law.
Employment effects	TSCA 24 [15 U.S.C. 2623] directs the EPA Administrator to continually evaluate the potential effects of specified rules, orders, and requirements under specified TSCA provisions on employment.	Proposed TSCA 24 is similar to current law, but directs the EPA Administrator to evaluate potential effects of the law as a whole, rather than specific provisions, and reporting is to be "periodic," rather than continual.

Table 6. (Continued)

Provision	15 U.S.C. 2601 et seq.	S. 847
Administration	TSCA 26(a) [15 U.S.C. 2625(a)] authorizes federal agencies, upon request from EPA, to provide services, personnel, facilities, and information to EPA to assist in implementation of TSCA. TSCA 26(b) [15 U.S.C. 2625(b)] authorizes EPA to collect fees from persons required to submit data under section 4 or 5 to defray the cost to EPA of administering the Act. Such fees may not exceed $2,500, or in the case of a small business $100. TSCA 26(c) [15 U.S.C. 2625(c)] authorizes EPA to impose regulatory controls on categories of chemicals, rather than on a case-by-case basis. Prohibits regulation of a group based solely on the fact that it consists of new chemical substances. TSCA 26(d) [15 U.S.C. 2625(d)] directs EPA to establish an office to assist the regulated community. TSCA 26(e) [15 U.S.C. 2625(e)] requires that EPA establish a procedure to ensure disclosure of financial interests in the regulated community by EPA employees. TSCA 26(f) [15 U.S.C. 2625(f)] provides that final orders issued under TSCA must contain a statement of basis and purpose. TSCA 26(g) [15 U.S.C. 2625(g)] requires appointment of an Assistant Administrator for Toxic Substances.	Proposed TSCA 26 is similar to current law, except for proposed subsections (b) and (c) and a new subsection (h). Proposed TSCA 26(b) authorizes collection of fees from any data submitter (not just those submitting under section 4 or 5) to defray the cost of administering TSCA. It removes the restrictions in the original TSCA 26(b) on the amount of such fees. Proposed TSCA 26(c) also authorizes the EPA Administrator to take an action with respect to a mixture if such action is authorized or required under any provision of the Act with respect to a chemical substance, if the Administrator determines it is "reasonable and efficient" to do so. New TSCA 26(h) authorizes the EPA Administrator to issue orders and prescribe regulations as necessary to carry out the law.
State programs	TSCA 28 [15 U.S.C. 2627] authorizes grants to states to establish and operate programs to prevent or eliminate unreasonable risks to health or the environment which EPA is unable or is not likely to address under TSCA.	Proposed TSCA 28 is similar to current law, but grants are authorized to prevent or eliminate any risks that EPA has not addressed. In addition, EPA is directed to establish a process to coordinate with the states "to share data and priorities relating to the management of chemical substances" under TSCA, as proposed, and under state programs.

Children's environmental health research	No comparable provision.	New TSCA 29(a) would establish a Children's Environmental Health Research Program at EPA and authorize the EPA Administrator to enter into contracts and make grants to conduct research that will "further understanding of the vulnerability of children to chemical substances and mixtures." Proposed TSCA 29(b) establishes an Interagency Science Advisory Board on Children's Health Research and makes it subject to the Administrative Procedure Act and Chapter 7 of Title 5 of the U.S. Code, which pertains to judicial review.
		The purpose of the Board is to provide independent advice upon request of the EPA Administrator or Congress relating to the implementation of the proposed TSCA "with respect to protecting children's health and research." The committee members would include representatives of the National Institute of Environmental Health Sciences, the Centers for Disease Control and Prevention, the National Toxicology Program, the National Cancer Institute, the National Tribal Science Council, and not fewer than 3 centers of children's health at leading institutions of higher education.
Monitoring exposures	No comparable provision.	New TSCA 29(c) would direct EPA to coordinate with the Secretary of Health and Human Services (HHS) to conduct a biomonitoring study to determine the presence of a chemical in human biological media in pregnant women and infants, if research has indicated that it may be present and may have adverse effects on development. Study results must be published. If the study finds that the chemical is present in human biological media, manufacturers and processors must disclose to EPA, commercial customers, consumers, and the public all known uses of the chemical and all articles in which the chemical is expected to be present.

Table 6. (Continued)

Provision	15 U.S.C. 2601 et seq.	S. 847
Animal-based testing	No comparable provision.a	New TSCA 30 would direct the EPA Administrator to minimize the use of animals in testing of chemical substances or mixtures. Establishes an Interagency Science Advisory Board on Alternative Testing Methods subject to Title 5, Chapter 5, Subchapter 11 and Chapter 7. The Board is directed to provide independent advice and peer review to the EPA Administrator and Congress and to publish a list of testing methods that reduce the use of animals in testing under proposed TSCA 4. Directs the EPA Administrator in consultation with the Board to develop a strategic plan, biennially report to Congress on progress in implementing this section, and fund and carry out research, development, performance assessment, and translational studies to accelerate the development of test methods and strategies for use in safety standard determinations under proposed TSCA 6(b). Authorizes the EPA Administrator, on request of a manufacturer or processor, to adapt or waive animal-based testing of a chemical substance or mixture under specific conditions.
Safer alternatives	No comparable provision.b	New TSCA 31(a) would establish a program to create market incentives for the development of safer alternatives to existing chemical substances that reduce or avoid the use and generation of hazardous substances. Requires that the program include expedited review of new chemical substances for which an alternatives analysis indicates it is a safer alternative, and recognition for a substance or product determined by EPA to be a safer alternative.

Green chemistry and green engineering	No comparable provision.b	New TSCA 31(b) would direct the EPA Administrator to establish a network of at least four green chemistry and engineering centers in various U.S. regions. New TSCA 31(c) would direct EPA to make grants to promote and support research, development, and adoption of safer alternatives. New TSCA 31(d) would create a program to facilitate the development of a workforce that produces safer alternatives to existing chemical substances.
International cooperation	No comparable provision.	New TSCA 32 would direct the EPA Administrator to cooperate with the Secretary of State and the head of any other appropriate federal agency "with international efforts as appropriate" to develop a common protocol or electronic database relating to chemical substances or to develop safer alternatives for chemical substances.
Reliable information and advice	No comparable provision.	New TSCA 33 would direct EPA by order to establish and implement procedures to ensure data reliability by annually inspecting laboratories and performing an annual data audit. Requires that EPA establish a registry of studies. Provides the EPA Administrator with access to all records of health and safety studies initiated in response to requirements of Title I, and requires each submitter of a research study conducted by a third party to disclose the sources of any funding used to conduct or publish the study.

Table 6. (Continued)

Provision	15 U.S.C. 2601 et seq.	S. 847
Hot spots	No comparable provision.	As proposed, a new TSCA 34 requires that EPA promulgate a rule to establish criteria to identify any locality that is disproportionately exposed. Defines "disproportionate exposure" to mean residential population exposure to one or more toxic chemical substances and mixtures at levels that are significantly greater than the average exposure in the United States. Directs EPA, within 120 days of promulgation of the rule, to identify localities subject to such exposure using data in EPA's National Air Toxic Assessment Database and other available data, and providing an opportunity for public nominations of localities.
		Requires EPA to publish a list of such localities, and to update it at least once every 5 years. The locations on the list are not subject to judicial review. Publication of a list is a nondiscretionary duty and subject to judicial review. Requires the EPA Administrator to develop and publish an action plan that includes an identification of the chemicals that contribute to the disproportionate exposure, and a description of actions to be taken to reduce exposure. Directs EPA to report annually to Congress.
Federal agencies subject to TSCA	No comparable provision.	New TSCA 35 would provide that all federal agencies are subject to the provisions of TSCA, as proposed, and expressly waive any immunity otherwise applicable to the United States. However, no agent, employee, or officer of the United States is personally liable for any civil penalty under TSCA with respect to any act or omission within the scope of the official duties of that person. Such persons are subject to any criminal sanction under proposed TSCA.

		The President is authorized to grant an exemption for any federal agency from compliance with any requirement of TSCA, as proposed, if "the President determines it is in the paramount interest of the United States."
		An exemption may be granted due to lack of appropriation if the President specifically requested such appropriation and Congress failed to make available such requested appropriation. Directs the President annually to report to Congress all exemptions granted during the previous year. Authorizes enforcement action against any federal agency, as well as voluntary resolution or settlement set forth in a consent order.
International agreements	No comparable provision	New TSCA 36 would provide authority for EPA to implement three international agreements: the Stockholm Convention on Persistent Organic Pollutants (Stockholm Convention), the Aarhus Protocol to the Convention on Long-Range Transboundary Air Pollution (LRTAP Protocol), and the Rotterdam Convention on the Prior Informed Consent Procedure for Certain Hazardous Chemicals and Pesticides in International Trade (PIC Convention).
		Directs the EPA Administrator to implement and support implementation of the provisions of the three agreements that have entered into force for the United States. Prohibits manufacture, processing, distribution in commerce, use, disposal, or any other action with respect to a covered chemical, mixture, or substance that is part of an article in a manner inconsistent with applicable international obligations.

Table 6. (Continued)

Provision	15 U.S.C. 2601 et seq.	S. 847
		Directs EPA to provide timely public notice and opportunity to comment on: a chemical proposed for listing, a recommendation made to list a chemical on any Annex in advance of any meeting of the Parties at which the recommendation is to be considered, and any decision by the Meeting of the Parties to list a chemical.
		Authorizes the EPA Administrator to prescribe regulations to carry out provisions of the three agreements or to ensure compliance with obligations under them. Prohibitions and other requirements shall be enforced in the same way as final rules or orders under proposed TSCA 6.
Authorization of appropriations	TSCA 29 [15 U.S.C. 2628] authorizes appropriations for implementation of specific TSCA provisions for 1982 and 1983. Prohibits expenditures of appropriated funds to construct laboratories.	New TSCA 39 (but identified as section 38 in the new Table of Contents) would authorize "such sums as are necessary" to carry out the law for 2011 through 2018, with no restriction on how those funds might be used.

[a] However, EPA has stated that it "is committed to examining alternative test methods that reduce the number of animals needed for testing, reduce pain and suffering of test animals, and whenever possible, replace animals in testing with validated in vitro (non-animal) test systems. EPA has released guidance on this issue. …" U.S. EPA, "Fact Sheet on Animal Welfare," April 2001, EPA 745-F-99-003, http://www.epa.gov/HPV/pubs/general/anfacs.pdf.

[b] Although there is no explicit authority in TSCA, EPA does promote green chemistry (http://www.epa.gov/greenchemistry/), safer products (http://www.epa.gov/dfe/product_label_consumer.html), green engineering (http://www.epa.gov/oppt/greenengineering/pubs/whats_ge.html), and other "green" initiatives.

End Notes

[1] For a summary of TSCA provisions and history, see CRS Report RL31905, *The Toxic Substances Control Act (TSCA): A Summary of the Act and Its Major Requirements*.

[2] For more information about issues revolving around TSCA, see CRS Report RL34118, *The Toxic Substances Control Act (TSCA): Implementation and New Challenges*.

[3] U.S. Congress, Senate, Committee on Environment and Public Works, Subcommittee on Superfund, Toxics and Environmental Health, Hearing, "Assessing the Effectiveness of U.S. Chemical Safety Laws." Feb. 3, 2011, http://epw.senate.gov/public/index.cfm?FuseAction=Hearings.Hearing&Hearing_ID eac94d1414b3.

[4] S. 906, which became P.L. 110-414.

In: Toxic Substances Control Act
Editors: Shannon M. McDonnery and Cindy L. Elroy
ISBN: 978-1-62100-783-8

Chapter 4

PROPOSED AMENDMENTS TO THE TOXIC SUBSTANCES CONTROL ACT (TSCA): SENATE AND HOUSE BILLS COMPARED WITH CURRENT LAW*

Linda-Jo Schierow

SUMMARY

On April 15, 2010, Senator Lautenberg introduced legislation (S. 3209) to amend the core provisions of the Toxic Substances Control Act (TSCA) Title I. Representatives Waxman and Rush introduced comprehensive legislation to amend TSCA (H.R. 5820) on July 22, 2010. This report compares key provisions of S. 3209, as introduced, H.R. 5820, as introduced, and current law (15 U.S.C. 2601 *et seq.*).

Both bills would amend the 35-year-old law to shift the burden of demonstrating safety for chemicals in commerce from the U.S. Environmental Protection Agency (EPA) to manufacturers and processors of chemicals. Both bills also would prohibit manufacture, processing, and distribution of any chemical substance or mixture for which safety has not been demonstrated. Although they propose somewhat different safety standards for EPA to enforce, both bills suggest a health-based standard. In contrast, current law requires that a chemical not pose "an unreasonable risk of injury to health or the environment," and that any regulation should control unreasonable risk to the extent necessary using the "least burdensome" means of available control. This TSCA standard has been interpreted to require cost-benefit balancing. To facilitate safety assessment, the proposals would require data development and submission to EPA for all chemicals in commerce.

TSCA amendments would direct EPA to target chemicals with particular characteristics (for example, persistence in the environment) for earlier evaluation and possible risk management. Any regulatory action would be expedited, for example, by

* This is an edited, reformatted and augmented version of a Congressional Research Service publication, CRS Report for Congress, R41335, from www.crs.gov, dated August 12, 2010.

allowing EPA to issue orders rather than rules. The bills also would add new sections to TSCA. Of particular significance is a section authorizing actions that would allow U.S. implementation of three international agreements, which the United States has signed but not yet ratified. Other new sections would provide authority for EPA to support research in so-called "green" engineering and chemistry, promote alternatives to toxicity testing on animals, encourage research on children's environmental health, and require biomonitoring of pregnant women and infants. A "hot spots" provision would require EPA to identify locations where residents are disproportionately exposed to pollution and to develop strategies for reducing their risks.

The proposals differ in many details and in several noteworthy ways. For example, for all existing chemicals that have not been placed on a priority list, data sets must be submitted within 14 years of the date of enactment of S. 3209, but within five years of enactment of H.R. 5820. The proposals also treat the identification of chemicals of highest concern differently. H.R. 5820 directs EPA to expedite action for 19 specified chemicals, while S. 3209 leaves identification of such chemicals to the Administrator's discretion. These and other provisions of the two legislative proposals are compared with current law in Tables 1 through 6.

INTRODUCTION

In 1976, President Gerald R. Ford signed the Toxic Substances Control Act (15 U.S.C. 2601 *et seq.*; TSCA).[1] Thirty-five years of experience with TSCA implementation and enforcement have demonstrated the strengths and weaknesses of the law and led many to propose legislative changes to TSCA's core provisions in Title I.[2] On April 15, 2010, Senator Lautenberg introduced comprehensive legislation (S. 3209) to amend TSCA, and Representatives Waxman and Rush posted draft TSCA reform legislation on the home page of the House Committee on Energy and Commerce. The latter House draft was subjected to stakeholder comments and critiques in a series of meetings during the spring. The proposal was revised and introduced July 22, 2010, as H.R. 5820.

This report compares key provisions of S. 3209, as introduced, H.R. 5820, as introduced, and current law. The major provisions of TSCA Title I are summarized in Tables 1 through 6. The first column of each table describes the provisions of TSCA Title I. The second and third columns summarize provisions of S. 3209 and H.R. 5820, respectively, that are related to the TSCA provisions in the first column. New provisions that would be added to the end of TSCA Title I by one or both proposals—for example, those related to reduced use of animals for toxicity testing—are summarized in Table 6.

EFFECTS OF THE PROPOSALS ON CURRENT LAW

The basic organization of TSCA would be unaffected by the proposals. For example, provisions related to testing would still be in Section 4, requirements for notifying EPA when a new chemical or new use is proposed would still be in Section 5, and regulatory authorities would remain in Section 6. Also unaffected would be recently enacted changes, such as a provision that bans exports of elemental mercury.

However, most of the original Title I provisions would be amended or deleted by the proposed legislation, and both proposals would make substantial changes to current law. For example, both proposals would shift the burden of demonstrating the safety of chemicals from the U.S. Environmental Protection Agency (EPA) to manufacturers and processors, and would prohibit manufacture, processing, and distribution of any chemical substance or mixture for any use for which safety had not been demonstrated to EPA's satisfaction. Exemptions from prohibitions would be allowed for particular uses only if a use was "in the paramount interest of national security"; lack of the chemical use "would cause significant disruption in the national economy"; the use was essential or critical and there was no safer feasible alternative; or the chemical use, relative to alternatives, provided a benefit to health, the environment, or public safety.

In addition, the proposals would require data development and submission to EPA for all chemicals in commerce, rather than only for chemicals that EPA has found "may present an unreasonable risk of injury to health or the environment" and for which EPA has demonstrated a data need, as required under current law. The proposed amendments to TSCA would increase public access to information about EPA's decisions as well as to some information about chemicals that currently is treated as confidential business information. Based on the data received, EPA would be directed to target chemicals with particular characteristics (for example, persistence in the environment) for early evaluation and possible risk management.

Once a chemical has been evaluated and EPA has determined whether (or under what conditions) use of the chemical was safe, the proposals would require risk management action to promptly reduce use of, or exposure to, the chemicals of highest concern, and to encourage development of "safer alternatives." Action would be expedited by allowing EPA to issue administrative orders instead of rules (which must be promulgated under current law), exempting certain EPA decisions from judicial review, and removing certain TSCA requirements that are in addition to requirements specified in the Administrative Procedure Act (5 U.S.C. 553) for notice and comment rulemaking.

The scope of EPA oversight also would be expanded by S. 3209 and H.R. 5820. Both include language that would allow EPA to define various distinct forms of substances that are the same in terms of molecular identity but differ in structure and function, such as manufactured nanoscale forms of carbon and silver. Both proposals also broaden the scope of environmental risks that EPA may manage to include risks found in the indoor environment; currently, TSCA applies only to chemicals in the ambient environment. The proposed amendments also appear to more clearly authorize EPA control of risks posed by articles formed from a substance.

Both proposals would authorize EPA activities not currently authorized under TSCA to allow implementation of international agreements pertaining to persistent organic pollutants and other hazardous chemicals. For example, the proposals would authorize EPA to regulate chemicals manufactured solely for export. The authority provided by S. 3209 is specific to three international agreements, while the authority provided by H.R. 5820 applies more generally to any international agreement concerning chemicals. Both proposals would prohibit production and use of some chemicals, but S. 3209 prohibits production and use when it is inconsistent with U.S. obligations under the treaties that have entered into force for the United States. H.R. 5820 directs EPA to ban activities only for specified chemicals that are intentionally produced and are not already regulated under U.S. law.

The effect of TSCA on state and local chemical laws also would be modified by the proposals. Current law, TSCA Section 18, generally does not preempt state laws. However, if EPA requires testing of a chemical under section 4, no state may require testing of the same substance for similar purposes. Similarly, if EPA prescribes a rule or order under section 5 or 6, no state or political subdivision may have a requirement for the same substance to protect against the same risk unless the state or local requirement is identical to the federal requirement, is adopted under authority of another federal law, or generally prohibits the use of the substance in the state or political subdivision. TSCA authorizes states and political subdivisions to petition EPA, and authorizes EPA to grant petitions, by rule, to exempt a law in effect in a state or political subdivision under certain circumstances. A petition may be granted if compliance with the requirement would not cause activities involving the substance to be in violation of the EPA requirement, and the state or local requirement provides a significantly higher degree of protection from the risk than the EPA requirement does, but does not "unduly burden interstate commerce." The proposed amendments would simplify this section of TSCA. S. 3209 provides that TSCA would not preempt laws relating to a chemical substance, mixture, or article unless they were less stringent than federal law. H.R. 5820 provides that the act does not affect the right of a state or locality to adopt or enforce its own requirements unless compliance with both the state or local requirements and TSCA is "impossible."

Several novel provisions are included in both legislative proposals. One provision, for example, would require definition and listing of localities with populations that are "disproportionately exposed" to toxic chemicals. EPA would be directed to develop an action plan to reduce exposure in such "hot spots." Another provision would direct the EPA Administrator to coordinate with the Secretary of Health and Human Services to conduct a biomonitoring study to determine whether a chemical that research has indicated may be present in human biological substances and that may have adverse effects on human development in fact is present in pregnant women and infants. If the chemical is found to be present, manufacturers and processors must disclose to EPA, commercial customers, consumers, and the general public all known uses of the chemical and all articles in which the chemical is expected to be present.

Children's environmental health also is addressed by the bills. Both proposals would establish a children's environmental health research program at EPA and an advisory committee to provide independent advice relating to implementation of TSCA and protection of children's health.

The proposals also would establish at least four research centers to encourage the development of safer alternatives to existing hazardous chemical substances. "Green chemistry and engineering" also would be promoted through grants.

Finally, the proposed amendments would direct EPA to minimize use of animals in toxicity testing. An advisory committee would be established to publish a list of testing methods that reduce use of animals. So-called "alternative testing methods" have been under development for many years, but remain a minor component of toxicity testing programs.

ALTERNATIVE APPROACHES TO REFORM

The proposals differ in many details (which will not be discussed here) and in several noteworthy ways that are summarized in Tables 1 through 6. One significant difference is the length of time each proposal allows before all chemicals in commerce must be tested for toxicity. For all existing chemicals that have not been placed on a priority list, data sets must be submitted within 14 years of the date of enactment of S. 3209. H.R. 5820 allows five years for data development.

Another difference that may spur debate is the definition of the safety standard that chemicals are required to meet. H.R. 5820 would require that a chemical substance or mixture "is not reasonably anticipated to present a risk of injury to health or the environment," "provides a reasonable certainty of no harm, including to vulnerable populations," taking into account aggregate and cumulative exposure to a chemical, "and protects the public welfare from adverse effects, including effects on the environment." S. 3209 would require that EPA ensure "aggregate exposure and cumulative exposure of the general population or of any vulnerable population to the chemical substance or mixture presents a negligible risk of any adverse effect." Although they propose somewhat different safety standards, both proposals propose a health-based standard, which might generally discourage consideration of other factors, such as benefits of chemical use or costs of alternative chemicals in similar applications. (However, EPA would be authorized to consider such benefits and costs under certain circumstances. See in Table 4 under the heading "Exceptions to prohibitions and other restrictions" the description of TSCA 6(e) as it would be amended.) In contrast, current law requires that a chemical not pose "an unreasonable risk of injury to health or the environment," and that regulation should control any unreasonable risk to the extent necessary using the "least burdensome" means of available control. This TSCA standard has been interpreted to require cost-benefit balancing.

The proposals also treat the identification of chemicals of highest concern differently. H.R. 5820 directs EPA to expedite action for 19 specified chemicals. S. 3209 leaves identification of such chemicals to the Administrator's discretion, directing her to "act quickly to manage risks from chemical substances that clearly pose the highest risks to human health or the environment."

Finally, only H.R. 5820 addresses "persistent, bioaccumulative, and toxic" chemicals (PBTs) directly. The bill directs EPA to promulgate a rule establishing criteria for identifying PBTs and requires listing of all PBTs within 18 months of enactment and every three years thereafter. EPA is required to impose conditions on the manufacture, processing, distribution, use, and disposal of PBTs to achieve the "greatest practicable reductions in exposure." EPA then is required to conduct the safety evaluation for all PBTs and to impose further risk management controls as needed.

These and other similarities and differences are summarized in Tables 1 through 6.

Table 1. Titles and Definitions in Selected Provisions of TSCA (15 U.S.C. 2601 et seq.), the Safe Chemicals Act (S. 3209), as Introduced, and the Toxic Chemicals Safety Act of 2010 (H.R. 5820), as Introduced

Provision	15 U.S.C. 2601 et seq.	S. 3209	H.R. 5820
Title	Toxic Substances Control Act (TSCA)	Safe Chemicals Act of 2010 (SCA)	Toxic Chemicals Safety Act of 2010 (TCSA)
Revised definitions	TSCA definitions are in alphabetical order in section 3 (15 U.S.C. 2602.)	S. 3209 section 4 amends definitions in TSCA section 3.	Section 3 of H.R. 5820 amends definitions in TSCA section 3.
Chemical substance	"[A]ny organic or inorganic substance of a particular molecular identity, including -(i) any combination of such substances occurring in whole or in part as a result of a chemical reaction or occurring in nature and (ii) any element or uncombined radical." The term does not include any mixture, pesticide, tobacco, nuclear material, firearms, shells or cartridges for firearms, food, food additive, drug, cosmetic, or devices regulated by other specified federal laws. [TSCA 3(2)]	Amended TSCA 3(2) is the same as 15 U.S.C. 2602(2), but also includes in the definition "any chemical substance contained in or formed into an article." In addition, adds a new subparagraph to the definition authorizing EPA to determine that "a variant of a chemical substance is a new chemical substance," notwithstanding molecular identity.	Amended TSCA 3(2) is the same as 15 U.S.C. 2602(2), but excludes alcoholic beverages and does not exclude pesticides, firearms, shells or cartridges for firearms, foods, food additives, drugs, cosmetics, or devices regulated under other federal laws. Does not include articles. New clause includes in the definition "any form of a substance determined by the Administrator to be a chemical substance under subsection (b)(1)" which refers to a new TSCA 3(b)(1).
Distribute in commerce / Distribution in commerce	"[T]o sell, or the sale of the substance, mixture, or article in commerce; to introduce or deliver for introduction into commerce, or the introduction or delivery for introduction into commerce of, the substance, mixture, or article; or to hold, or the holding of, the substance, mixture, or article after its introduction into commerce." [TSCA 3(4)]	Amends the TSCA 3(4) definition to include "to export or offer for export the substance, mixture, or article."	Amended TSCA 3(4) is the same as S. 3209, but excepts export of a substance "for demonstrated use solely as a pesticide, … food, food additive, drug, cosmetic, or device ..."
Environment	"[I]ncludes water, air, and land and the interrelationship which exists among and between water, air, and land and all living things." [TSCA 3(5)]	Amends the TSCA 3(5) definition to include "ambient" and "indoor air."	Amended TSCA 3(5) is the same as S. 3209.
Health and safety study	"[S]tudy of any effect of a chemical substance or mixture on health or the environment or on both, including underlying data and epidemiological studies, studies of occupational exposure to a chemical substance or mixture, toxicological, clinical, and ecological studies of a chemical substance or mixture, and any test performed pursuant to this chapter" [which corresponds to TSCA]. [TSCA 3(6)]	Amends the TSCA 3(6) definition to specifically include any test that relates to a chemical substance or mixture or to a specific chemical identity.	Same as S. 3209.

Manufacture	To import into the United States, produce, or manufacture. [TSCA 3(7)]	Same as TSCA 3(7).	U.S.C. 2602(7) "except for demonstrated use solely as a pesticide, … food, food additive, drug, cosmetic, or device …"
Mixture	"[A]ny combination of two or more chemical substances if the combination does not occur in nature and is not, in whole or in part, the result of a chemical reaction; except that such term does include any combination which occurs, in whole or in part, as a result of a chemical reaction if none of the chemical substances comprising the combination is a new chemical substance and if the combination could have been manufactured for commercial purposes without a chemical reaction at the time the chemical substances comprising the combination were combined." [TSCA 3(8)]	Same as TSCA 3(8) [15 U.S.C. 2602(8)] but amends the definition to include any mixture contained in or formed into an article.	H.R. 5820, section 10(a) amends TSCA 3(8) [15 U.S.C. 2602(8)] to authorize the Administrator to determine different mixtures comprised of the same chemical substances to be the same mixture if the substance characteristics of the mixtures are identical.
New chemical substance	"[A]ny chemical substance which is not included in the chemical substance list compiled and published under section 2607(b) of this title, [corresponding to TSCA section 6(b)]." [TSCA 3(9)]	Revises the definition of TSCA 3(9), eliminating reference to listing under 15 U.S.C. 2607(b) and instead referring to any chemical substance that does not have a submitted declaration under amended TSCA section 8(a).	Amended TSCA 3(9) is the same as S. 3209, "except that, with respect to the first year after the date of enactment … such term shall not include a chemical substance distributed in commerce as of such date of enactment."
Process	Preparation of a chemical, after its manufacture, for distribution in commerce. [TSCA 3(10)]	Same as TSCA 3(10).	Amended TSCA 3(10) is the same as 15 U.S.C. 2602(10) but excepts preparation for use as a pesticide, food, food additive, drug, cosmetic, or device. Also states that relabeling, redistributing, or repackaging an article does not constitute processing.
Standards for the development of test data	A "prescription of (A) the - (i) health and environmental effects, and (ii) information relating to toxicity, persistence, and other characteristics which affect health and the environment, for which test data for a chemical substance or mixture are to be developed and any analysis that is to be performed on such data, and (B) to the extent necessary to assure that data respecting such effects and characteristics are reliable and adequate (i) the manner in which such data are to be developed,	Eliminates this definition.	Same as S. 3209.

Table 1. (Continued)

Provision	15 U.S.C. 2601 et seq.	S. 3209	H.R. 5820
	(ii) the specification of any test protocol or methodology to be employed in the development of such data, and (iii) such other requirements as are necessary to provide such assurance." [TSCA 3(12)]		
New definitions			
Adverse effect	No comparable definition.	"A biochemical change, anatomic change, functional impairment, or pathological lesion, or its known precursor, that" either (a) "affects or alters performance of an anatomic structure of a vital system of an organism or progeny"; (b) "causes irreversible change in homeostasis of an organism"; (c) "increases the susceptibility of an organism or progeny … to other chemical or biological stressors or reduces the ability of an organism or progeny of an organism to respond to additional health or environmental challenges"; or (d) "affects, alters, or harms the environment such that the health of humans or other organisms is directly or indirectly threatened." [Amended TSCA 3(14)]	Amended TSCA 3(14) is similar to S. 3209, except that the effect is one that "has the potential to impair" rather than one that "affects or alters" the performance of an anatomic structure of a vital system of an organism or progeny of an organism. The definition does not specify that it includes a "pathological lesion." Finally, H.R. 5820 authorizes the Administrator to revise this definition, by rule, to reflect the state of the science and provide for equal or greater protection of health and the environment.
Aggregate exposure	No comparable definition.	Total exposure to a chemical substance or mixture regardless of the source of exposure, including activities involved in the manufacture, processing, distribution, use, or disposal of chemicals used in food, cosmetics, or medical devices. [Amended TSCA 3(15)]	Amended TSCA 3(15) is similar to S. 3209, but omits mention of exposure from mixtures and explicitly includes exposure from contamination of food, air, water, soil, house dust, and any other environmental media from current or prior uses or activity.

Bioaccumulative	No comparable definition.	entitled "Category for Persistent, Bioaccumulative, and Toxic New Chemical Substances" (64 Federal Register 60194, Nov. 4, 1999). EPA is authorized to revise this definition. [Amended TSCA 3(16)]	highly likely to accumulate in biota. EPA is authorized by rule to revise the definition to reflect the state of the science and to provide "equal or greater protection of health and the environment." [Amended TSCA 3(16)]
Chemical identity	No comparable definition.	Each common and trade name, the most current internationally standardized name, the Chemical Abstracts Service registration number, and the molecular structure of a chemical substance, and for a mixture, the chemical identities and proportions of the components. [Amended TSCA 3(17)]	Amended TSCA 3(17) is similar to S. 3209, but refers to the 9th Collective Index of the internationally standardized name (rather than the most current index) and the molecular identity, as well as the molecular structure, and does not specifically refer to chemical identities in a mixture.
Cumulative exposure	No comparable definition.	The sum of aggregate exposure to each chemical substance that is known or suspected to contribute "appreciably to the risk of an adverse effect," and mixtures containing those chemical substances. [Amended TSCA 3(18)]	Amended TSCA 3(18) is similar to S. 3209, but exposure is cumulative across chemical substances and mixtures that are known or, "where supported by scientific consensus, suspected to contribute appreciably to the risk of the same adverse effect."
End consumer	No comparable definition.	An "individual or other entity that purchases and uses or consumes a chemical substance, mixture, or article." [Amended TSCA 3(19)]	No comparable definition.
Federal agency	No comparable definition.	"[A]ny department, agency, or other independent agency or establishment of the Federal Government including any Government corporation, and the Government Printing Office." [Amended TSCA 3(20)]	Amended TSCA 3(19) is similar to S. 3209, but also refers to any "other instrumentality" of the Federal Government.
Importer	No comparable definition.	No comparable definition.	"[A]ny person who imports a chemical substance or mixture, or any article containing a chemical substance or mixture, for distribution in commerce." [Amended TSCA 3(20)]

Table 1. (Continued)

Provision	15 U.S.C. 2601 et seq.	S. 3209	H.R. 5820
Persistent	No comparable definition.	As defined in the policy statement entitled "Category for Persistent, Bioaccumulative, and Toxic New Chemical Substances" (64 Federal Register 60194, Nov. 4, 1999). Authorizes EPA to revise this definition by rule. [Amended TSCA 3(21)]	Significantly persists in one or more environmental media, as indicated by monitoring data or other evidence. Authorizes EPA to revise the definition by rule to reflect the state of the science and provide for equal or greater protection of health and the environment. [Amended TSCA 3(21)]
Person	No comparable definition.	An "individual, trust, firm, joint stock company, corporation (including a government corporation), partnership, association, State, municipality, commission, political subdivision of a State, or any interstate body and shall include each Federal agency and any officer, agent, or employee thereof." [Amended TSCA 3(22)]	No comparable definition.
Reasonable certainty of no harm	No comparable definition.	"[I]n establishing whether a chemical substance or mixture meets the safety standard under this subchapter, aggregate exposure and cumulative exposure of the general population or of any vulnerable population to the chemical substance or mixture presents a negligible risk of any adverse effect …"[Amended TSCA 3(23)]	No comparable definition.
Special substance characteristics	No comparable definition.	Defines "special substance characteristics" to mean "such physical, chemical, or biological characteristics, other than molecular identity, that the Administrator determines, by order or rule, may significantly affect the risks posed by substances exhibiting those characteristics." Allows consideration of size, shape, reactivity, and any other properties that may significantly affect risks posed. [Amended TSCA 3(24)]	Defines "substance characteristic" as "the physical and chemical characteristics that may vary for such substance, and whose variation may bear on the toxicological properties or the exposure potential of the chemical substance." Includes structure and composition, size, shape, surface structure, reactivity, and "other characteristics that may bear on toxicological properties." [Amended TSCA 3(22)]

		meeting criteria for Category 1 or 2 for any toxicity endpoint established by the Globally Harmonized System for the Classification and Labeling of Hazardous Substances; "causes an adverse effect that has been demonstrated in humans or other exposed organisms";	
		or "the weight of evidence … demonstrates the potential for an adverse effect in humans or other exposed organisms." [Amended TSCA 3(25)]	Similar to S. 3209, but includes a metabolite or degradation product of a substance or mixture and omits the first condition—that is, it does not define the term by reference to the categories of the Globally Harmonized System for the Classification and Labeling of Hazardous Substances. Also, the word "exposed" is omitted from the third defining condition. [Amended TSCA 3(23)]
Toxicological property	No comparable definition.	"[A]ctual or potential toxicity or other adverse effects of a chemical substance or mixture, including actual or potential effects of exposure" on mortality, morbidity, reproduction, growth and development, the immune system, the endocrine system, brain or nervous system, other organ systems, or "any other biological functions in humans or nonhuman organisms." [Amended TSCA 3(26)]	Amended TSCA 3(24) is similar to S. 3209 but includes established precursors to such toxicity or adverse effects and explicitly includes effects on genetics, including mutagenicity, genotoxicity, and epigenetics.
Use	No comparable definition.	No comparable definition.	Any utilization of a chemical substance or mixture that is not otherwise covered by the terms manufacture or process, such as "any composition of the chemical substance with other chemical substances" or any group of utilizations determined by EPA to be a single use under new TSCA 3(b)(2). [Amended TSCA 3(25)]

Table 1. (Continued)

Provision	15 U.S.C. 2601 et seq.	S. 3209	H.R. 5820
Vulnerable population	No comparable definition.	A "population that is subject to a disproportionate exposure to, or potential for a disproportionate adverse effect from exposure to, a chemical substance or mixture …" and includes those who work with chemical substances and mixtures, individuals with preexisting medical conditions, the elderly, pregnant women, infants, children, adolescents, and "members of any other appropriate population identified by the Administrator." [Amended TSCA 3(27)]	Amended TSCA 3(26) is similar to S. 3209, except that workers are included in the definition without regard to their work with chemicals and effects on pregnant women include effects on fetal development. Other appropriate populations may be identified based on consideration of socioeconomic status, racial or ethnic background, cultural practices, or similar factors identified by the Administrator.
EPA authority to define	No comparable provision.	No comparable provision.	Adds a new subsection (b) to TSCA section 3 (15 U.S.C. 2602). New TSCA 3(b)(1) authorizes the Administrator to determine different forms of a chemical substance with a particular molecular identity to be different chemical substances for purposes of the act based on variations in the substance characteristics. Such distinct substances are to be considered new chemical substances. New TSCA 3(b)(2) authorizes the Administrator to determine different uses of a chemical substance or mixture to be the same use for purposes of the act, based on industry classification systems or factors determined by the Administrator to indicate similarity in use and exposure.

Provision	15 U.S.C. 2601 et seq.	S. 3209	H.R. 5820
Testing authorities and requirements	TSCA 4(a) [15 U.S.C. 2603(a)] directs the EPA Administrator to promulgate a rule requiring that testing be conducted on a substance or mixture to develop health and environmental effects data if: (1) the manufacture, processing, distribution, use, or disposal of the chemical "may present an unreasonable risk of injury to health or the environment," or (2) the chemical is produced in very large volume and there is a potential for a substantial quantity to be released into the environment or for substantial or significant human exposure. In either case, EPA also must find that (a) existing data are insufficient to resolve the question of safety, and (b) testing is necessary to develop the data.	S. 3209, section 5, amends TSCA 4. Amended TSCA 4(a) directs the EPA Administrator within one year of enactment of S. 3209 to promulgate a rule establishing a minimum data set and requiring submission to EPA of such data by manufacturers and processors of new chemical substances or existing chemical substances on a priority list [established in amended TSCA 6(a)]. Also requires updates of minimum data set submissions. Amended TSCA 4(b) authorizes EPA to require, by rule or by order, testing and submission of test results by a specified date "as necessary for making any determination or carrying out any provision" of TSCA. Authorizes EPA to require submission of a sample of any chemical for the purpose of conducting tests and making a determination or carrying out any provision of the act.	H.R. 5820, section 4, amends TSCA 4. Similar to S. 3209, but amended TSCA 4(a) requires manufacturers and processors to submit a minimum data set for mixtures as well as chemical substances. In addition, the Administrator is required to update the rule establishing the minimum data set at least once every 5 years. Amended TSCA 4(a)(3) excepts several categories of chemical substances (see Exemptions below). Amended TSCA 4(b) explicitly authorizes EPA to issue a rule or order, after notice and opportunity for comment, for collection of data in addition to the minimum data set, but the bill does not authorize chemical sample collection (except for enforcement purposes under amended TSCA 11).
Test rule requirements	TSCA 4(b) [15 U.S.C. 2603(b)] requires EPA in any test rule to identify the chemical substance or mixture for which testing is required, specify standards for the development of test data, and specify the period during which test results must be submitted.	Amended TSCA 4(c) is similar to 15 U.S.C. 2603(b), but is applicable to EPA orders as well as rules.	Like S. 3209 in applying to orders as well as rules, but EPA is authorized rather than required to specify test protocols and methodology, and the bill does not refer to "standards for the development of test data."
Deadlines for data submission	No comparable provision.	Amended TSCA 4(a) requires submission to EPA of the minimum data set within 18 months of the date that EPA places a chemical on the chemical substance priority list, or at the time notice is provided to EPA [under revised TSCA section 5(a)] that a new chemical will be manufactured. Amended TSCA 6(b)(2) requires submission of the minimum data set within 30 months of the date that EPA places a chemical on the chemical substance priority list, or for existing chemicals not placed on the priority list, within 14 years of the date of enactment of S. 3209.	Amended TSCA 4(a) requires minimum data set submission within 18 months of the date that EPA places a chemical or mixture on the chemical substance priority list; at the time notice is provided to EPA that a new chemical will be manufactured; or, for existing chemicals (but not mixtures) not placed on the priority list, within 3 years of the date of enactment of H.R. 5820 for high production volume chemicals, within 4 years for chemicals produced in moderate volumes, and within 5 years for chemicals produced in low volumes, as determined by the Administrator.

Table 2. (Continued)

Provision	15 U.S.C. 2601 et seq.	S. 3209	H.R. 5820
Persons required to submit data	TSCA 4(b) [15 U.S.C. 2603(b)] requires manufacturers and processors to conduct tests in response to a rule issued by EPA, but allows EPA to permit such persons to designate one person or a qualified third party to conduct such tests and submit data on their behalf.	Amended TSCA 4(c) directs EPA to specify in any rule or order persons required to conduct tests and submit data, but allows designation of a single data provider, as is allowed under current law. In the event that a single data provider is designated, all parties remain individually liable for testing requirements	Amended TSCA 4(b)(5) is the same as S. 3209.
Failure to submit data	No comparable provision.	Amended TSCA 4(b)(3) authorizes EPA to, by order, prohibit manufacture, processing, or distribution in commerce for a chemical if a manufacturer or processor fails to submit required data.	Amended TSCA 4(a)(4) authorizes penalties for noncompliance as provided in amended TSCA section 16, or imposition of conditions, by order, including prohibitions on the manufacture, processing, or distribution in commerce of the chemical substance, mixture or article containing the substance. Failure to submit required information is grounds for determining that the chemical substance or mixture does not meet the safety standard under amended TSCA 6(b)(3)(D).
Data exemption	TSCA 4(c) [15 U.S.C. 2603(c)] allows manufacturers and processors to request an exemption, and directs EPA to grant an exemption if data would be duplicative. Provides for reimbursement by the exempted persons to manufacturers and processors who collected and submitted data. EPA is required to order a manufacturer or processor who is exempt to reimburse the entity that submitted data. Such an order is a final agency action for the purpose of judicial review.	Amended TSCA 4(d) would have the same effect as TSCA, except exemptions could apply to orders as well as rules, and the bill does not provide that the Administrator's order to reimburse is a final agency action for the purpose of judicial review.	Similar to 15 U.S.C. 2603(c), but amended TSCA 4(c) applies to orders as well as rules. In addition, amended TSCA 4(a)(3) exempts from data requirements: (1) chemicals for which EPA first is required to make a safety determination under amended TSCA 6(a)(1)(A); (2) chemicals determined by the Administrator to be persistent, bioaccumulative, and toxic and to which people are exposed; (3) chemicals EPA exempts because, due to their intrinsic properties, they do not pose any risk of injury to health or the environment; and (4) chemicals that EPA determines are safer substitutes for chemicals already in commerce.

processing		has submitted a declaration of cessation of manufacture or processing of a chemical substance.	permanent cessation.
Contents of minimum data set	No comparable provision.	Amended TSCA 4(a) directs EPA to include in the minimum data set information on substance characteristics and on hazard, exposure, and use of chemical substances and mixtures, information that the EPA anticipates will be useful in conducting safety standard determinations as required by amended TSCA section 6(b). Allows EPA to provide for varied or tiered testing for different chemicals or categories of chemicals.	Similar to S. 3209, but amended TSCA 4(b)(3) also requires that the set include information on chemical identity; biological and environmental fate and transport; toxicological properties; volume manufactured, processed, or imported; intended uses; and "exposures from all stages of the chemical substance or mixture's lifecycle that are known or reasonably foreseeable to the party submitting the data set."
Prescribed data needs	TSCA 4(b) [15 U.S.C. 2603(b)] authorizes EPA to prescribe data development standards for effects which may present an unreasonable risk of injury to health or the environment and for characteristics of chemical substances and mixtures which may present such a risk, as well as for methodologies including epidemiological studies, serial or hierarchical tests, in vitro tests, and whole animal tests.	Amended TSCA 4(c) authorizes EPA to prescribe data development standards for effects which may be considered in a safety determination, assessing exposure, including presence in human tissues and fluids, and characteristics of chemicals that may present an adverse effect. Also authorizes EPA to prescribe biomonitoring studies, in addition to methodologies already permitted under 15 U.S.C. 2603(b).	Similar to 15 U.S.C. 2603(b) but amended TSCA 4(b)(4)(A) does not refer to test standards, and it provides broad authority to prescribe testing for "any toxicological property and any other adverse effect which may be considered in a safety standard determination under [amended TSCA] section 6(b)." Specifies exposure information for which testing may be prescribed, and explicitly authorizes testing for bioaccumulation, biomonitoring studies, and in amended TSCA 4(b)(4)(B), industrial hygiene surveys.
Petition for standards for development of test data	TSCA 4(g) [15 U.S.C. 2603(g)] authorizes manufacturers to petition EPA to prescribe standards for the development of test data for a new chemical.	Eliminates this provision.	Same as S. 3209.
Alternatives to animal testing	No comparable provision.3	Requires that animal tests are consistent with provisions of amended TSCA section 31, promoting alternatives to animal testing.	Amended TSCA 4(b)(4)(B) requires that whole animal studies be consistent with amended TSCA section 34.

Table 2. (Continued)

Provision	15 U.S.C. 2601 et seq.	S. 3209	H.R. 5820
Biomonitoring by the Centers for Disease Control and Prevention	No comparable provision.	No comparable provision.	New TSCA 4(b)(6) requires that any biomonitoring study of the public regarding a chemical substance or any metabolite or degradation byproduct be conducted by the Director of the Centers for Disease Control and Prevention in collaboration with the Administrator at the expense of the manufacturers and processors of the substance.
Review and revision of data needs	TSCA 4(b) [15 U.S.C. 2603(b)]requires annual review and revision, if necessary, of standards for the development of data.	Changes the interval between required reviews and revisions, if necessary, from one to 3 years.	Similar to 15 U.S.C. 2603(b), but amended TSCA 4(b)(4)(C) refers to "methodology" rather than "standards for the development of test data."
Rulemaking process	TSCA 4(b) [15 U.S.C. 2603(b)] directs EPA to issue test rules pursuant to 5 U.S.C. 553 (Administrative Procedure Act, procedures for informal notice and comment rulemaking). In addition, persons must be given an opportunity for oral presentation of data, views, or arguments and to make written submissions; a transcript must be made of oral presentations; and the Administrator must publish findings required by TSCA 4(a)(1)(A) or (B).	Amended TSCA 4(c) omits TSCA requirements for rulemaking that go beyond the requirements of 5 U.S.C. 553. Amended TSCA 4(b) authorizes EPA to issue orders in lieu of rules.	Amended TSCA 4(b)(8) is the same as S. 3209.
Interagency testing committee	TSCA 4(e) [15 U.S.C. 2603(e)] establishes the Interagency Testing Committee (ITC) to advise the Administrator regarding chemicals that should receive priority consideration for promulgation of a test rule [under subsection (a)].	Amended TSCA 6(a)(3) establishes the Interagency Prioritization and Testing Committee, which is similar to the ITC in composition.	Amended TSCA 4(e) is similar to current law, but amended TSCA 4(e) directs the ITC also to make recommendations for listing chemical substances and mixtures under amended TSCA 6(a)(1). The bill raises the number of committee members from 8 to 10, including a representative of the Food and Drug Administration and one from the Consumer Product Safety Commission.

for testing	prioritized list of chemicals for the Administrator to consider testing and to designate up to 50 chemicals on the list as the highest priority. In selecting chemicals, the committee is authorized to consider all relevant factors, including "the extent to which the substance or mixture is closely related to a chemical substance or mixture which is known to present an unreasonable risk of injury to health or the environment."	recommendations for issuance of test rules or orders. The committee is directed to make recommendations for issuance of test rules or orders based on "all factors relevant to risk" including presence in biological and environmental media, use, production volume, toxicity, persistence, or bioaccumulation.	chemicals posing a "substantial risk" rather than those posing "an unreasonable risk" of injury to health or the environment, and directs the committee to provide priority attention to chemicals suspected of causing or contributing to "adverse effects on health or the environment" rather than those that might cause or contribute to cancer, gene mutations, or birth defects.
	Priority attention is to be given to chemicals "known to cause or contribute to or which are suspected of causing or contributing to cancer, gene mutations, or birth defects."	The committee also is to make recommendations for placement of chemical substances on the priority list based on criteria identified pursuant to amended TSCA 6(a)(1). Recommendations are to be in the form of one or more lists of chemical substances and mixtures and are to be updated annually, if necessary. The Administrator is directed to provide reasonable opportunity to any interested person to file written comments on the recommendations.	The requirement that the list of chemicals designated for testing should remain less than 50 is eliminated. The chemicals listed are to be those that should be subject to test rules or orders, in the view of the committee.
Public notice of receipt of data	TSCA 4(d) [15 U.S.C. 2603(d)] requires that EPA provide public notice of receipt of data and make data available for examination by any person (subject to section 14).	Amended TSCA 4(e) is similar to 15 U.S.C. 2603(d) in requiring public notice of the receipt of data, but applies also to data submitted in accord with an EPA order, and requires that data be made available on the internet.	Similar to 15 U.S.C. 2603(d), but amended TSCA 4(d) applies also to data submitted in accord with an EPA order and requires that notices be added to the public database established in amended TSCA 8(d).
Judicial review prohibited for committee recommendations	No comparable provision.	Amended TSCA 6(a)(4) protects from judicial review recommendations by the Interagency Prioritization and Testing Committee.	No comparable provision.
Required agency actions	TSCA 4(f) [15 U.S.C. 2603(f)] requires the EPA Administrator to respond within 180 days to new information indicating "that there may be a reasonable basis to conclude that a chemical substance or mixture presents or will	Eliminates this provision, but TSCA 4(a) as amended requires EPA, within 180 days of receipt of a data submission, to determine, by order, whether the manufacturers and processors of the substance have established that the substance meets the safety standard. If data are not submitted, S.	Eliminates this provision, but amended TSCA 6(b)(3)(D) requires that the Administrator complete and publish the safety standard determination within 30

Table 2. (Continued)

Provision	15 U.S.C. 2601 et seq.	S. 3209	H.R. 5820
	present a significant risk of serious or widespread harm to human beings from cancer, gene mutations, or birth defects." Requires EPA to "initiate appropriate action under section 5, 6, or 7 to prevent or reduce to a sufficient extent such risk or publish in the Federal Register a finding that such risk is not unreasonable." A finding that a risk is not unreasonable is a final agency action for purposes of judicial review.	3209 authorizes EPA to prohibit, by order, manufacture, processing, or distribution in commerce of the substance, mixture, or article containing the substance.	months of the date on which the chemical substance or mixture is placed on the priority list, or, within 18 months of the date of enactment of H.R. 5820 for chemicals listed in amended TSCA 6(a)(1)(A). However, if additional information is needed, the determination must be completed and published within 12 months after submission of all required information.
Requests from other federal agencies	No comparable provision.	Amended TSCA 4(f) authorizes any federal agency to request that EPA seek information unavailable to that other agency which it has determined would assist it in carrying out its duties or exercising its authority. Requires EPA to collect and provide such information to the requesting agency or to publish in the Federal Register the reason for not doing so.	Amended TSCA 4(f) is the same as S. 3209.
Certification of data submitted	No comparable provision.	Amended TSCA 4(g) requires that each submission of information under a rule or order be accompanied by a certification of the accuracy, reliability, and completeness (to the extent reasonably ascertainable) of the information provided. Such certification must be signed by a responsible official of the manufacturer or processor.	Amended TSCA 4(a)(2)and 8(i) require each submission of a minimum data set to be accompanied by a certification of the accuracy, reliability, and completeness (to the extent reasonably ascertainable) of the information provided. Such certification must be signed by a responsible official of the manufacturer or processor.

Provision	15 U.S.C. 2601 et seq.	S. 3209	H.R. 5820
Notices concerning new chemicals or uses	TSCA 5(a)(1) [15 U.S.C. 2604(a)(1)] prohibits manufacture of a new chemical and prohibits manufacture or processing of any chemical for a use which is a significant new use unless notice is submitted to EPA 90 days prior to such manufacture or processing.	Amended TSCA 5(a)(1)-(3) is similar to current law, but it also requires notice prior to processing of a new chemical substance or mixture. Requires notice prior to manufacture or processing of an existing chemical that has met the safety standard for a use, at a production volume, or in a manner other than specified in the safety determination. It is unclear whether notice is required for an existing chemical for which EPA has not made a safety determination when a new use is proposed. However, it appears that the law would require a new declaration under amended TSCA 8(a) and data submission under amended TSCA 5(b) prior to manufacturing or processing.	Amended TSCA 5(a) is similar to S. 3209 in that it prohibits manufacturing and processing of new chemical substances and mixtures unless notice is provided to EPA. H.R. 5820 also requires notice prior to manufacture or processing of a new mixture or an existing chemical or mixture for a use that EPA determines is a new use [see "New use determination" below].
New use determination	TSCA 5(a)(2) [15 U.S.C. 2604(a)(2)]directs EPA to designate a significant new use of an existing chemical by promulgating a rule after considering "all relevant factors, including—(A) the projected volume of manufacturing and processing of a chemical substance, (B) the extent to which a use changes the type or form of exposure of human beings or the environment to a chemical substance, (C) the extent to which a use increases the magnitude and duration of exposure of human beings or the environment to a chemical substance, and (D) the reasonably anticipated manner and methods of manufacturing, processing, distribution in commerce, and disposal of a chemical substance."	Amended TSCA 5(a)(2) and (3) designate use of an existing chemical as new if at the time of enactment of S. 3209—such use was not ongoing, use would be at a significantly increased volume, or the person who would be manufacturing or processing the chemical had not previously done so.	Amended TSCA 5(a)(2) designates a use as new if—1) the substance or mixture already received a safety standard determination which did not include the use; or (2) the proposed use will result in manufacturing or processing of the chemical substance or mixture at a significantly increased volume from that previously considered in the safety determination made under amended TSCA 6(b).
Special substance characteristics	No comparable provision.	Amended TSCA 5(a)(6) directs Administrator to determine by order or rule that a variant of a chemical substance exhibiting one or more "special substance characteristics" [such as size or reactivity, as defined in amended TSCA 3(24)] is a new use or a new chemical substance.	No comparable provision.

Table 3. (Continued)

Provision	15 U.S.C. 2601 et seq.	S. 3209	H.R. 5820
Notice content	TSCA 5(d) [15 U.S.C. 2604(d)] requires that notices contain the information required by TSCA 8(a)(2)(A)-(D), (F), and (G). [See “Reporting and record keeping” below.]	Amended TSCA 5(c) requires a notice to include the declaration made under amended TSCA 8(a)(2), the minimum data set, and a statement that the chemical will meet the safety standard.	Amended TSCA 5(c) is similar to S. 3209, but the statement required is that the chemical is “reasonably anticipated to meet the safety standard under section 6(b),” and H.R. 5820 requires a justification for such statement.
Certification	No comparable provision.	Amended TSCA 5(e) requires that each submission of information under a rule or order be accompanied by a certification of the accuracy, reliability, and completeness (to the extent reasonably ascertainable) of the information provided. Such certification must be signed by a responsible official of the manufacturer or processor.	Amended TSCA 8(i) requires each submission of information that is required pursuant to “this title” to be accompanied by a certification of the accuracy, reliability, and completeness (to the extent reasonably ascertainable) of the information provided. Such certification must be signed by a responsible official of the manufacturer or processor.
Submission of test data with notice	TSCA 5(b) [15 U.S.C. 2604(b)] requires persons who propose to manufacture a new chemical or to manufacture or process a chemical for a significant new use to submit with such notice any test data that are required by rule under TSCA 4(a). If no test data are required under TSCA 4(a), but the chemical has been listed under TSCA 5(b)(4), indicating that the Administrator has determined that it “presents or may present an unreasonable risk,” manufacturers and processors must submit data showing that manufacture, processing, distribution in commerce, use, and disposal (in the case of a new chemical or mixture), or the new use (in the case of a significant new use), “will not present an unreasonable risk of injury to health or the environment.”	Amended TSCA 5(b) requires submission to EPA of any data required for a chemical under a test rule or order, as well as the declaration and minimum data set at the time notice is provided to EPA. With respect to a new use of a chemical for which the Administrator previously has made the safety determination, manufacturers must provide an update for the minimum data set. With respect to a new use of a chemical which has not been evaluated for safety, manufacturers must submit to EPA a new or updated declaration under amended TSCA 8(a) and comply with amended TSCA 5(b).	Amended TSCA 5(b) is similar to S. 3209 in requiring data submission for chemicals subject to test rules or orders at the time notice is provided, but requires submission for new mixtures as well as new chemical substances. H.R. 5820 also requires submission of the declaration and minimum data set when notice is provided regarding production of a chemical substance or mixture. Also requires that any chemical substance subject to a Significant New Use Rule as of the date of enactment of H.R. 5820 remain subject to that rule until it receives a safety standard determination and any conditions are imposed.

data	subject to protections for confidential business information in section 14.	TSCA 14.	manufacture notice. Also requires that EPA publish notice regarding the chemical identity, intended uses, the nature and results of tests performed, and availability of the declaration under amended section 8(a) and the minimum data set under amended TSCA 4(a). Internet publication is not explicitly required.
EPA's response to notice	No comparable provision, but EPA has 90 days to decide whether the chemical or chemical use may present an unreasonable risk of injury to health or the environment.	Amended TSCA 5(a)(4) requires EPA to determine within 180 days after receiving notice and data whether it has been established that the chemical substance or mixture meets the safety standard under amended TSCA section 6(b).	Requires EPA to determine within 90 days after receiving notice and data whether the use is a critical use or whether a safety standard determination is required by amended TSCA 5(a)(1)(B). Within 9 months of that determination, the Administrator is required to "complete any such required safety standard determination."
Extension of the notice period	TSCA 5(c) [15 U.S.C. 2604(c)] authorizes EPA to extend the period between notice and manufacture for additional periods of up to a total of 90 days "for good cause."	Eliminates this provision.	Same as S. 3209.
Publication of notice	TSCA 5(d) [15 U.S.C. 2604(d)(1)] requires notice to be available for examination by interested persons, subject to disclosure restrictions at TSCA 14 [15 U.S.C. 2613]. [See "Disclosure of data" section below.] Directs EPA to publish a notice identifying the chemical, listing the intended uses, and describing the nature of tests performed and data that were developed pursuant to a rule.	Amended TSCA 5(b)(3)-(4) is similar to current law [TSCA 5(d)(1)], but specifies that EPA must make notices available on the internet and requires disclosure of the availability of the minimum data set. In addition, requires EPA to make available on the internet a list of chemical substances for which notice has been received monthly. [Also, see "Disclosure of data" section below.]	Amended TSCA 5(c)(3) is similar to current TSCA 5(d), but H.R. 5820 specifies that data must be placed in the public database established pursuant to amended TSCA 8(d). Eliminates specific content requirements for published notices. [Also, see "Disclosure of data" section below.]
"Manufacture" and "process"	TSCA 5(i) [15 U.S.C. 2604(i)] defines "manufacture" and "process" as used in TSCA section 5 to mean manufacturing and processing for commercial purposes.	Amended TSCA 5(f) provides the definition as current law.	Same as current law [TSCA 5(i)].

Table 3. (Continued)

Provision	15 U.S.C. 2601 et seq.	S. 3209	H.R. 5820
Safety determination for new chemical or new use	No specific provision, but TSCA requires an EPA finding that manufacture, processing, distribution in commerce, use, and disposal of a chemical “may present an unreasonable risk of injury to health or the environment,” when the agency issues a test rule under TSCA 4(a). Similarly, EPA must find that a chemical substance “presents an unreasonable risk” before EPA can issue a rule to ensure that risks are adequately regulated.	Amended TSCA 5(a) prohibits manufacture and processing of a chemical for which notice is required unless the Administrator finds either: (1) that the manufacturers and processors have established that the chemical meets the safety standard under proposed TSCA 6(b), or (2) that the new chemical substance or its metabolite or degradation product is not, and is not expected to be—manufactured in a volume of more than one million pounds annually or released into the environment in a volume of more than 100,000 pounds annually; a known, probable, or suspected reproductive, developmental, neurological, or immunological toxicant, carcinogen, mutagen, or endocrine disruptor, or has other toxicological properties of concern; persistent and bioaccumulative; found in human cord blood, or otherwise found in human blood, fluids, or tissue, unless it is naturally present at the level commonly found in that medium; or found in food, drinking water, ambient or indoor air, residential soil, or house dust, unless it is naturally present at the level commonly found in that medium. With respect to a new use of a chemical for which the Administrator previously has made the safety determination, manufacturers must provide evidence that permits the Administrator to amend the safety determination.	Amended TSCA 5(a) imposes an additional condition on any new chemical or use: manufacture or processing is permitted only if the Administrator finds—the use is a critical use as determined pursuant to amended TSCA 6(e), or the substance or mixture meets the safety standard for all intended uses under amended TSCA 6(b).
Protection against unreasonable risks	TSCA 5(f) [15 U.S.C. 2604(f)] directs EPA to control an unreasonable risk posed by a new chemical or a significant new use of a chemical in the interim between the expiration of the notification period and the effective date of a rule that is being developed to control such risk.	This provision is eliminated. S. 3209 requires risk management prior to production and distribution.	Same as S. 3209.

	rule, it is effective on the date it is issued.		
Regulation pending development of information	TSCA 5(e) [15 U.S.C. 2604(e)] authorizes the Administrator to issue a proposed order to prohibit or limit manufacture, processing, distribution in commerce, use, or disposal of a new chemical or significant new use in the event that the Administrator determines that: the information available "is insufficient to permit a reasoned evaluation of the health and environmental effects" of the chemical; and either the chemical may present an unreasonable risk, or it will be produced in substantial quantities and "may reasonably be anticipated to enter the environment in substantial quantities or there is or may be significant or substantial human exposure to the substance." If EPA makes such a determination but no order is issued or objections are filed to the order, then EPA must apply to the District Court to prohibit or limit activities with respect to the chemical, unless EPA finds on the basis of the objections that the determination cannot be made.	This provision is eliminated. Amended TSCA 5(a) requires submission of data and a safety determination prior to production and distribution of a new chemical or of an existing chemical for a new use.	Same as S. 3209.
Statement of reasons for not taking action	If EPA does not take action with respect to a chemical covered by a test rule [under TSCA 4(a)], a significant new use rule [under TSCA 5(a)(1)(B)], or listed under TSCA 5(b)(4), then TSCA 5(g) directs the Administrator to publish a statement of reasons for not taking action.	This provision is eliminated.	This provision is eliminated.
Exemptions from notice requirements General authority	TSCA 5(h)(4) [15 U.S.C. 2604(h)(4)] authorizes EPA upon application and by rule to exempt a manufacturer of a new chemical substance from notification and data requirements, if the Administrator determines it will not "present an unreasonable risk of injury to health or the environment." Any such rule must be promulgated in accord with TSCA section 6(c)(2) and (3) (see below).	Eliminates this provision.	Same as S. 3209, but amended TSCA 39(d) directs EPA to review existing exemptions granted under TSCA 5(h)(4) within a year of enactment of H.R. 5820 to determine whether chemicals exempted under current law meet the "intrinsic properties" requirements to qualify for an exemption under amended TSCA 39(d).

Table 3. (Continued)

Provision	15 U.S.C. 2601 et seq.	S. 3209	H.R. 5820
Intermediate production chemicals	TSCA 5(h)(5) [15 U.S.C. 2604(h)(5)] authorizes exemptions upon application for production-related (temporary, so-called "intermediate") chemicals when no human or environmental exposure will occur.	Amended TSCA 5(d)(4) is the same as current law.	Same as current law.
Test marketing	TSCA 5(h)(1) [15 U.S.C. 2604(h)(1)] authorizes EPA to exempt any person from notification or data requirements so as to permit manufacture or processing for test marketing purposes, if the person applies for such exemption and demonstrates the chemical will not present an "unreasonable risk."	Amended TSCA 5(d)(1) is similar to current law but a person must show that it "will not endanger the health [sic] or the environment." "Test marketing" is defined in amended TSCA 5(f) to exclude provision of a chemical or article containing a chemical to an end consumer.	Amended TSCA 5(d)(1) is similar to current law but specifies that exemptions are made "by order," authorizes exemptions for mixtures as well as chemical substances, and requires that the applicant show the chemical or mixture will not present "a substantial" risk.
Equivalent chemicals and duplicative data	TSCA 5(h)(2) [15 U.S.C. 2604(h)(2)] allows manufacturers and processors of new chemicals or chemicals with significant new uses that are on the priority list but are not subject to a section 2603 data submission requirement to request from EPA an exemption from the requirement in 2604(b)(2) that they submit data	Amended TSCA 5(d)(2) allows manufacturers and processors of new chemicals or chemicals with new uses to request, and EPA to grant, full or partial exemption from data submission requirements if the chemical is equivalent to a chemical substance for which data have been submitted and submission would be duplicative of data previously submitted to EPA.	Amended TSCA 5(d)(2) concerns any new use of a chemical substance or mixture subject to a data collection rule or order under section 4. H.R. 5820 directs the Administrator upon application to exempt the manufacturer or processor of such a chemical or mixture from the amended TSCA 5
	showing that manufacture, processing, distribution in commerce, use, and disposal of the chemical substance, or the significant new use, will not present an unreasonable risk. Directs EPA to grant such exemption if the chemical is equivalent to a substances for which data has been submitted and data would be duplicative. Provides for reimbursement by the exempted persons to manufacturers and processors who collected and submitted data. EPA is required to order a manufacturer or processor who is exempt to reimburse the entity that submitted data. Such an order is a final agency action for the purpose of judicial review.	Provides for reimbursement by the exempted persons to those who collected and submitted data in the same manner as current law.	requirement to submit data along with the required new use notice, if the chemical is equivalent to a substance for which data have been submitted previously and submission would be duplicative. Provides for reimbursement by the exempted persons to those who collected and submitted data in the same manner as current law.

Small quantities	manufacturing and processing of small quantities for purposes of scientific experimentation or chemical research on, or analysis of, such substances or another substance, including product development.	Amended TSCA 5(d)(3) is the same as current law.	Amended TSCA 5(d)(3) is similar to current law, but it also applies to mixtures.
EPA response to exemption requests	TSCA 5(h)(6) [15 U.S.C. 2604(h)(6)] requires EPA to publish notices of, and request comments on, requests for exemptions that the agency receives. EPA must issue an approval or disapproval within 45 days.	Amended TSCA 5(d)(5) is the same as current law.	Same as current law.
Safer chemical substances or mixtures	No comparable provision.	No comparable provision.	Amended TSCA 5(d)(1) exempts from section 5 requirements any new chemical substance or mixture approved pursuant to amended TSCA 35 as a safer alternative. Amended TSCA 5(d)(2) authorizes the Administrator to exempt any new chemical substance or new use of a chemical substance or mixture from the requirements of amended TSCA section 5 pursuant to section 39, based on intrinsic properties which render the substance harmless.
Chemicals of concern list (priority list)	TSCA 5(b)(4) [15 U.S.C. 2604(b)(4)] authorizes EPA to "by rule, compile and keep current a list of chemical substances with respect to which the Administrator finds that the manufacture, processing, distribution in commerce, use, or disposal, or any combination of such activities, presents or may present an unreasonable risk of injury to health or the environment." In listing decisions the Administrator is directed to consider "all relevant factors, including	Amended TSCA 6(a) directs EPA by order to develop and publish a priority list of not less than 300 chemical substances "for which safety standard determinations shall first be made" within 18 months of S. 3209 enactment. Failure of EPA to establish the priority list or to update it is defined to be a failure to perform a nondiscretionary duty and subject to judicial review.	Amended TSCA 6(a) establishes a list of 19 specified chemical substances for which safety standards must first be made. Twelve months after H.R. 5820 is enacted, the Administrator must update the list to consist of at least 300 chemical substances. Listing is at the

Table 3. (Continued)

Provision	15 U.S.C. 2601 et seq.	S. 3209	H.R. 5820
	—(I) the effects of the chemical substance to health and the magnitude of human exposure to such substance; and (II) the effects of the chemical substance on the environment and the magnitude of environmental exposure to such substance."	Chemicals must be selected based on: available scientific evidence, relative risk, presence in biological and environmental media, use, production volume, toxicity, persistence, bioaccumulation, "or other properties indicating risk." Requires removal of a substance from the list only after a safety standard determination has been made for it. Requires EPA to add chemical substances or mixtures periodically to keep the number greater than 300 at all times until all substances and mixtures distributed in commerce have had a safety standard determination.	Administrator's discretion, "based on available scientific evidence and consideration of their hazard, exposure, or risk relative to other chemical substances, aggregate or cumulative exposure, evidence of exposure to humans including presence in human or animal biological and environmental media including in the workplace, use, volume of manufacture, toxicological properties, persistence, bioaccumulation, or other properties indicating risk." Otherwise similar to S. 3209, but does not require the list to be developed and published "by order" and may include mixtures.
	Any rule listing a chemical must identify "uses that the Administrator determines, by rule under subsection (a)(2), would constitute a significant new use of such substance." Any rulemaking under this provision must be promulgated pursuant to the procedures specified in 5 U.S.C. 553 and must provide opportunity for oral and written presentation of data, views, or arguments. In addition, a transcript must be kept of any oral presentation and the Administrator must make and publish with the rule the finding that an activity related to the chemical "presents or may present an unreasonable risk of injury to health or the environment."	EPA must give due consideration in listing decisions to recommendations provided by the Interagency Prioritization and Testing Committee which is to base its recommendations on the criteria listed (above) in amended TSCA 6(a). Amended TSCA 6(a)(4) protects from judicial review EPA's decisions about whether to place particular chemicals on the priority list, including any EPA response to a petition to list a particular chemical substance.	H.R. 5820 also does not explicitly require that EPA consider listing recommendations provided by the Interagency Prioritization and Testing Committee.

Provision	15 U.S.C. 2601 et seq.	S. 3209	H.R. 5820
Regulation	TSCA 6(a) [15 U.S.C. 2605(a)] directs EPA by rule to apply one or more requirements "to the extent necessary to protect adequately against" an "unreasonable risk" "using the least burdensome requirements," if EPA finds that "there is a reasonable basis to conclude that the manufacture, processing, distribution in commerce, use, or disposal of a chemical substance or mixture … presents or will present an unreasonable risk of injury to health or the environment." Specifies various regulatory options. Authorizes regulations to—prohibit or limit the amount of substance manufactured, processed, or distributed in commerce, generally or for a specific use; require labeling, recordkeeping, provision of notice to distributors and to the public of unreasonable risk of injury, or replacement or repurchase of a substance; and specify methods of disposal.	S. 3209 does not require rulemaking, but section 7 amends TSCA 6(b) and (c) to authorize EPA to specify allowed uses of any substance that meets the safety standard and to impose conditions on its manufacture, processing, use, distribution in commerce, or disposal to "ensure the safety standard is met." Many of the conditions that EPA is authorized to impose are the same as the regulatory options listed in current law, but S. 3209 also authorizes EPA to impose a requirement that the manufacturers and processors of a chemical substance or mixture or article containing it develop a risk reduction management plan to achieve a risk reduction specified by the Administrator. The bill does not authorize the option of requiring manufacturers or processors to give notice of unreasonable risk of injury to distributors or the public or to replace or repurchase a substance.	Amended TSCA 6(c)(2) is similar to S. 3209, but the bill authorizes prescription for specific control measures to reduce occupational exposures and requires that any such measures must reflect the industrial hygiene hierarchy of controls. Any warnings or instructions required must be consistent with the Globally Harmonized System of Labeling and Classification of Chemicals. In determining the conditions necessary to ensure the substance or mixture meets the safety standard, the Administrator must "consider human health and the environment as the primary and paramount concern, and shall also consider the technological feasibility of compliance, the economic impact of compliance, and benefits of earlier compliance, and other relevant considerations."
	TSCA 6(c) [15 U.S.C. 2605(c)] specifies procedures for rulemaking that allow for informal hearings and requires EPA to publish a statement describing the health and environmental effects, level of exposure, benefits of the substance, and "reasonably ascertainable economic consequences of the rule, after consideration of the effect on the national economy, small business, technological innovation, the environment, and public health." Requires that EPA's decisions be based on the rulemaking record. Directs EPA to promulgate needed rules under other environmental laws, unless it is in the public interest to issue rules under TSCA.	In addition, S. 3209 differs from current law in that the bill does not authorize limiting conditions to specified geographic areas, nor does it prohibit requiring a person to take an action that would be in violation of a law or requirement of a state or political subdivision.	

Table 4. (Continued)

Provision	15 U.S.C. 2601 et seq.	S. 3209	H.R. 5820
General process for safety determinations	No comparable provision.	Amended TSCA 6(b)(1) requires that EPA produce a risk assessment addressing health and environmental impacts using "the best available science" in support of any determination that a manufacturer or processor of a chemical substance has met the burden of proof. Risk assessments must be transparent and understandable to the public and to risk managers.	Amended TSCA 6(b)(1) requires the Administrator to apply a safety standard that "takes into account aggregate exposure to a chemical substance or mixture and ensures that, for all intended uses—(
		No risk assessment is required when EPA determines that the burden of proof has not been met, and such determination is not subject to judicial review. Amended TSCA 6(b)(1) also establishes that manufacturers and processors of a chemical substance are responsible for proving that the substance meets the applicable safety standard, and that the EPA Administrator has the responsibility of determining within 180 days of data submission whether the manufacturers and processors have met the burden of proof.	i) with regard to public health, there is a reasonable certainty that no harm will result, including to vulnerable populations; and (ii) the public welfare is protected." The Administrator is required to consider the lifecycle of the substance or mixture and "available information concerning the cumulative effects of exposure to chemical substances or mixtures." H.R. 5820 is similar to S. 3209 in that amended TSCA 6(b)(2) assigns the burden of proving that a chemical meets the safety standard to manufacturers and processors. Amended TSCA 6(b)(3) requires the Administrator to "determine whether the chemical substance or mixture meets the safety standard, taking into account any existing conditions or controls already in effect, or can be made to meet the safety standard through the imposition of additional conditions … and whether intended uses that do not meet the safety standard are critical."

			30 months after the date on which a chemical is placed on the priority list, or within 18 months of the date of enactment for the 19 chemicals listed in amended TSCA 6(a)(1)(A). The determinations must be made in keeping with "standards for assessment" developed by the Administrator under amended TSCA 6(b)(4).
Scientific standards for data assessment	No comparable provision.	Amended TSCA 6(b)(1)(C) requires The Administrator to "use the best available science" in conducting a risk assessment considering the most recent recommendations of the National Academy of Sciences "on ways to better protect people, including pregnant women, infants, children and other vulnerable populations from harm by exposure to toxic substances when assessing such potential risks."	Within 18 months of the date of enactment of H.R. 5820, amended TSCA 6(b)(4) directs the Administrator, after providing for notice and opportunity for comment, to develop and publish guidance regarding the use of science in making safety determinations. Requires that the Administrator rely on the recommendations of the National Academy of Sciences report entitled Science and Decisions. Such guidance must be reviewed and may be revised to reflect new scientific developments or understanding at least once every 5 years.
Safety of chemicals for export	No comparable provision.	Directs EPA to consider risks that a chemical manufactured for export may pose in the United States during production and distribution in commerce, including in imported products containing the substance.	No comparable provision.
Safety determinations for existing chemicals			
EPA's determination	No comparable provision.	Within 180 days of receipt of a data submission, EPA is directed to determine, by order, whether the manufacturers and processors of the substance have established that the substance meets the safety standard.	Amended TSCA 6(b)(3)(D) requires that the Administrator complete and publish the safety standard determination within 30 months of the

Table 4. (Continued)

Provision	15 U.S.C. 2601 et seq.	S. 3209	H.R. 5820
			date on which the chemical substance or mixture is placed on the priority list, or, within 18 months of the date of enactment of H.R. 5820 for chemicals listed in amended TSCA 6(a)(1)(A). However, if additional information is needed, the determination must be completed and published within 12 months after submission of all required information.
Failure to submit data	No comparable provision.	If data are not submitted, amended TSCA 6(b)(2) authorizes EPA to prohibit, by order, manufacture, processing, or distribution in commerce of the substance, mixture, or article containing the substance.	Amended TSCA 6(b)(3) provides that failure to submit required information is grounds for determining that the chemical substance or mixture does not meet the safety standard.
Failure by EPA	No comparable provision.	If EPA fails to meet the deadline for a safety determination, amended TSCA 6(b)(2) provides that manufacturers and processors are required to notify EPA, the public, their employees, and customers written notice that a determination by EPA of the safety of the chemical is pending.	Amended TSCA 6(b)(7) requires EPA promptly to publish notice of a failure to publish or renew a determination by the applicable deadline. Directs the Administrator to prohibit new manufacturers or processors or new uses of the chemical substance or mixture until the determination is published and requires manufacturers and processors to provide written notice to the public, their employees, and their commercial customers that a safety standard determination is pending.
Resubmission	No comparable provision.	Amended TSCA 6(b)(2) provides that at least every 15 years, manufacturers and processors of each chemical substance must submit the minimum dataset and indicate whether the substance and specified uses meet the safety standard.	Amended TSCA 6(b)(6) provides that a safety determination remains in effect for up to 15 years, if no new use or information warrants a redetermination.

Redetermination	No comparable provision.	information raises a question in that regard, on the receipt of a renewal submission, or 15-years following the previous determination.	periods but the burden of proof for renewal remains with the manufacturers and processors.
Petition for redetermination	No comparable provision.	Authorizes any person to petition the Administrator for a redetermination. The Administrator must decide whether to make the requested redetermination and publish the decision and its basis in the Federal Register within 180 days.	No comparable provision.
Restrictions on substances that do not meet the safety standard	No comparable provision, but TSCA 6(a) directs EPA by rule to apply one or more requirements (such as labeling or banning particular uses) "to the extent necessary to protect adequately against" an "unreasonable risk" "using the least burdensome requirements," if the Administrator finds that "there is a reasonable basis to conclude that the manufacture, processing, distribution in commerce, use, or disposal of a chemical substance or mixture, or that any combination of such activities, presents or will present an unreasonable risk of injury to health or the environment."	Amended TSCA 6(b)(3) prohibits manufacture, processing, and distribution in commerce of a chemical substance, mixture, or article if EPA makes a safety determination and does not determine that a substance meets the safety standard. Such prohibition is effective immediately for a new chemical or after one year for any other chemical.	Amended TSCA 6(c)(3) is similar to S. 3209 but also immediately prohibits activities with respect to a new use of an existing substance, mixture, or article if EPA determines that the manufacturers and processors have not shown that the use meets the safety standard.
Unrestricted distribution in commerce	No comparable provision, but current law allows unrestricted distribution in commerce of chemicals and mixtures unless EPA determines that a substance presents an unreasonable risk and then promulgates a rule to regulate it.	No comparable provision. If EPA determines that the substance meets the safety standard, the allowed uses of the substance must be specified as well as any conditions on those specified uses to ensure that the safety standard is met. S. 3209 prohibits manufacture, processing, and distribution in commerce of a chemical substance, mixture, or article for uses not specified in the safety determination.	Amended TSCA 6(c)(1) authorizes manufacture, processing, and distribution in commerce for any chemical substance or mixture that EPA determines meets the safety standard without imposition of conditions for uses identified and included in the safety standard determination. EPA is authorized to make the determination contingent on the continuation of conditions or controls already in effect.

Table 4. (Continued)

Provision	15 U.S.C. 2601 et seq.	S. 3209	H.R. 5820
Uses restricted for substances meeting the safety standard	No comparable provision.	Amended TSCA 6(b) prohibits manufacture, processing, and distribution in commerce of a chemical substance, mixture, or article for any use not specified in the safety determination if EPA determines that the chemical and its specified uses meet the safety standard.	Amended TSCA 6(c)(2) requires EPA to impose conditions on manufacture, processing, use, distribution in commerce, or disposal of a chemical substance or mixture to ensure that it meets the safety standard. Such conditions must "be identified in a manner that ensures effective and efficient protection of health and the environment."
Effective date of Section 6 rules	TSCA 6(d) [15 U.S.C. 2605(d)] directs EPA to make such rules effective "as soon as feasible," and allows EPA to make a proposed rule effective upon publication until the effective date of the final rule if there is an unreasonable risk of serious or widespread injury to health or the environment and a court has granted relief under section 7.	Amended TSCA 6(i) directs EPA to specify a date on which a rule or order shall take effect and that such date should be "as soon as feasible."	Amended TSCA 6(c)(2)(H) requires that conditions be met within one year after publication of the determination, or as quickly as feasible and in no case later than 3 years after publication. Prohibits activities with respect to a chemical if such conditions are not met by the applicable deadline.
Quality control	TSCA 6(b) [15 U.S.C. 2605(b)] authorizes EPA to review and regulate a manufacturer's or processor's quality control procedures if there is "a reasonable basis to conclude" that the manner of manufacturing or processing "unintentionally causes a chemical … to present or which will cause it to present an unreasonable risk of injury to health or the environment."	Amended TSCA 6(d) is similar to current law but applies when there is "a reasonable basis to conclude" that the manner of manufacturing or processing "may present a substantial endangerment to health or the environment." Does not require such determination to be made on the record after opportunity for hearing.	Amended TSCA 6(d) is similar to current law but applies when there is a reasonable basis to conclude that the manner of manufacturing or processing "causes the chemical substance or mixture to present or which will cause it to present a significant risk of injury to health or the environment."
	EPA also is authorized to order the manufacturer or processor to provide notice to its customers of such risk and to replace or repurchase the substance as is necessary to adequately protect health or the environment. Requires any determination that a chemical presents an unreasonable risk to be made on the record after opportunity for hearing.		

Resale of used articles	No comparable provision.	[illegible] or 29 do not apply to resale of an article subject to a restriction under amended TSCA 6(b) if the article has previously been used.	No comparable provision.
Delay of effective date of restrictions	No comparable provision.	Authorizes EPA to order delay in the effective date of a restriction for 3 years for retail sales to an end consumer of a chemical substance, mixture, or article subject to a restriction under sections 4(a)(3), 4(b)(3), 6(b)(2)(A)(iv), 6(b)(3), 8(b)(6), 8(c)(3), or 29, if necessary and appropriate, if it "will not present a substantial endangerment to human health or the environment." EPA authority does not extend to any retailer who has failed to comply with an order requesting information under amended TSCA section 8.	No comparable provision, but conditions may be imposed up to 3 years after they are established (see above "Effective date of Section 6 rules").
Exemptions from prohibitions and other restrictions	No comparable provision.	Amended TSCA 6(e) authorizes EPA to grant, by order, exemptions (and renewals of exemptions) to restrictions established under sections 4(a)(3), 4(b)(3), 6(b)(2)(A)(iv), 6(b)(3), 8(b)(6), 8(c)(3), and 29 for particular uses. Exemptions and renewals may be granted for up to 5 years, if manufacturers and processors "have established by clear and convincing evidence that the uses to be exempted meet the exemption criteria." Those criteria are: (1) that the exemption is in the paramount interest of national security; (2) lack of availability would cause significant disruption in the national economy; or (3) the use is a critical or essential use, and there is no safer feasible alternative, or the specified use compared to available alternatives provides benefit to health, the environment, or public safety.	Amended TSCA 6(e) authorizes manufacturers and processors to request exemptions from restrictions under amended TSCA 6(c) for a specific use by a manufacturer or processor. The procedure for granting exemptions is the same as under S. 3209, but H.R. 5820 requires that EPA impose conditions on any use receiving an exemption "to reduce risk from the chemical substance or mixture to the greatest extent feasible."

Table 4. (Continued)

Provision	15 U.S.C. 2601 et seq.	S. 3209	H.R. 5820
		The manufacturer or processor must notify customers and the public of any exemptions granted. EPA is directed to impose any condition on a granted exemption that is necessary to ensure the protection of human health and the environment.	
Certification of the quality of submitted information	No comparable provision.	Amended TSCA 6(h) requires that each submission of information under a rule or order be accompanied by a certification of the accuracy, reliability, and completeness (to the extent reasonably ascertainable) of the information provided. Such certification must be signed by a responsible official of the manufacturer or processor.	Amended TSCA 8(i) requires each submission of information that is required pursuant to "this title" or pursuant to a rule or order issued under this title to be accompanied by a certification of the accuracy, reliability, and completeness (to the extent reasonably ascertainable) of the information provided. Such certification must be signed by a responsible official of the manufacturer or processor.
Mercury	15 U.S.C. 2605(f) prohibits federal agencies from conveying, selling, or distributing elemental mercury to any federal agency, state or local government, or private entity, except to facilitate storage at a federal agency.	Amended TSCA 6(g) is the same as current law.	Amended TSCA 6(g) is the same as current law.
Polychlorinated biphenyls (PCBs)	TSCA 6(e) [15 U.S.C. 2605(e)] directs EPA to prescribe methods of disposal for PCBs and to require PCBs to be marked with clear and adequate warnings and instructions regarding processing, distribution in commerce, use, or disposal. Prohibits use of any PCB other than "in a totally enclosed manner," unless EPA finds that such activity "will not present an unreasonable risk of injury to health or the environment."	Amended TSCA 6(f) is similar to existing law but authorizes the Administrator to act by order or rule, and to grant exemptions from the general prohibitions when the activities "will not present a substantial endangerment to health or the environment" rather than when activities "will not present an unreasonable risk."	Amended TSCA 6(f) is similar to current law, but authorizes EPA to grant exemptions if activities will not "present a substantial risk to health or the environment" and will comply with section 37 (concerning data quality).

	person to petition for an exemption and authorizes EPA to grant such exemption if EPA finds that an unreasonable risk would not result, and "good faith efforts have been made to develop a chemical substance which does not present an unreasonable risk … and which may be substituted for such [PCB]." Requires use of rulemaking procedure in TSCA 6(c).		
Imminent hazards			
Relief	Authorizes an appropriate district court to grant relief necessary to protect health or the environment from unreasonable risk.	Similar to current law, but authorizes court to grant relief necessary to protect health or the environment from "the risk associated with the activity involved in the action."	Similar to current law, but authorizes court to grant relief necessary to protect health or the environment from "imminent and substantial endangerment."
Civil actions	TSCA 7(a) [15 U.S.C. 2606(a)] authorizes EPA to begin a civil action: for seizure of "an imminently hazardous" chemical substance, mixture, or article; for relief against any person who manufactures, processes, distributes in commerce, or uses, or disposes of such chemical or article; or for both seizure and relief. Requires EPA to commence such civil action if the agency has not made a rule under TSCA 6(a) effective immediately. Requires that EPA "where appropriate, concurrently with the filing of an action … initiate a proceeding for the promulgation of a rule" under TSCA 6(a). Defines "imminently hazardous chemical substance or mixture" to mean a chemical that "presents an imminent and unreasonable risk of serious or widespread injury to health or the environment."	Similar to current law, but authorizes EPA action against a person when a chemical, mixture, or article "may present an imminent and substantial endangerment to health or the environment." S. 3209 does not require EPA to commence action if the agency has not made a rule effective immediately concerning the chemical. S. 3209 also authorizes EPA to issue orders to protect health or the environment from a chemical substance or mixture or article containing such substance or mixture that may present an imminent and substantial endangerment to health or the environment. Eliminates authority concurrently to initiate a proceeding for the promulgation of a rule under TSCA 6(a) [15 U.S.C. 2605(a)]. Also eliminates the definition for "imminently hazardous chemical substance or mixture."	Amended TSCA 7 is similar to S. 3209, but amended TSCA 7(d) directs the Administrator, as appropriate, concurrently with the filing of an action under amended TSCA 7(a)(1), to add the chemical substance or mixture to the priority list under amended TSCA 6(a) or to initiate a redetermination of whether the substance meets the safety standard under amended TSCA 6(b).

Table 5. Reporting Requirements in Selected Provisions of TSCA (15 U.S.C. 2601 et seq.), the Safe Chemicals Act (S. 3209), as Introduced, and the Toxic Chemicals Safety Act of 2010 (H.R. 5820), as Introduced

Provision	15 U.S.C. 2601 et seq.	S. 3209	H.R. 5820
Reporting and record keeping (declaration)	TSCA 8(a) [15 U.S.C. 2607(a)] authorizes EPA, to the extent necessary for the effective enforcement of the law, to promulgate rules requiring maintenance of records and submission of reports to EPA by persons who manufacture or process or who propose to manufacture or process a chemical substance. Prohibits a rule requiring maintenance of records or submission of reports with respect to changes in the proportions of the components of a mixture unless necessary for effective enforcement.	Amended TSCA 8(a) requires each manufacturer and processor of a chemical substance to submit a declaration of current manufacturing or processing for each substance, mixture, or article manufactured or processed containing information that will assist the Administrator in making a safety determination or otherwise in administering the law. Each declaration must be accompanied by certification of its accuracy, reliability, and comprehensiveness. Amended TSCA 8(b) authorizes EPA by rule or order to require any person who manufactures, processes, distributes in commerce, uses, or disposes of a chemical substance, mixture, or article to maintain records of and report any information that would assist the Administrator in administering TSCA. Authorizes EPA to require information concerning chemical identity.	Amended TSCA 8(a) is the same as S. 3209, but in addition authorizes EPA to require submission of a declaration by manufacturers and processors of mixtures, when the Administrator determines that the substance characteristics of the mixture are different from those of the constituent chemical substances, "in kind or in degree." Amended TSCA 8(b) is similar to S. 3209.
Failure to submit declaration	No comparable provision.	EPA may by order prohibit manufacture, processing, or distribution of any substance if a manufacturer or processor violates EPA requirements for submitting or updating declarations.	Amended TSCA 8(a)(6) authorizes the Administrator to impose penalties pursuant to section 16 or, by order, prohibit, or otherwise impose conditions under amended TSCA 6(c) on a manufacturer or processor in violation of an 8(a) reporting requirement.
Information submitted	TSCA 8(a) authorizes collection of information including: trade name or common name, chemical identity, categories of use, amount of each chemical manufactured or processed, byproducts resulting from such manufacture or processing, "all existing data concerning the environmental and health effects," number of individuals exposed, and, in the initial report, the manner of disposal.	Amended TSCA 8(a) requires the declaration to state: the chemical identity and substance characteristics; name and location of each facility where the substance is manufactured or processed or from which it is distributed; a list and copies of health and safety studies that are reasonably ascertainable; and all other information not previously submitted to EPA regarding the physical, chemical, and toxicological properties of the substance, the annual production volume and known uses of, exposure and fate information, and the name and location of each facility to which the substance is sent for processing, distribution, or use.	Similar to S. 3209, but also requires information regarding the number of individuals exposed, classification of the toxicity of the chemical, categories of intended use of the substance or mixture, total amount of substance and mixture manufactured or processed, byproducts resulting from manufacture, processing, use, or disposal, exposure information, any condition currently placed on the substance or mixture due to regulation under any federal law or due to voluntary action, and for a processor of a chemical substance, information indicating that the mixture has substance characteristics that are different from

		has ceased or will cease within 180 days. Declarations must be updated and submitted at least every 3 years, and immediately when new information becomes available regarding a physical, chemical, or toxicological property or use of, or exposure to the substance.	adverse effect of the chemical substance or mixture, suggesting an adverse effect at a lower dose than previously demonstrated, or otherwise reasonably relevant to an analysis of whether the chemical substance or mixture meets the safety standard under section 6."
Inventory	TSCA 8(b) [15 U.S.C. 2607(b)] directs EPA to compile, keep current, and publish an inventory of each chemical manufactured or processed in the United States. New chemicals are to be listed when manufacture or processing begins. The list should exclude chemicals produced in small quantities for purposes of scientific experimentation, analysis, or research. Authorizes EPA to list chemicals by category rather than individually.	Amended TSCA 8(c) is the same as TSCA 8(b), except that it omits the authority in current law to list chemicals by category rather than individually. In addition, S. 3209 requires that EPA publish in the Federal Register a list of all chemical substances distributed in commerce that categorizes the substances based on existing information available into categories based on known health or environmental effects, exposure, insufficient data, or other category that EPA considers appropriate.	Amended TSCA 8(c)(1) directs the Administrator to compile, keep current, publish and enter into the public database established under amended TSCA 8(d) a list of each chemical substance and mixture for which a declaration (under amended TSCA 8(a)) is received which is manufactured or processed in the United States. Omits the authority in current law to list chemicals by category rather than individually. The list shall not include any chemical substance or mixture for which all manufacturers and processors have submitted declarations of permanent cessation. Also requires the categorization of substances as in S. 3209, but includes mixtures.
Small quantities for research and development	TSCA 8(a)(3) [15 U.S.C. 2607(a)(3)] explicitly authorizes EPA to require by rule reporting from small manufacturers and processors of chemicals substances or mixtures subject to a rule proposed or promulgated under TSCA 4, 5(b)(4), or 6 or an order under TSCA 5(e) or with respect to which relief has been granted under TSCA 5 or 6. Reporting also may be required once under TSCA 8(b) for the original inventory (see below) from processors and manufacturers who are small (as determined by the Administrator after consultation with the Small Business Administration).	Amended TSCA 8(b)(2) authorizes EPA by rule to define manufacture, processing, distribution in commerce, use, or disposal of a chemical substance in small quantities solely for purposes of research, and to issue a rule or order under this subsection only if EPA determines maintenance of records or submission of reports is necessary for effective enforcement of the law.	Amended TSCA 8(b)(2) is the same as S. 3209.

Table 5. (Continued)

Provision	15 U.S.C. 2601 et seq.	S. 3209	H.R. 5820
	TSCA 8(b) [15 U.S.C. 2607(b)]directs EPA to limit record keeping and reporting requirements for those who manufacture or process a chemical in small quantities solely for purposes of scientific experimentation or analysis of a chemical substance.		
Public access	No comparable provision.	Amended TSCA 8(d) directs EPA to establish an electronic database of information relating to the toxicity and use of and exposure to chemical substances. It is required to include descriptions of "all significant decisions made by the Administrator" and significant information submitted under TSCA Title I.	Same as S. 3209.
Records of significant adverse reactions	TSCA 8(c) [15 U.S.C. 2607(c)] requires all manufacturers and processors to keep records of all reports of significant adverse reactions to health or the environment alleged to have resulted from exposure to a chemical substance.	Amended TSCA 8(e) is similar to TSCA but also requires submission of such records to EPA.	Similar to S. 3209 but requires submission to EPA annually or immediately upon request by the Administrator, while current law and S. 3209 do not require reports at specific times.
Disclosure to commercial purchasers	No comparable provision.	No comparable provision.	Amended TSCA 8(f) requires all manufacturers and processors of chemical substances and mixtures to provide to all known commercial purchasers, with shipment or promptly thereafter, and by request, a disclosure, subject to amended TSCA 14
			(which protects confidential business information), of the chemical identity of the substances or mixture ingredients, their toxicological properties, health and safety studies submitted to EPA, and records of significant adverse reactions submitted under amended TSCA 8(e).
Information from other federal agencies	No comparable provision.	Amended TSCA 8(f) requires each federal agency and institution to submit to EPA a synopsis of the data and records in its control that may be useful to EPA in carrying out TSCA Title I. Such synopsis shall be updated and resubmitted at least once every 3 years.	Similar to S. 3209, but agencies are to respond to a request from EPA, not to submit reports every 3 years, and the bill directs EPA to prescribe by order the format, content, and level of detail of the requested report.

		to hazard, use, exposure, or risk of a chemical substance or mixture.	Administrator reasonably expects may have information on chemical substances or mixtures that would assist in making a safety standard determination. Requests must be issued no more than 12 months after a substance or mixture is added to the priority list under amended TSCA 6(a) or within 12 months of enactment of H.R. 5820 for substances listed in amended TSCA 6(a)(1)(A).
Health and safety studies	TSCA 8(d) [15 U.S.C. 2607(d)] directs EPA to require manufacturers, processors, and distributors to submit lists and copies of health and safety studies for each chemical manufactured or processed.	S. 3209 requires submission of such studies as part of the declaration under amended TSCA 8(a).	Same as S. 3209.
Substantial risk notice	TSCA 8(e) [15 U.S.C. 2607(e)] requires manufacturers, processors, and distributors who obtain information "which reasonably supports the conclusion" that a chemical substance or mixture "presents a substantial risk of injury to health or the environment" to inform EPA.	Amended TSCA 8(g) is the same as current law.	Amended TSCA 8(h) is the same as current law.
Certification	No comparable provision.	Amended TSCA 8(h) requires that each submission of information under a rule or order be accompanied by a certification of the accuracy, reliability, and completeness (to the extent reasonably ascertainable) of the information provided. Such certification must be signed by a responsible official of the manufacturer or processor.	Amended TSCA 8(i) requires each submission of information that is required pursuant to "this title" or pursuant to a rule or order issued under this title, other than a submission under section 8(g) (relating to submissions from federal agencies),
			to be accompanied by a certification of the accuracy, reliability, and completeness (to the extent reasonably ascertainable) of the information provided. Such certification must be signed by a responsible official of the manufacturer or processor.

Table 5. (Continued)

Provision	15 U.S.C. 2601 et seq.	S. 3209	H.R. 5820
"Manufacture" and "process"	TSCA 8(f) [15 U.S.C. 2607(f)] defines "manufacture" and "process" to mean manufacture or process for commercial purposes.	Amended TSCA 8(i) is the same as current law.	Amended TSCA 8(j) is the same as current law.

Table 6. Other Selected Provisions of TSCA (15 U.S.C. 2601 et seq.), the Safe Chemicals Act (S. 3209), as Introduced, and the Toxic Chemicals Safety Act of 2010 (H.R. 5820), as Introduced

Provision	15 U.S.C. 2601 et seq.	S. 3209	H.R. 5820
Action under laws administered by other federal agencies	If EPA has a reasonable basis to conclude that activities with respect to a chemical substance or mixture present or will present an unreasonable risk, and EPA determines that such risk may be prevented or reduced to a sufficient extent by action taken under a federal law not administered by EPA, then TSCA 9(a) [15 U.S.C. 2608(a)] directs EPA to submit to the agency which administers such law a report describing the risk and activities that present such risks. The EPA report must request that the other federal agency (1) tell EPA whether the risk may be prevented or reduced under the law the agency administers, and (2) issue an order declaring whether the activities present a risk. If EPA makes a report and the other agency either (1) issues an order declaring that the activities do not present the risk, or (2) initiates action to protect against such risk, then EPA may not take regulatory action under TSCA 6 or 7.	Amended TSCA 9(a) is similar to current law, but the criterion for EPA action differs. If the Administrator determines "that the manufacture, processing, distribution in commerce, use, or disposal of a chemical … either does not meet the safety standard … or requires conditions or restrictions" to do so, and "that action may be taken under a Federal law not administered by the Administrator" then EPA must submit a report to the other agency describing the activities that prevent the chemical from meeting the safety standard or restrictions or conditions required to meet the safety standard. The report must request that the other agency (1) determine if the action may be taken under a law administered by the agency, and if so, (2) initiate such action and provide a timetable for action, and (3) respond to EPA's report. If the other agency initiates action within the timeframe specified, EPA may not take regulatory action, except under TSCA 7. If the other agency determines that action cannot be taken under its authorities; does not initiate action or complete action within the timeframe provided; or fails to respond, then EPA may, by order, initiate action to ensure compliance with the safety standard.	Similar to current law, except that EPA must submit a report to another agency if "the Administrator has reasonable basis to conclude that a chemical substance or mixture does not meet the safety standard under section 6(b)." Also, information that is to be published in the Federal Register must be entered into the public database established in amended TSCA 8(d).

other EPA administered laws	taken under other federal laws administered by EPA.	Same as current law.	
Occupational safety and health	TSCA 9(c) states that any EPA exercise of authority under TSCA is deemed to be exercising statutory authority to prescribe or enforce standards or regulations affecting occupational safety and health.	Same as current law. In addition, S. 3209 directs EPA to ensure that any EPA actions to address workplace exposures "are consistent with the industrial hygiene hierarchy of controls."	Same as current law.
Coordination	TSCA 9(d) directs EPA to consult and coordinate with appropriate federal agency heads to achieve "maximum enforcement" "while imposing the least burdens of duplicative requirements" on those being regulated.	S. 3209 strikes the requirement that coordination for the purpose of enforcement should impose the least burdens of duplicative requirements.	Same as S. 3209.
Mixture survey	No comparable provision.	No comparable provision.	Amended TSCA 8(c)(3) directs EPA to characterize the number of mixtures introduced into commerce and the number of such mixtures that may have different substance characteristics from the constituent chemical substances. Such survey shall be based on declarations and a survey of processors. The characterization of mixtures in commerce must be published in the Federal Register and entered into the public database established in amended TSCA 8(d).
Subpoenas and warrants	TSCA 11(c) [15 U.S.C. 2610(c)] authorizes EPA to require by subpoena attendance and testimony of witnesses, production of reports, documents, answers to questions, and other information. Authorizes district courts to order compliance in the event of contumacy, failure, or refusal to obey.	Amended TSCA section 11(c) authorizes EPA to require attendance, testimony, and production of documents, items, answers to questions and other information deemed necessary. In the event that "there is reason to believe that the provisions" of the law have been violated, EPA is empowered to obtain and to execute warrants authorizing entry, inspection, and copying of records, or seizures of any chemical in violation.	Amended TSCA 11 is the same as current law.

Table 6. (Continued)

Provision	15 U.S.C. 2601 et seq.	S. 3209	H.R. 5820
Inspections	TSCA 11 [15 U.S.C. 2610] authorizes EPA to inspect premises in which chemicals are manufactured, processed, stored, or held before or after distribution in commerce and any conveyance used to transport chemicals in commerce. Limits inspections by requiring presentation of appropriate credentials and written notice to the person in charge of the premises or conveyance to be inspected on each occasion of inspection. Requires inspections to begin and end with reasonable promptness and to "be conducted at reasonable times, within reasonable limits, and in a reasonable manner." Prohibits inspection of financial, sales, pricing, personnel, or research data, unless they are described specifically in the required written notice.	Similar to TSCA but also applies to premises and conveyances handling articles subject to TSCA, and S. 3209 does not limit inspections by requiring presentation of credentials or provision of written notice. Additionally authorizes EPA to inspect any place where records relating to compliance with the law are held and to inspect and obtain samples of any chemicals, containers, or labeling. Does not prohibit inspection of any data.	Amended TSCA 11 is similar to current law, but also applies to commercial premises in which articles containing such substances or mixtures are manufactured, processed, stored, or held, and to any place where records relating to such substances or mixtures or articles are held. Like S. 3209, authorizes EPA to inspect and obtain samples. The bill also authorizes EPA to collect containers and labeling of substances, mixtures, products, or articles.
Exports			
Exclusion from requirements	TSCA 12(a) [15 U.S.C. 2611(a)] excludes chemical products manufactured for export (other than elemental mercury) from TSCA requirements except for reporting and record keeping requirements in Section 8. This exclusion applies as long as the products are labeled for export only and their manufacture, processing, and distribution do not pose an unreasonable risk within the United States. EPA may require testing to allow assessment of the risk within the United States.	Amended TSCA 12 eliminates the current exclusion from requirements for chemicals manufactured, processed, or distributed in commerce solely for the purpose of export.	Same as S. 3209.
Mercury	TSCA 12(c) [15 U.S.C. 2611(c)] prohibits the export of elemental mercury (but not of coal). Authorizes exemptions from this prohibition for essential uses.	Same as current law.	Same as current law.
Notice of export	TSCA 12(b) [15 U.S.C. 2611(b)] requires anyone who exports or intends to export a substance that is subject to a test rule or order under section 4 or a proposed or final rule under section 5 or 6, or for which action is pending or relief has been granted under section 5 or 7, to notify EPA of such exportation or intent, and	Amended TSCA 12(a) is similar to current law, but excludes from requirements those who "intend" to export, and applies only to exports of chemicals subject to data submission requirements under amended TSCA 5 or 6(b), or for which action has been taken under TSCA 6 or 7.	Similar to S. 3209, but requires exporters of substances contained in Annex III of the Rotterdam Convention on Prior Informed Consent Procedure for Certain Hazardous Chemicals and

	EPA must then notify the countries that will be receiving the substance that data are available or that restrictions are in place in the United States for such substance.	of export for providing notice to EPA, and specifies that EPA must provide notice to countries "promptly thereafter." Requires exporters to notify EPA, and EPA to notify receiving countries, of any change in the status of a chemical. EPA also must notify receiving countries that it has received new data or if there is any change in risk management action taken under section 6 or 7. Requires EPA to maintain copies of current notices provided to other governments and to make them available to the public electronically.	Pesticides in International Trade (including any amendment or protocol) to file notice of export at least 30 days prior to the date of exportation. (Note that the United States has not yet ratified this treaty.)
Imports	TSCA 13 [15 U.S.C. 2612] directs the Secretary of the Treasury to refuse entry into the United States of chemicals that fail to comply with a rule under TSCA or that are in violation of TSCA.	Amended TSCA 13 is similar to current law but transfers authority to the Secretary of the Department of Homeland Security.	Amended TSCA 13 is similar to S. 3209, but requires importers of substances, mixtures, or articles to satisfy all requirements under amended TSCA 4, 5, 6, and 8.
Disclosure of data	TSCA 14 [15 U.S.C. 2613] provides broad protection of proprietary confidential information about chemicals in commerce. Disclosure by EPA employees of such information generally is not permitted, except to other federal employees or when relevant in any proceeding under TSCA.	Amended TSCA 14 requires conformance to the standards of the Freedom of Information Act (FOIA). Like current law, S. 3209 prohibits disclosure of proprietary confidential information by EPA employees except to other federal agencies and EPA contractors, but it specifically directs	Amended TSCA 14 is similar to S. 3209 in that it requires conformance to the standards of the FOIA and allows disclosure to state, tribal, and municipal governments.
	Disclosure of information is required when "necessary to protect health or the environment against an unreasonable risk of injury to health or the environment." Manufacturers, processors, or distributors in commerce may designate data that they believe is entitled to confidential treatment. If EPA proposes to release such data the Administrator must notify the manufacturer, processor, or distributor who designated the data.	EPA to disclose information upon request to a state, tribal, or municipal government for the purpose of administration or enforcement of a law if an agreement ensures that the recipient government will take appropriate steps to maintain the confidentiality of the information in accordance with amended TSCA 14 and 40 CFR 350.27, which refers to the substantiation form to accompany claims of trade secrecy under the Emergency Planning and Community Right-to-Know Act.	It also generally prohibits disclosure by EPA employees, but only if the designation is not determined to be inappropriate. Like S. 3209, H.R. 5820 provides for disclosure to state, tribal, and municipal governments. Directs EPA to release information if it is necessary to protect health and the environment from a "substantial" risk of injury.

Table 6. (Continued)

Provision	15 U.S.C. 2601 et seq.	S. 3209	H.R. 5820
		Directs EPA to release information if it is necessary to protect health or the environment against "an imminent and substantial endangerment" to health or the environment. Requires those designating data as confidential to justify such claims and to certify that the information is not otherwise publicly available. The Administrator is required to by order develop standards for justifying claims and necessary documentation. Requests must be reviewed by EPA within 90 days. If approved, submitted information will be protected from disclosure for up to 5 years.	The procedure in amended TSCA 14(f) for requesting and receiving designation of information as confidential is similar to that in S. 3209, but submitters must pay a fee, and the Administrator is not required to approve each request. Rather the Administrator is required to review and approve a representative sample of requests.
Health and safety information	Disclosure of health and safety information is not prohibited when it relates to a chemical which has been offered for commercial distribution, or for which testing is being required under section 4, or for which notification is required under section 5, unless data disclosure would reveal a chemical process or chemical proportion in a mixture.	Amended TSCA 14 specifies data that are not to be protected, including the identity of a chemical, any safety standard determination, and information "indicating the presence of a chemical in a consumer article intended for use or reasonably expected to be used by children or to which children can otherwise be reasonably expected to be exposed."	Similar to S. 3209. In addition, H.R. 5820 denies protection for information about the components of a mixture, when included in a health and safety study, safety standard determination, or information indicating presence in a consumer article intended for use or reasonably expected to be used by children or indicating exposure to the mixture in children. Any other information indicating exposure to a chemical substance or mixture in children also is denied disclosure protection.
Penalties for disclosure and inappropriate designation	TSCA 14(d) provides that knowing and willful disclosure of protected information by a federal employee may result in a fine of up to $5,000 or imprisonment for up to one year, or both.	Amended TSCA 14(f) is the same as current law.	Amended TSCA 14(g) retains the penalties for disclosure in current law. In addition, it authorizes administrative penalties for a manufacturer or processor whose designation of information is found not to have met the criteria for protection. Knowing and willful designation of information that does not meet the criteria may result in a fine of not more than $5,000 or imprisonment for up to one year, or both.

designating information confidential	No comparable provision.	No comparable provision.	payment of a reasonable fee from any person designating information for protection or seeking to renew such designation.
Risk information for workers	No comparable provision.	Amended TSCA 14(h) requires EPA to provide standards for and facilitate sharing with each certified or recognized bargaining agent information regarding chemical identity, safety standard determination, and health and safety data that pertains to substances that workers may come into contact with or otherwise be exposed to during the course of work.	Amended TSCA 14(j) is the same as S. 3209.
Prohibited Acts	TSCA 15 [15 U.S.C. 2614] prohibits any person from failing or refusing to comply with rules, orders, or other requirements of TSCA, using for commercial purposes a chemical substance or mixture that was known to be manufactured, processed, or distributed in commerce in violation of the law, failing or refusing to establish and maintain records, submit reports, notices, or other information, or to permit access to or copying of records, or failing or refusing to permit entry or inspection.	Amended TSCA 15 is similar to current law and prohibits all the same actions, but also prohibits manufacturing, processing, distributing in commerce, or disposing of a chemical or article or using an article that was known to have been manufactured, processed, or distributed in commerce in violation of the law. S. 3209 also prohibits failing or refusing to establish and maintain "accurate and complete" records, reports, notices, information, disclosures, declarations, certifications, or other information. Prohibits submitting information "that is materially false, in whole or in part," or falsifying or concealing "any material fact." Prohibits taking any action prohibited by amended TSCA.	Similar to S. 3209, but also prohibits failing or refusing to permit access to or copying of records and introducing or knowingly distributing in commerce a substance or mixture, or an article containing a substance or mixture, that lacks or fails to comply with labeling requirements, or that has misleading advertising or labeling. It also prohibits making or employing without proper authority any identification device authorized or required under TSCA.
Penalties	TSCA 16 [15 U.S.C. 2615] authorizes civil penalties, not to exceed $25,000 per violation per day, and affords the defendant an opportunity to request a hearing before an order is issued and to petition for judicial review of an order after it is issued with the U.S. Court of Appeals for the District of Columbia circuit or for any other circuit in which the person resides or transacts business.	Amended TSCA 16 increases the maximum per violation per day civil penalty to $37,500 and authorizes EPA to commence a civil action in an appropriate U.S. district court to assess penalties. Changes the court in which a person may file a petition for judicial review to eliminate jurisdiction in any federal circuit court, instead vesting jurisdiction in the appropriate district court for the district in which the person resides or transacts business.	Similar to S. 3209 for civil penalties and criminal penalties, but as in current law, criminal penalties apply to persons who "knowingly or willfully" violate the act.

Table 6. (Continued)

Provision	15 U.S.C. 2601 et seq.	S. 3209	H.R. 5820
	Criminal penalties of up to $25,000 per day of violation or up to one year of imprisonment, or both, also are authorized for knowing or willful violations.	Removes criminal sanctions for "willfully" violating any provision of TSCA, as amended, but increases the maximum penalty for "knowing" violations to $50,000 per day of violation or up to 5 years of imprisonment, or both. Adds a provision that any person who knowingly violates any provision of the law and "who knows at the time that he thereby places another person in imminent danger of death or serious bodily injury to any person shall upon conviction be subject to a fine of not more than $250,000 or imprisonment of not more than 15 years, or both." A person who is not an individual is subject to a fine of not more than $1,000,000.	
Seizure	TSCA 17 [15 U.S.C. 2616] makes substances produced in violation of Title IV (Lead Exposure Reduction) liable to be proceeded against, by process of libel, for seizure and condemnation in any district where the substance is found.	Amended TSCA 17 is similar to current law but in addition to substances and mixtures, S. 3209 applies to "articles" rather than "products" and to any such items that are subject to any title of TSCA.	Same as S. 3209.
Enforcement	TSCA 17 [15 U.S.C. 2616] provides jurisdiction to district courts over civil actions to restrain any violation or any person from taking any action prohibited, to compel the taking of any action required, or to direct any manufacturer or processor in violation of section 5 or 6 or of Title IV (or a rule or order under those provisions): to give notice to distributors and to others in possession of the substance, to give public notice of risk, and to replace or repurchase the substance. Authorizes civil actions brought in the U.S. district court for the judicial district wherein any violation occurred or where the defendant is found or transacts business.	Amended TSCA 17 authorizes the EPA Administrator to commence a civil action in the appropriate district court to compel compliance of any person with any provision of TSCA or any rule or order promulgated pursuant to it. Authorizes EPA to seek civil or criminal penalties, enjoin any violation, or order compliance, through an administrative proceeding, with any provision of TSCA or with any rule or order issued under it. Gives district courts jurisdiction over civil actions to seek penalties or enjoin violations in the U.S. district court for the judicial district wherein any violation occurred or where the defendant is found or transacts business. Gives jurisdiction over civil actions ordering compliance to the U.S. district court for the judicial district where the defendant is found or transacts business.	Same as S. 3209.

Preemption of state law	testing of a chemical under section 4, no state may require testing of the same substance for similar purposes; and (2) if EPA prescribes a rule or order under section 5 or 6 to protect against a risk, no state or political subdivision may have a requirement for such substance to protect against such risk unless it is identical to the EPA requirement, is adopted under authority of the Clean Air Act or another federal law, or prohibits the use of such substance in such state or political subdivision (other than use in manufacture or processing of other substances or mixtures).	Amended TSCA 18 would not preempt laws relating to a chemical substance, mixture, or article of states or political subdivisions unless they were less stringent than federal law.	Amended TSCA 18 provides that the act does not affect the right of a state or political subdivision to adopt or enforce its own laws or requirements with regard to a chemical unless compliance with both the requirement and TSCA is "impossible."
Exemption from preemption	TSCA 18 [15 U.S.C. 2617] authorizes EPA, upon application by a state or political subdivision, by rule to exempt a law in effect in the state or political subdivision, if compliance with the requirement would not cause activities involving the substance to be in violation of the EPA requirement,	No comparable provision. (Since state laws are not preempted, there is no need for an exemption.)	Same as S. 3209.
	and the requirement of the state or political subdivision provides a significantly higher degree of protection from the risk than the EPA requirement does and does not "unduly burden interstate commerce."		
Standard for judicial review	TSCA 19 [15 U.S.C. 2618] authorizes any person to file a petition with the U.S. Court of Appeals for the District of Columbia Circuit or for the circuit in which such person resides or in which the person's principal place of business is located, for judicial review of rules promulgated under TSCA sections 4(a), 5(a)(2), 5(b)(4), 6(a), 6(e), or 8. within 60 days of issuance. The appropriate district court is directed to set aside specified rules if they are not supported by "substantial evidence in the rulemaking record … taken as a whole" which is defined in TSCA 19(a)(3).	Similar to current law, but TSCA 19, as amended, authorizes filing a petition for judicial review of any rule or order issued under TSCA, as amended, rather than only specified rules, and eliminates the directive in current law to the court (to set aside a rule not supported by substantial evidence in the rulemaking record taken as a whole).	Same as S. 3209.

Table 6. (Continued)

Provision	15 U.S.C. 2601 et seq.	S. 3209	H.R. 5820
Citizen suits	TSCA 20 [15 U.S.C. 2619] authorizes civil suits by any person against any person in violation of TSCA or rules or orders promulgated under specified sections of TSCA. It also authorizes suits against EPA to compel performance of nondiscretionary actions under TSCA.	Amended TSCA 20 is similar to current law, but authorizes suits against any person in violation of rules or orders promulgated under any provision of TSCA, as amended.	Same as S. 3209.
Citizen petitions	TSCA 21 [15 U.S.C. 2620] provides the public with the right to petition EPA to initiate rulemaking or repeal of specified rules. Requires the Administrator to grant or deny the petition within 90 days of its filing.	Amended TSCA 21 is similar to current law, but authorizes petitions for EPA to initiate any action authorized under the law.	Amended TSCA 21 is the same as S. 3209.
Employee protection	TSCA 23 [15 U.S.C. 2622] prohibits employers from discriminating against an employee because the employee has acted or is about to act in a way that would further the purposes of TSCA. Authorizes filing of complaints by employees who believe they have been discriminated against. Describes remedies, procedures, and enforcement.	Same as current law.	H.R. 5820, section 22 amends TSCA 23 to elaborate the procedures, authorize protection for employees who refuse to violate TSCA or who share information about violations of TSCA with government officials, shorten the time between the filing of a complaint and issuance of a preliminary order by the Secretary of Labor, and describe the criteria that are to be used by the Secretary to deal with complaints.
Employment effects	TSCA 24 [15 U.S.C. 2623] directs the Administrator to continually evaluate the potential effects of specified rules, orders, and requirements under specified TSCA provisions on employment.	Amended TSCA 24 is similar to current law, but directs the Administrator to evaluate potential effects of the law as a whole, rather than specific provisions, and reporting is to be "periodic," rather than continual.	Same as S. 3209.
Administration	TSCA 26(a) [15 U.S.C. 2625(a)] authorizes federal agencies, upon request from EPA, to provide services, personnel, facilities, and information to EPA to assist in implementation of TSCA. TSCA 26(b) [15 U.S.C. 2625(b)] authorizes collection of fees for EPA processing of data submitted in response to an order under Section 4 or 5.	Amended TSCA 26 is similar to current law, except for subsection (b) and a new subsection (h). Amended TSCA 26(b) authorizes collection of fees from data submitters to defray the cost of administering TSCA, as amended. It removes the restrictions in the original TSCA 26(b) on the amount of such fees. New TSCA 26(h) authorizes the Administrator to issue orders and prescribe regulations as necessary to carry out the law.	H.R. 5820, section 24 is similar to current law, except that it amends TSCA 26(b) in the same way as S. 3209. In addition, the bill amends TSCA 26(d) to direct the Administrator to take actions by order when the action applies to a single chemical substance or single category of chemical substances.

	impose regulatory controls on categories of chemicals, rather than on a case-by-case basis. Prohibits regulation of a group based solely on the fact that it consists of new chemical substances. TSCA 26(d) [15 U.S.C. 2625(d)] directs EPA to establish an office to assist the regulated community. TSCA 26(e) [15 U.S.C. 2625(e)] requires that EPA establish a procedure to ensure disclosure of financial interests in the regulated community by EPA employees. TSCA 26(f) [15 U.S.C. 2625(f)] provides that final orders issued under TSCA must contain a statement of basis and purpose. TSCA 26(g) [15 U.S.C. 2625(g)] requires appointment of an Assistant Administrator for Toxic Substances.		Amended TSCA 26(e) also provides that no action will apply to articles already introduced or delivered for introduction into commerce, unless the action is taken to address an imminent hazard and is necessary to protect health or the environment. Finally, amended TSCA 26(j) authorizes the Administrator to prescribe regulations as are necessary to carry out the act.
State programs	TSCA 28 [15 U.S.C. 2627] authorizes grants to states to establish and operate programs to prevent or eliminate unreasonable risks to health or the environment which EPA is unable or is not likely to address under TSCA.	Amended TSCA 28 is similar to current law, but grants are authorized to prevent or eliminate any risks that EPA has not addressed. In addition, EPA is directed to establish a process to coordinate with the states "to share data and priorities relating to the management of chemical substances" under TSCA, as amended, and under state programs.	Amended TSCA 28 is similar to S. 3209 except that tribes are eligible for grants, and the specific reference to "cancer, birth defects, and gene mutations" is eliminated. Amended TSCA 28(b) also specifies the areas for coordination.
Children's environmental health research	No comparable provision.	New TSCA 30 establishes a Children's Environmental Health Research Program at EPA and authorizes the Administrator to enter into contracts and make grants to conduct research that will "further understanding of the vulnerability of children to chemical substances and mixtures." Establishes an Interagency Science Advisory Board on Children's Health Research subject to the Federal Advisory Committee Act (FACA) to provide independent advice upon request of the Administrator or Congress relating to the implementation of the amended TSCA "with respect to protecting children's health and research."	New TSCA 33 is similar to S. 3209, but does not establish a research program at EPA. It does direct the Administrator to enter into contracts and make grants, subject to amounts made available in advance in appropriations acts.

Table 6. (Continued)

Provision	15 U.S.C. 2601 et seq.	S. 3209	H.R. 5820
		The committee members would include representatives of the National Institute of Environmental Health Sciences, the Centers for Disease Control and Prevention, the National Toxicology Program, the National Cancer Institute, the National Tribal Science Council, and not fewer than 3 centers of children's health at leading universities.	Establishes the Science Advisory Board on Children's Health and Toxic Substances, an advisory committee subject to FACA, to consult with the Administrator on the scientific and technical aspects of issues relating to the implementation of the amended TSCA. Membership is the same as for the interagency committee established by S. 3209. The appointment process for members of the committee is to be publicly disclosed. A transcript or audio or video recording of each advisory committee meeting must be made available electronically on the EPA website within 30 days of the meeting.
Monitoring exposures	No comparable provision.	New TSCA 30 directs EPA to coordinate with the Secretary of Health and Human Services (HHS) to conduct a biomonitoring study to determine the presence of a chemical in human biological media in pregnant women and infants, if research has indicated that it may be present and may have adverse effects on development. Study results must be published. If the study finds that the chemical is present in human biological media, manufacturers and processors must disclose to EPA, commercial customers, consumers, and the public all known uses of the chemical and all articles in which the chemical is expected to be present.	New TSCA 33(c) is similar to S. 3209, except that a study need not be conducted if the Administrator determines that the substance already is subject to equivalent testing or meets the safety standard, or a safety standard determination is pending and a study is not required to complete the determination.
Animal-based testing	No comparable provision.4	New TSCA 31 directs the Administrator to minimize the use of animals in testing of chemical substances or mixtures. Establishes an Interagency Science Advisory Board on Alternative Testing Methods subject to FACA.	New TSCA 34 is similar to S. 3209, but does not require EPA to fund and carry out research, development, performance assessment, and translational studies to accelerate development of test methods and strategies.

		and peer review to the Administrator and Congress and to publish a list of testing methods that reduce the use of animals in testing under amended TSCA 4. Directs the Administrator in consultation with the Board to develop a strategic plan, biennially report to Congress on progress in implementing this section, and fund and carry out research, development, performance assessment, and translational studies to accelerate the development of test methods and strategies for use in safety standard determinations under amended TSCA 6(b). Authorizes the Administrator, on request of a manufacturer or processor, to adapt or waive animal-based testing of a chemical substance or mixture under specific conditions.	new interagency advisory board, instead directing EPA to consult with the Interagency Coordinating Committee on the Validation of Alternative Methods, which already is established (P.L. 106-545, 42 U.S.C. 2851-3). Specifies that a waiver of animal-based testing does not waive the duty of the manufacturer or processor to demonstrate that the substance or mixture meets the safety standard.
Safer alternatives	No comparable provision.5	New TSCA 32 establishes a program to create market incentives for the development of safer alternatives to existing chemical substances that reduce or avoid the use and generation of hazardous substances. Requires that the program include expedited review of new chemical substances for which an alternatives analysis indicates it is a safer alternative, and recognition for a substance or product determined by EPA to be a safer alternative.	New TSCA 35 is similar to S. 3209, except that it: requires the program to apply to mixtures as well as chemical substances; requires the Administrator to provide notice and an opportunity for public comment prior to establishment of the program; and omits the requirement that the program include expedited review of new chemical substances that may be safer alternatives. Also, the Administrator is directed to establish by rule the data that constitute a safer alternative data set to be used in seeking approval for designation as a safer alternative for a particular use. Requires inclusion of specified information. Directs the Administrator to approve an applicant alternative for a proposed use if the manufacturer or processor shows that the product is effective and provides a reasonable certainty of no harm from aggregate exposure through intended uses, protects the public welfare,

Table 6. (Continued)

Provision	15 U.S.C. 2601 et seq.	S. 3209	H.R. 5820
			and reduces the potential for harm relative to the substance it is meant to replace. Such safer alternatives are exempt for 15 years from requirements of amended TSCA 4, 5, and 6 for the uses approved.
Green chemistry and green engineering	No comparable provision.6	Directs the Administrator to establish a network of at least four green chemistry and engineering centers in various U.S. regions. Directs EPA to make grants to promote and support research, development, and adoption of safer alternatives. Creates a program to facilitate the development of a workforce that produces safer alternatives to existing chemical substances.	Similar to S. 3209, but directs the Administrator within 2 years of the date of enactment of H.R. 5820 to establish an interdisciplinary network of an unspecified number of regional centers to support research, development, and adoption of safer alternatives. All these requirements are made subject "to amounts made available in advance in appropriations Acts."
Reliable information and advice	No comparable provision.	New TSCA 34 directs EPA by order to establish and implement procedures to ensure data reliability by annually inspecting laboratories and performing an annual data audit. Requires that EPA establish a registry of studies.	New TSCA 37 is similar to S. 3209, but does not direct EPA to establish a registry of health and safety studies and requires notice and an opportunity to comment on procedures to ensure data reliability.
		Provides the Administrator with access to all records of health and safety studies initiated in response to requirements of Title I, and requires each submitter of a research study conducted by a third party to disclose the sources of any funding used to conduct or publish the study.	
Hot spots	No comparable provision.	New TSCA 35 requires that EPA promulgate a rule to establish criteria to identify any locality that is disproportionately exposed. Defines "disproportionate exposure" to mean residential population exposure to one or more toxic chemical substances and mixtures at levels that are significantly greater than the average exposure in the United States.	New TSCA 38 is similar to S. 3209, but does not address judicial review or state that listing is a nondiscretionary duty. Requires EPA to initially identify at least 20 localities.

		rule, to identify localities subject to such exposure using data in EPA's National Air Toxic Assessment Database and other available data, and providing an opportunity for public nominations of localities. Requires EPA to publish a list of such localities, and to update it at least once every 5 years. The locations on the list are not subject to judicial review. Publication of a list is a nondiscretionary duty and subject to judicial review. Requires the Administrator to develop and publish an action plan that includes an identification of the chemicals that contribute to the disproportionate exposure, and a description of actions to be taken to reduce exposure. Directs EPA to report annually to Congress.	
Federal agencies subject to TSCA	No comparable provision.	New TSCA 36 provides that all federal agencies are subject to the provisions of TSCA, as amended, and expressly waives any immunity otherwise applicable to the United States. However, no agent, employee, or officer of the United States is personally liable for any civil penalty under TSCA with respect to any act or omission within the scope of the official duties of that person. Such persons are subject to any criminal sanction under amended TSCA. The President is authorized to grant an exemption for any federal agency from compliance with any requirement of amended TSCA if "the President determines it is in the paramount interest of the United States." An exemption may be granted due to lack of appropriation if the President specifically requested such appropriation and Congress failed to make available such requested appropriation.	New TSCA 40 is the same as S. 3209.
		Directs the President annually to report to Congress all exemptions granted during the previous year. Authorizes enforcement action against any federal agency, as well as voluntary resolution or settlement set forth in a consent order.	

Table 6. (Continued)

Provision	15 U.S.C. 2601 et seq.	S. 3209	H.R. 5820
International cooperation	No comparable provision.	New TSCA 33 directs the Administrator to cooperate with the Secretary of State and the head of any other appropriate federal agency with international efforts to develop a common protocol or electronic database relating to chemical substances or to develop safer alternatives for chemical substances.	New TSCA 36 is similar to S. 3209, but directs the Administrator to cooperate with any international effort that "the Administrator determines has broad international support and a reasonable expectation of success" to develop "safer alternatives for chemical substances and mixtures."
Provision Persistent, bioaccumulative, toxic substances (PBTs)	15 U.S.C. 2601 et seq. No comparable provision.	S. 3209 No comparable provision.	H.R. 5820 New TSCA 32 directs the Administrator within one year of enactment of H.R. 5820 to establish criteria by rule to identify chemical substances and mixtures that are persistent, bioaccumulative, and toxic, (PBTs), or are degraded or metabolized into PBTs, and for which there is documented evidence of exposure to humans or the environment. Within 6 months of the promulgation of such rule, and every 3 years thereafter, the Administrator is directed to publish a list of all PBTs based on "available scientific information."
			The bill requires EPA, within 18 months of listing a PBT, to impose conditions under amended TSCA 6(e), (which provides for critical use exemptions), on its manufacture, processing, use, distribution in commerce, and disposal "to achieve the greatest practicable reductions in exposure."

			of such conditions, the Administrator is directed to determine whether the PBT meets the safety standard with the conditions imposed, and to impose any further conditions authorized under amended TSCA 6(c) to ensure that it meets the safety standard. Manufacturers and processors of PBTs are not required to submit a minimum data set, unless requested to do so. However, the declaration required by amended TSCA 8(a)(2) must be submitted within 6 months of PBT listing.
Exemption based on intrinsic properties	No comparable provision.	No comparable provision.	New TSCA 39 authorizes the Administrator to determine that "scientific consensus exists that the intrinsic properties of a chemical substance or mixture are such that it does not and would not pose any risk of injury to health or the environment under any current, proposed, or anticipated levels of production, patterns of use, or exposures arising at any stage across the lifecycle of the substance or mixture."
			Authorizes the Administrator, by order, to exempt from requirements of amended TSCA 4, 5, 6, and 8 such substance or mixture, or particular uses of it. Exemptions granted pursuant to TSCA 5(h)(4) prior to enactment of H.R. 5820 may remain in effect but must be reviewed by EPA within one year of enactment.
Authorization of appropriations	TSCA 29 [15 U.S.C. 2628] authorizes appropriations for implementation of specific TSCA provisions for 1982 and 1983. Prohibits expenditures of appropriated funds to construct laboratories.	New TSCA 39 authorizes "such sums as may be necessary" to carry out the law for 2011 through 2013, with no restriction on how those funds might be used.	New TSCA 29 is the same as S. 3209.

End Notes

[1] For a summary of TSCA provisions and history, see CRS Report RL31905, *The Toxic Substances Control Act (TSCA): A Summary of the Act and Its Major Requirements*.

[2] For more information about issues revolving around TSCA, see CRS Report RL34118, *The Toxic Substances Control Act (TSCA): Implementation and New Challenges*.

[3] However, EPA "is committed to examining alternative test methods that reduce the number of animals needed for testing, reduce pain and suffering of test animals, and whenever possible, replace animals in testing with validated in vitro (non-animal) test systems. EPA has released guidance on this issue ..." (U.S. EPA, "Fact Sheet on Animal Welfare," April 2001, EPA 745-F-99-003, http://www.epa.gov/HPV/pubs/general/anfacs.pdf.

[4] However, EPA "is committed to examining alternative test methods that reduce the number of animals needed for testing, reduce pain and suffering of test animals, and whenever possible, replace animals in testing with validated in vitro (non-animal) test systems. EPA has released guidance on this issue ..." U.S. EPA, "Fact Sheet on Animal Welfare," April 2001, EPA 745-F-99-003, http://www.epa.gov/HPV/pubs/general/anfacs.pdf.

[5] Although there is no explicit authority in TSCA, EPA does promote green chemistry (http://www.epa.gov/greenchemistry/), safer products (http://www.epa.gov/dfe/product_label_consumer.html), green engineering (http://www.epa.gov/oppt/greenengineering/pubs/whats_ge.html) and other "green" initiatives.

[6] Ibid.

INDEX

A

B

C

D

E

N

O

P

T

U

V

W